World's Fair Gardens

World's Fair Gardens

CATHY JEAN MALONEY

Shaping American Landscapes

University of Virginia Press CHARLOTTESVILLE AND LONDON

University of Virginia Press

© 2012 by the Rector and Visitors of the University of Virginia

All rights reserved

Printed in China on acid-free paper

First published 2012

9 8 7 6 5 4 3 2 1

Library of Congress Cataloging-in-Publication Data

Maloney, Cathy Jean.

World's fair gardens : shaping American landscapes / Cathy Jean Maloney.

p.   cm.

Includes bibliographical references and index.

ISBN 978-0-8139-3311-5 (cloth : acid-free paper)

1. Gardens—United States—History—19th century. 2. Gardens—United States—History—20th century.
 3. Exhibitions—United States—History—19th century. 4. Exhibitions—United States—History—20th
century. 5. Landscape design—United States—History—19th century. 6. Landscape design—
United States—History—20th century. 7. Landscape architecture—United States—History—19th
century. 8. Landscape architecture—United States—History—20th century. I. Title.

SB466.U6M225 2012

635—dc23

2012005561

For my family

Contents

 Acknowledgments

Thank you to the alchemists at the University of Virginia Press who turned my words into a beautiful book. Among the many fine editors and staff at the Press, in particular I'd like to thank Boyd Zenner, who championed and polished the manuscript. As always, I am grateful to the librarians and archivists across the United States who helped me track down elusive world's fair source documents.

Mike and Tom support me in so many ways I lose track, but I am so glad they are in my life. My extended family provides encouragement, inspiration, and humor.

This book was supported by a grant from the Graham Foundation for Advanced Studies in the Fine Arts. I am indebted to the Foundation for its early and sustained commitment to this project.

World's Fair Gardens

 Introduction

What do zippers, telephones, Ferris wheels, and X-ray machines have in common? All formally debuted at a United States world's fair, like thousands of other innovations and works of art. In their heyday, between 1850 and 1940, world's fairs offered millions of people a first look at important discoveries and trends in science, agriculture, art, industry, and the humanities. These international expositions brought exhibitors and visitors from around the globe to a host city. Civic pride and boosterism ballooned with each new fair as each city sought to outdo the previous show.

The impact of world's fairs is hard to fathom in our current hypernetworked society. Before the advent of radio and television, a world's fair offered the best way to showcase national pride. In one designated city, typically over a period of months, people gathered to see, touch, hear, smell, and taste the world's newest products. Fairs drew millions of visitors: attendance ranged from more than six million at the pioneering 1851 "Great Exhibition" in London, to nearly forty-five million at New York's 1939–1940

World's Fair.[1] Familiar icons of world's fairs include the Ferris wheel, the Corliss engine, the Trylon and Perisphere, and other demonstrations of engineering prowess.

Equally familiar and well documented are examples of world's fair architecture, from the 1893 White City of Chicago to the World of Tomorrow in 1939 New York. Today, although most buildings from these expositions are long gone, the legacies of world's fairs in the United States can be found directly underfoot in the greenery of cherished parks and public spaces. Although individual garden features may be lost, the broad outlines of many major U.S. urban green spaces can be traced directly to a world's fair.

Frequently overshadowed by the fanfare around exposition buildings and exhibits, an exposition's landscapes and grounds often were its only vestiges within the host city. Civic leaders' rationales for hosting a world's fair varied from city to city, from bolstering sagging economies to increasing railroad travel to improving civic reputations. Every world's fair needed a fairground, however, and the opportunity to convert undeveloped land to prime real estate attracted many exposition investors. City boosters used world's fairs as catalysts for urban renewal or the creation of public parks. Fair sites were carefully chosen—often amid much controversy—with a speculative eye toward future value and use. Many of these major green spaces remain today as integral elements of urban life. Thus, a former swamp in Chicago became the lakefront jewel Jackson Park, and an erstwhile landfill became the beautiful park in New York's Flushing Meadows.

Landscaping and horticulture at world's fairs demanded innovative design, creative technical solutions, and scientific prowess. Consider the challenges of preparing a world's fair site. In a matter of months, the illusion of mature landscapes had to be created to complement building styles ranging from Beaux-Arts to baroque. A fair site needed to handle a crush of pedestrian traffic, yet also provide for delicate ornamental gardens. Countries from around the world expected a suitable showcase for their native plantings and produce, often in climates completely unlike their own. At U.S. world's fairs, problems like these were creatively solved by some of the preeminent landscape designers of the day, whose work then became accessible to visitors unable to afford private residential designs. Professionals in horticulture and allied disciplines also benefited from the exchange and communication of new ideas. Through this confluence of technology, high-profile landscaping, and information sharing, the floral displays at U.S. world's fair gardens had an immediate impact on public and private gardens. Even though, by nature, world's fair gardens were ephemeral, their influence was both widespread and permanent.

Horticultural feats were achieved not only in the selection and shaping of world's fair sites, but also in their exquisite horticultural palaces, which housed exciting exhibits of floriculture, pomology, and viticulture from around the world. Each decade brought dramatic changes in garden styles and technology, all showcased in spirited competition among participating nations. Long after the other world's fair buildings were demolished, horticulture halls remained standing in, for example, Philadelphia's Fairmount Park and New Orleans's Audubon Park.

U.S. world's fairs not only created public parks from former wastelands, but also showcased city planning, horticultural societies, commerce, and the emerging profession of landscape architecture.[2] Integrating landscapes with buildings became a city planning ideal as exemplified by the City Beautiful movement, which had its genesis in Chicago's 1893 World's Fair. Horticultural societies frequently convened at the fairs, and many, including the American Horticultural Society, debuted at or were reinvigorated by an exposition's Horticultural Congress.[3] Technology and horticultural business processes, such as shipping methods for live plants or produce, cold storage, tree transplantation, and more, were tested at world's fairs and then adopted in day-to-day commerce.

The Evolution of World's Fairs from Europe to the United States

World's fairs originated in Europe and quickly spread to other countries. The United States, an early exhibitor at European fairs, quickly assumed the role of host. In the late nineteenth century, as the landscape architecture profession began to emerge in America, world's fair landscapes mirrored and even anticipated changes in garden design. During the first half of the twentieth century, technology and horticultural discoveries accelerated in businesses and nurseries across the country, and these became integral elements of world's fairs.

In 1851, London sponsored the first world's fair, styled "The Great Exhibition of the Works of Industry of All Nations." An outgrowth of local artisan fairs, this ambitious exposition had the full support of Prince Albert and Queen Victoria. Horticulture was the predominant feature at this inaugural fair when Sir Joseph Paxton won the building design competition with his spectacular plan for the Crystal Palace, a magnificent glasshouse that encompassed all of the exhibits. The tremendous success of the London exposition fueled the world's fair mania over the next several decades—a mania that persists in many parts of the world today.[4]

Each decade since 1851 has produced at least four world's fairs.[5] In the 1880s, seventeen major international expositions were held, and multiple fairs were hosted within the same year during the 1900s. It became clear that a mediating authority should regulate the frequency and venue of world's fairs, and thus the Paris-based Bureau of International Expositions (BIE) was formed in 1928. The BIE officially sanctions world's fairs and, ideally, ensures that no single country has a monopoly on expositions and that sufficient time elapses between them to prevent fair fatigue.

As expositions proliferated throughout the years, separate buildings were constructed to display the escalating number and variety of exhibits. The fairs outgrew single exhibition halls such as London's Crystal Palace and expanded into clusters of buildings on a landscaped campus. As the preference for such a campus setting grew, so did the need for landscapes to unify the buildings and offer scenic or utilitarian circulation routes. Unlike their European counterparts, many cities in the United States, unconstrained by city limits, still had room to grow. U.S. venues thus offered ideal sites for the creation of large, landscaped campuses.

Landscape designers for U.S. world's fairs often took fact-finding trips to European fairs for inspiration. Thus, Herman Schwarzmann and other planners of Philadelphia's 1876 Centennial Exhibition visited the 1873 Vienna International Exposition. Frederick Law Olmsted, the "Father of American Landscape Architecture," and U.S. delegates toured Paris's 1889 Exposition Universelle in advance of the World's Columbian Exposition.[6] Participation in international world's fairs influenced U.S. gardening styles first in exposition fairgrounds and then in individual backyards. Cosmopolitan and influential members of U.S. world's fair management teams often championed foreign gardening trends by appointing foreign landscape designers for individual exhibits.[7]

Paradoxically, world's fairs also provided Americans with opportunities to rethink their dependence on European gardening trends. Plants and styles that worked well in foreign locales might prove unsuitable for American soils and climates such as certain types of rhododendrons from England and many Japanese bonsai plants. American judges for the 1876 Centennial Horticulture Department noted, "Those who follow the examples given in European horticultural works and journals, will be greatly disappointed, as many of the plants most useful there are quite worthless with us."[8]

The Golden Age of American Exposition Landscapes

An awareness of the historical context surrounding world's fairs helps explain how their remnant green spaces still affect us today. World's fairs reflected and in some cases anticipated America's evolution from agrarian to industrial nation. As the country's horticultural interests evolved from a desire to grow the best potato to a more sophisticated concern with landscape design and environmental issues, exposition green spaces evolved accordingly.

The first world's fair in the United States, the Exhibition of the Industry of All Nations held in New York in 1853–54, included utilitarian exhibits of agrarian implements such as reapers, corn shellers, churns, and threshing machines, but no horticultural or

▲ The Crystal Palace, with its
greenhouse construction built
around living trees, highlighted
the importance of horticulture at
the 1851 World's Fair in London.
(Author's collection)

landscape displays. A single building housed this entire world's fair: dubbed the Crystal Palace, it—like its London namesake—resembled an overgrown greenhouse. The footprint of the New York Crystal Palace consumed virtually all of the exhibition's land (now Bryant Park) and left little room for exterior landscaping.[9] The author Horace Greeley, an ardent supporter of and visitor to the 1854 World's Fair, described his unsatisfactory search for agricultural produce:

> Our first survey of the Exhibition gave us the impression that there was absolutely no display of the agricultural productions of the United States, in the raw or natu-

ral condition of their growth . . . The first articles in this collection that you will be likely to notice, are a baker's dozen of very large and very ancient-looking edible roots. There is no name, nor anything to indicate what they are, or where they are from, or why they are there . . . We happened to be able to tell sundry inquirers that they were California potatoes; whereat they stared and wondered amazingly.[10]

Of this sorry display, he complained: "And this is the New York World's Fair Exhibition of Industry and Production of American Farmers! Can anything more disgraceful to that class of our citizens, upon whom all other classes are dependent, be conceived?"[11]

It was not until the 1876 Exhibition in Philadelphia that Greeley's message was heard. During the two intervening decades, the United States was preoccupied with the Civil War and subsequent reconstruction, and it hosted no major fairs. In Europe, however, exhibitions continued with marked advances in horticulture. The 1867 Exposition Universelle in Paris was the first to recognize horticulture as a separate exhibition category, a hard-won distinction that underscored the growing importance of the field.[12]

Taking cues from the preceding fairs in Paris and Vienna, the Philadelphia Centennial Exhibition of 1876 offered a freestanding Horticultural Palace and extensive landscaped grounds. While the 1876 Centennial introduced horticulture as a sign of sophistication, Chicago's 1893 World's Columbian Exposition confirmed landscape architecture's status as an art form. City leaders in Chicago commissioned Frederick Law Olmsted to design the Columbian fairgrounds in the city's then undeveloped Jackson Park, and Olmsted enjoyed equal status with the fair's architects. The three disciplines of agriculture, horticulture, and landscape architecture frequently overlapped in early U.S fairs, but became more distinct as the nineteenth century closed.

Just as labor specialization emerged in the newly industrialized United States, responsibilities for creating increasingly complex world's fair landscapes expanded from single practitioners to teams of experts. Relatively unknown local landscape designers such as the Philadelphian H. J. Schwarzmann at the 1876 Centennial may have had sufficient expertise to design for early fairs, but later exhibitions demanded the combined talents of teams working for such nationally known figures such as Olmsted and his sons, John C. and Frederick Law Olmsted Jr., Warren Manning, William Le Baron Jenney, and George Kessler. In designing the fairgrounds, these men not only influenced contemporary garden styles but also shaped the public green spaces we enjoy today.

During this golden period of exposition landscaping, leading horticulturists, seedsmen, and nurserymen brought their latest plant introductions to the fairs. Venerable seedsmen such as Peter Henderson's of New York, J. C. Vaughan of Chicago, James Vick & Sons, and Stark Brothers were consistent exhibitors. Their latest plant introduc-

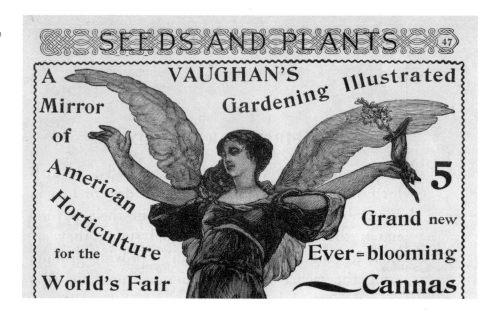

tions and floral displays influenced outdoor gardens and tabletop vases from the humblest cottage to the grandest mansion.

Regionalism, especially as showcased through gardens surrounding individual state buildings, contributed greatly to the diversity of expositions, adding a delightfully personal, informative dimension to the exhibits. Inside the horticultural palaces, different states developed signature exhibition styles. California was known for its flamboyant, larger-than-life sculptures made from local produce: elephants sculpted from walnuts, for example, and pyramids of oranges. Florida often planted demonstration citrus groves, while conservative midwestern states such as Missouri and Illinois sought gold medals with carefully arranged plates of polished apples. In later fairs, as sponsorship of the horticulture departments shifted from states to private entities, more homogenized displays evolved.

Horticulturists constantly sought better methods of cold storage for plant material both when it was in transit and while on the fairgrounds. Before the advent of air transport, any live plant material shipped from overseas went by slow boat, and frequently incurred damage en route. Within the United States, railroad companies—huge supporters of world's fairs—offered significant fare discounts to visitors and exhibitors, thus fueling demand for train transport. Exhibitors and railway companies alike strove to improve shipping techniques. Horticulture officials in early fairs in New Orleans, Chicago, Buffalo, and St. Louis garnered and shared advice from around the nation on the best storage practices.

Technical advances affected the landscape design as well as horticultural displays. Trees, critical landscape elements needed to bring a sense of maturity to the grounds, posed some of the most vexing problems for world's fair landscape designers. There were either not enough trees on the fair site or too many in the wrong spot. Tree-transplantation technologies burgeoned from 1876 through 1940 as flatbed trucks replaced horse-drawn carts, and methods of digging and wrapping trees were perfected to improve survival rates.

Site preparation and maintenance posed other challenges. Early fairs relied on teams of horses and manual labor

to clear and prepare the land. In many instances, the labor pool was untrained and unskilled. Rudolph Ulrich, superintendent of landscaping for the 1893 World's Columbian Exposition, complained that "the resources available in any large capital of Europe were not at command in Chicago, and the work had to be pushed rapidly with unknown and untrained men."[13] Manual irrigation systems increased labor costs and produced inconsistent results, until an advanced sprinkling system was introduced at San Francisco's Panama-Pacific International Exposition. All pruning, trimming, and weeding was done by hand. Natural, organic methods of fertilizing and pest prevention predominated in the 1800s, but by the 1930s, world's fairs touted artificial pesticides that ultimately found their way into America's backyards.

Landscape lighting, water features, and circulation paths all evolved parallel with technological changes. As electrification became more prevalent, outdoor lighting options expanded. Initially utilitarian, outdoor lighting enabled fairs to stay open longer, and soon included special effects to highlight plantings and aquatic displays such as the rainbow-hued "singing fountains" of the 1930 fairs. Water features also benefited from improved pumping mechanisms that allowed fountains to spring higher and manmade streams to circulate farther. Designs for footpaths gave way to vehicular traffic by the 1940s as automotive technology became commonplace and buses toured the fairgrounds.

In an age before mass communication, networking opportunities were key benefits of world's fairs. Professionals in the horticulture, seed, florist, and landscape design business could only benefit from proximity and discussions with others in their fields. Warren H. Manning, an esteemed landscape architect and protégé of Frederick Law Olmsted, wrote glowingly of the knowledge-sharing opportunities at these conventions: "The bringing together of widely separated men and women representing all the activities of a nation, or of the world, in organized conferences or even in accidental meetings will do more to promote these activities than will a large amount of correspondence and reading."[14] World's fairs thus served not only to entertain and inform the public about new gardening ideas, but also to help landscape designers and nurserymen strengthen the bonds of their own professions.

U.S. world's fairs succumbed to a dry spell after the bicoastal fairs in New York and San Francisco in 1939–40. The exigencies of World War II reduced interest in and diverted focus from international festivals. In one dramatic example, the exquisite wrought-iron gate from the New York World's Fair's "Gardens on Parade" exhibit was melted down for the war effort.[15] It wasn't until the 1960s that enthusiasm for the fair reawakened in the United States.[16] In the postwar era, U.S. fairs' horticultural and landscape efforts seemed to have lost the dynamism that had characterized them in earlier fairs. In these later fairs, exhibits from corporations such as Firestone, Kodak, IBM, Westinghouse, and others largely overshadowed foreign- and state-sponsored buildings. Corporate displays, while beautifully executed, lacked the unique regionalism that made the horticulture of earlier fairs so interesting.

Almost ninety years had elapsed between the first world's fair in New York in 1854 and the fair's return to the city in 1939 for the World of Tomorrow Exposition. In the intervening years, American life was modernized by the telephone, automobile, airplane, household refrigerator, and countless other scientific advances. The United States grew from thirty-three to forty-eight states, each of which contributed something unique to the world of gardening. America had survived the Civil War, World War I, Spanish flu pandemic of 1918–19, and other national and international crises. Throughout these nine decades, world's fair horticulture and landscape artistry both shared and showcased garden trends.

United States World's Fair Sampler

Choosing which among the many world's fairs to include in this book was a challenge, since every exposition offered something new. Fairs profiled in this book met these criteria:

* Included significant international representation
* Offered a substantial horticultural component
* Represented a particular era (approximately one fair per decade between 1870 and 1930)
* Were designed by an influential or promising landscape designer
* Some remnant of the fairgrounds exists today

The table lists the fairs featured in this work in chronological order, and includes statistics on each fair's size and attendance.[17]

Inevitably, exceptions were made. For example, while the 1907 World's Fair in Jamestown, Virginia, did not have its own horticulture building, it was sufficiently important as a preplanned residential community to warrant inclusion. Because the period from 1900 through 1910 featured numerous American world's fairs, only representative fairs are included.[18] Nonetheless, the fairs included here offer a rich sampler that demonstrates the progress in American horticulture and landscape design throughout the decades.

World's fairs are still popular today, and horticultural progress continues, particularly in the areas of ecology and environmentalism. Still, it was in earlier times, when travel was an adventure and gardens were dreams of chromolithography, that the landscapes of world's fairs made the most impact on American gardens. World's fairs spawned the development of many of the country's most beautiful public spaces. Understanding the original design intent for world's fair landscapes—and the technological constraints under which they were created—may allow for a greater appreciation

Featured U.S. World's Fairs

FAIR NAME	LOCATION/TIME FRAME	TOTAL ATTENDANCE (thousands)	SIZE OF GROUNDS (acres)	PROFIT OR LOSS (thousands USD)
Centennial Exhibition	Philadelphia May 10–November 10, 1876	9.7	285	-$4.5
World's Industrial and Cotton Centennial Exposition	New Orleans December 16, 1884–June 1, 1885	1.2	249	-$470
World's Columbian Exposition	Chicago May 1–October 30, 1893	27.5	686	$1.4
Pan-American Exposition	Buffalo, New York May 1–November 1, 1901	8.1	350	-$3.0
Louisiana Purchase Exposition	St Louis April 30–December 1, 1904	19.7	1,272	$1.02
Jamestown Exposition	Jamestown, Virginia April 26–November 30, 1907	2.8	400	-$2.5
Panama-Pacific International Exposition	San Francisco February 20–December 4, 1915	18.9	635	$2.4
Century of Progress Exposition	Chicago May 27–November 12, 1933, and May 26–October 31, 1934	48.7 (both years)	427	$160
World of Tomorrow	New York City April 30–October 31, 1939, and May 11–October 27, 1940	44.9 (both years)	1,217	-$18.7

of the remnant sites and perhaps encourage their preservation. Comparing world's fair landscapes among cities, both as originally conceived and as repurposed today, helps us to better understand regional differences and similarities in urban planning. Across the country, from Flushing Meadows to Golden Gate Park, many of America's best-known green spaces, and their innovative technologies and horticultural societies, persist as beautiful souvenirs of expositions past.

 Centennial Exhibition

PHILADELPHIA, 1876

The Debut of American Horticulture on the World Stage

The decades between the 1854 New York World's Fair and 1876 Centennial Exhibition encompassed some of the most dramatic changes in U.S. history. The catastrophic Civil War and its aftermath, along with the completion of the Transcontinental Railroad in 1869, transformed American life. The shift from agrarian to industrial-based economies was well under way, and a rising middle class coupled with swelling immigrant populations significantly altered the demographics not only of most major U.S. urban centers but of the nation in general.

The pace of change had also intensified in horticulture and landscape design. The historian U. P. Hedrick claims that the decades between 1830 and 1860 saw more horticultural progress than the combined years previous.[1] Amateur botanists and plant hunters discovered new plants in the Plains states and western territories, even as state and local horticulture societies sprang up across the country.

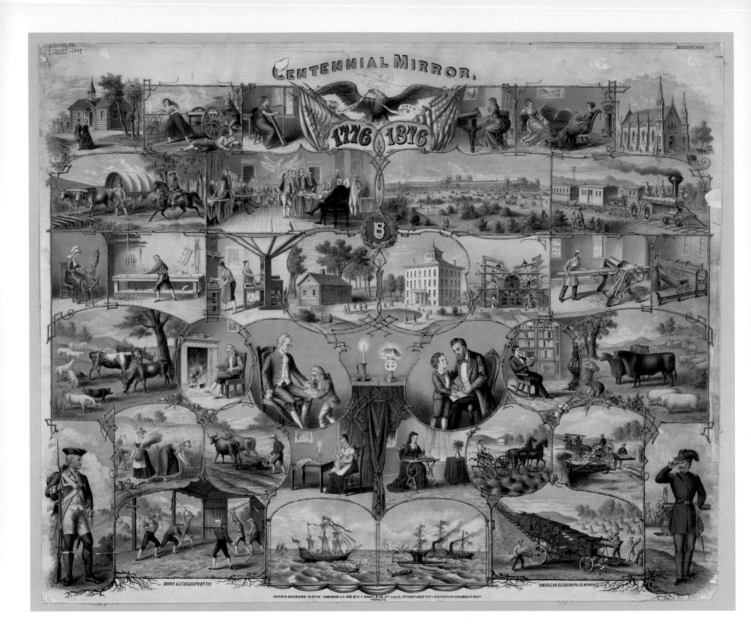

The theme and displays of the 1876 Centennial Exhibition reflected the excitement of the new industrial and transportation age. The main icon of the exhibition, the massive Corliss steam engine, powered the exhibits in the great Machinery Hall, a fitting symbol of its era. Consistent with the emphasis on progress, exhibitors of Centennial horticulture displays and landscapes sought to show new trends and technologies in their fields.

Philadelphia was selected as the Centennial site not only for its patriotic history and transportation access, but also for its horticultural renown: Andrew Jackson Downing once called it "the first city in point of horticulture in the United States."[2] When William Penn charted the city in the 1600s, he designed it as a "greene country town, gardens round each house, that it might never be burned, and always be wholesome."[3] The idea of hosting an exposition in such an established, cosmopolitan city appealed to fair organizers who particularly wanted to impress visitors.

The Centennial grounds layout marked a significant departure from most previous European world's fairs and provided a template for future U.S. fairs in that it was hosted in several buildings rather than a single large exhibition hall.[4] Multiple buildings offered exhibitors more flexibility and also provided architects with the opportunity to design structures better suited to and reflective of the exhibits within.

At the Centennial, the public encountered extensive use of carpet bedding, a garden style limited mostly to public parks and, in the United States, to private estates of the wealthy. In his 1847 Dictionary of Modern Gardening, the Philadelphian seedsman David Landreth described "bedding out" as the practice of "removing plants from the pots in which they have been raised, into the beds which they are intended to adorn during summer and autumn."[5] The style flourished with the publication of Frank J. Scott's popular 1870 book Suburban Home Grounds, in which the author presented nineteen patterns for bedding out designs in his chapter entitled "Flowers and Bedding Plants, and Their Settings."[6] Scott's designs, based on succession plantings of spring bulbs followed by seed-sown summer bloomers, suited smaller properties that may not have had expensive greenhouses for growing tropical plants.

Carpet bedding is best displayed against a manicured lawn, but at the time of the exhibition, grassy lawns required maintenance with scythes or horse-drawn rollers. Although the Englishman Edwin Budding invented the lawn mower in 1830, Virginia Scott Jenkins notes in The Lawn (1994) that no lawn mowers were exhibited at the Centennial, and that "lawns were just becoming a subject of general interest and were still unusual."[7] Carpet bedding on any sort of large-scale basis was thus limited to those with means.

With the expansion of railroads, tourism in the United States boomed in the last quarter of the nineteenth century. The Centennial was one of the earliest event-based destinations that attracted a huge number of visitors arriving by rail. For years, wealthy tourists had taken the waters at Saratoga Springs or traveled to Yosemite. Democratized travel, however, arrived with the railroad, and more middle-class travelers from across the country could afford a Centennial trip. Nearly 10 million people attended the fair—an average of fifteen thousand per day in July.[8]

The popular Centennial offered visitors an unparalleled opportunity to take in new ideas in landscape design and to challenge traditional definitions of engineering and architecture as well as landscape design. The Centennial Exhibition also drew attention to the emerging role of landscape designers: here the general public could see exhibits of landscape plans by designers such as the Olmsted protégé Jacob Weidenmann or installed flower beds by William Saunders. The new role of landscape gardeners (later redefined as landscape architects) caused controversy in the crowded field of entrepreneurial growers and nurserymen. Indistinct boundaries separated the professions of civil engineers, gardeners, architects, and nurserymen and caused territorial skirmishes. Engineers were often criticized as sacrificing aesthetics for practicality. Nurserymen derided landscape gardeners and architects as lacking practical experience, whereas the latter dismissed hands-on gardeners as untutored in the finer points of artistic composition.

Reflecting this public squabbling, an 1876 issue of the Philadelphia-based Gardener's Monthly asked its readers, "Who shall lay out our ornamental grounds?" One subscriber responded that some practitioners "were actually ashamed of the term gardener. They had themselves printed [cards] and called [themselves] landscape architects, landscape engineers, rural architects, artists in grounds, etc., etc.,; anything but landscape gardeners."[9] Another reader countered, "we want no more of jobbing gardeners, who work physically, and claim to be landscapists; nor do we want engineers, who perhaps are capable of running a straight line, but know no more of a graceful curve than the mule Nebuchadnezzar . . . Let us trust and hope . . . that a man must be taught to form a beautiful landscape place in conformity to the surrounding lay of the country, the style of architecture . . . and know just what trees and grades to place and make in it."[10]

RUSTIC ARBOR

> The rustic beauty of pre-Centennial Fairmount Park included characteristic rugged rock outcroppings and follies such as this gazebo. (From John C. Sinclair's *Views of Fairmount Park in Philadelphia*, ca. 1870. Courtesy Library of Congress Prints and Photographs Division, Washington, D.C. LC-DIG-ppmsca-24828)

Schwarzmann Creates the Fair in Fairmount Park

Philadelphians' commitment to gardens and nature was never so evident as in the purchase and development of Fairmount Park, the site ultimately chosen for the Centennial. At the time of the exhibition, Fairmount Park comprised more than 2,700 acres, making it the fourth-largest park in the world, and the largest in the United States. A delightful patchwork of designed landscapes interspersed with natural areas, the park encompassed country villas such as Lemon Hill and Sweet Briar.[11] As the park grew, these estates, along with their mature plantings, were deeded as public grounds.[12] The villas in Fairmount Park became de facto outdoor museums of garden design styles for Centennial visitors.

Belmont Mansion, with its labyrinthine cedar and spruce hedge, broad allée of English cherry trees, summerhouses, and statuary, was one such villa. Incorporated into the park in the 1860s, Belmont led local design trends by decades through its combination of naturalistic elements such as "the wood" with formal avenues and allées reflecting the influence of English aesthetic concepts.[13]

Setting a precedent for the U.S. world's fairs that followed, the Centennial's planners recognized that the fairgrounds' design needed to accommodate the eventual development of the park. Accordingly, and consistent with the value placed on horticulture and art, Philadelphia and the State of Pennsylvania paid for the erection of two permanent buildings, Horticultural Hall and Memorial Hall. All other buildings were to be of temporary construction, with only the roads, parkways, and some plantings designated as permanent. On July 4, 1873, amid much fanfare, the City of Philadelphia transferred a portion of Fairmount Park to the Centennial Commission for the purpose of creating the exhibition grounds and buildings. The chosen tract comprised about 450 acres in the southwest quadrant of the park. Roughly triangular in shape, the parcel of land, formerly the Lansdowne Estate,[14] was bordered on the east by the Schuylkill River, and sloped gradually downward for about 200 feet from George's Hill eastward to the floodplain of the river.

With less than two years to Opening Day, the Centennial Commission did not yet have a viable master plan of the grounds, so they announced an architectural competition to design the Centennial buildings. Renowned firms from across the nation submitted bids, but a young park employee, the German immigrant Hermann Schwarzmann, developed a pragmatic design that eventually prevailed over entries from such luminaries as Olmsted and Vaux.[15] Schwarzmann's background lay in engineering and architecture, with landscape and gardening duties a distant second. The Centennial plan showed this bias toward buildings and infrastructure, with garden features delegated to others.

Once work began, individual areas of the grounds were landscaped in piecemeal fashion; as buildings were finished, trees, shrubs, or flower plots were hastily arranged as needed. Until the 1893 World's Columbian Exposition, this is the process that was followed for landscape installation at American world's fairs. Unfortunately, difficulties in obtaining consensus on building locations and sizes plagued construction timetables. Every building sponsor wanted the most favorable location on the grounds,

and significant lobbying ensued before final decisions were made. Grounds layout became a puzzle-solving exercise—and the puzzle pieces continually changed shape. There were weather delays and contractors who were "much amazed by water and quicksand" in Fairmount Park, and after only a month, Schwarzmann had to report that work was already behind schedule.[16] Nonetheless, on July 4, 1874, the mayor of Philadelphia officiated at a groundbreaking ceremony near Memorial Hall.

Manual labor constituted the bulk of the landscaping effort, augmented by horse-power where possible. Horse-drawn rollers were used to level the walkways, with hand-pushed rollers used in smaller areas. Miscommunication and the occasional fracas erupted among superintendents, threatening the work effort. When the Conservatory heating contract was awarded, for example, Schwarzmann was not involved. He protested to the Committee of Plans and Designs: "I request to be furnished with the necessary plans and specifications that I may know what to do. I regret that this whole matter has been decided by [chief of the Horticulture Department] Mr. Miller without myself being consulted on the subject, and I take this opportunity of requesting your Committee to give such instructions to Mr. Miller as will secure to me the full control of this building as long as it is in the course of construction."[17]

Schwarzmann noted in his report to the Centennial Commission: "Two weeks before the opening of the Exhibition, the grounds were finally closed to the public. All such minor works as planting, seeding, sodding, paving, etc. were completed by the opening day . . . and, on May 10, 1876 [Opening Day], I had the honor to hand over the work to the Building Committee in a finished condition."[18] The efforts of Schwarzmann and his crew were monumental: crews moved more than 500,000 cubic yards of earth, erected 2.78 miles of wooden fence, and laid 16 miles of roads, avenues, and walks. Seven miles of drainpipes, 9 miles of water pipes, and more than 7 miles of gas pipes were installed, and three major bridges and eleven footbridges were built. This work and more was accomplished with an average of 600 men laboring on the grounds each day—with the workforce peaking at 1,100 men.[19] At last, almost two years after groundbreaking, the Centennial Exhibition was ready to welcome the public.

Bird's-Eye View of the Grounds

Sepia-toned stereoviews provide most of today's insight into the Centennial landscape. While interesting and appealing, these views cannot possibly convey the overall effect of what must have been a brilliantly colorful scene. Carnival-style tents and concessionaire kiosks dotted the avenues; handsome new exhibition halls were offset by tessellated parterres; water features ornamented the landscape and mirrored impressive sculptures. The 5-acre Centennial Lake, excavated to provide drainage for the grounds, boasted a central fountain that created cooling breezes. Numerous other fountains offered fresh drinking water to parched fairgoers and alleviated the monotony of such broad boulevards as the nearly mile-long Avenue of the Republic.

One such fountain marked the intersection of north-south Belmont Avenue and east-west Fountain Avenue. The latter, the most intensively landscaped thoroughfare on the grounds, terminated at the raised terraces of Horticultural Hall. Fountain Avenue featured not only the fountains for which it was named but also shrub collections and colorful parterres of annuals displayed by the nurserymen of the country and the world. One of the most photographed garden features, Fountain Avenue became emblematic of Centennial landscaping, along with the grounds immediately surrounding Horticultural Hall. Annual flowers highlighted these designs: as the *American Agriculturist* newspaper advised gardeners, "To produce striking effects, plants . . . are set out in masses, in separate beds all of one color, or a few contrasting kinds in the same bed, arranged in circles or other well defined patterns."[20]

North and south of Horticultural Hall, the ground dipped into two preexisting wooded ravines: Belmont Valley to the north and Lansdowne Valley to the south. Small streams ran through each of the ravines and connected them with the Schuylkill

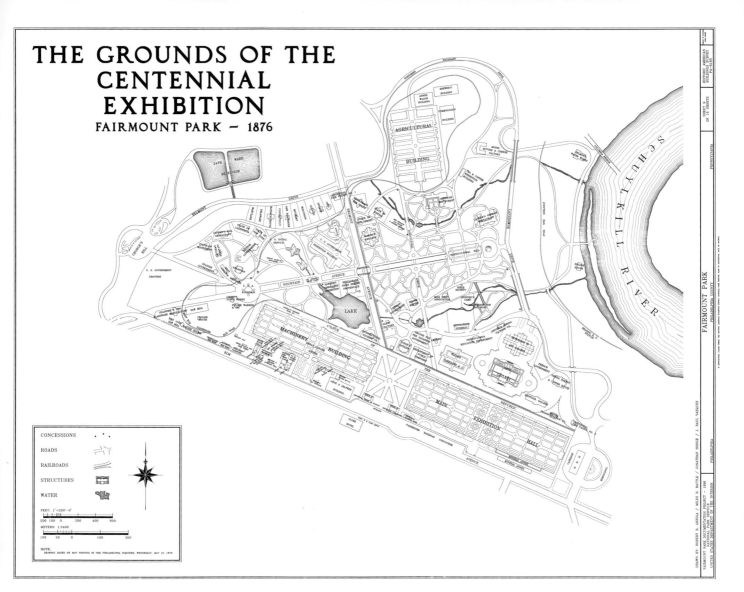

THE GROUNDS OF THE
CENTENNIAL
EXHIBITION
FAIRMOUNT PARK ~ 1876

CONCESSIONS

ROADS

RAILROADS

STRUCTURES

WATER

FEET: 1"=200'-0"
200 100 0   200   400   600
METERS: 1:2400
100   50   0   100   200

NOTE:
DRAWING BASED ON MAP PRINTED IN THE PHILADELPHIA INQUIRER, WEDNESDAY, MAY 10, 1876.

▲ The triangular-shaped Centennial grounds plan centered on the intersection of Belmont and Fountain Avenues. Horticultural Hall is in the upper middle. (Author's collection)

River. In the natural rugged beauty of the valleys, mature existing trees thrived. These cool, shaded glens, untouched by Schwarzmann and the grounds crew save for some newly built rustic footbridges, offered visitors a picturesque "wild" landscape that contrasted with formal bedding-out designs.

In the southwestern quadrant of the exposition grounds, the majority of state, federal, and foreign government buildings had been hastily constructed before the fair opened. In contrast with later expositions, few attempts were made to regionalize the architecture or surrounding gardens.[21] Only the Japanese displayed gardens representative of their national style. Japan would be a major and consistent exhibitor in America's world's fairs, and the Centennial launched this long relationship. Japan sponsored two freestanding exhibits at the 1876 Fair, in addition to displays in the Main Exhibition Building. The Japanese dwelling, representing a typical home, was located in the southwest quadrant of the fair, with state and other governmental buildings. The Japanese government building and grounds, called the "Japanese Bazaar" in contemporary reports, occupied a prime site just across from the Esplanade at the Centennial's main entrance.

During construction of both buildings, Japanese workers were ridiculed in the local press for their nontraditional building techniques, but the completed buildings, with their elegant simplicity, amazed the visiting public. Similarly, the gardens around the Japanese Bazaar, while simple by today's standards, were fresh and "exotic" and sparked a long-standing love of things Japanesque in American design.[22] One visiting journalist reported:

▲ Japan's long-standing participation in U.S. world's fairs began with the Japanese Bazaar at the Centennial. (Library of Congress Prints and Photographs Division, Washington, D.C., LC-USZ62-125801)

> In one corner of the back yard adjoining the bazaar was the Japanese horticultural display. Young bamboo, flowers and stunted trees and shrubbery were exhibited. In a box of blue porcelain, with white raised imitations of beets, carrots, etc., on the outer surface and having porcelain supports of the size, shape and color of turnips, was a stunted cedar tree sixty years old and not more than thirty-two inches in height. The spread of its branches was four and a half feet in the widest part. The trunk was eight inches in diameter. The principal blooming plant shown was the tiger lily (*Lilium auratum*).[23]

Horticultural Hall and Gardens

Situated high atop a hill presiding over Fountain Avenue, Horticultural Hall epitomized floral achievement. Touted as the largest conservatory in the world, Horticultural Hall, almost 75,000 square feet and nearly 70 feet tall, attracted professional and amateur gardeners alike. The smallest of the five main exhibition halls, with its Moorish arches and colorful tiled mosaics, it was perhaps the most highly ornamented.

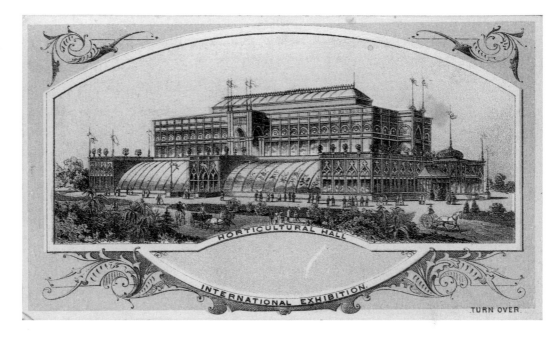

Inside, nurserymen, florists, and novice landscape designers exhibited a variety of tropical plants, garden equipment, and garden plans. In dramatic fashion, the Centennial introduced the general public to the notion of landscape design, as exemplified by the grounds surrounding Horticultural Hall and inside the building itself. The New York landscape designer Jacob Weidenmann displayed topographical and drainage maps that, according to the judges' report, were "very complete in engineering details, and the drawings carefully executed and neatly finished."[24] Philadelphian Charles H. Miller also displayed working plans and a planting map for laying out the grounds of a country residence. Examples of tasteful garden ornament inspired visitors with aquaria, flower stands, and ferneries from companies such as Racine Hardware Manufacturing of Wisconsin. Various floral handcrafts were displayed including waxwork models of fruit, preserved flowers, and herbaria.

Plants, of course, took center stage in four large brick-edged beds or in stand-alone containers in the main conservatory. Eleven countries exhibited indoors, with the United States, as might be expected, sponsoring the most attractions.[25] Tropical plants comprised most of the displays. Favored by the burgeoning Victorian middle class, tropical plants signified exotic travel and the wealth needed to undertake it. Having a home conservatory indicated the leisure time available for a gardening hobby. Thomas Meehan opined, "[The Centennial's] collection of palms is perhaps one of the most valuable ever seen at any great exposition, and surprises those of our English friends who fancied Americans far behind in these tasteful luxuries."[26]

Australian tree ferns, contributed by the nurserymen Miller & Sievers of San Francisco, dominated the center of the house, although some critics observed that they had suffered much during transport.[27] Other exhibitors brought banana plants, camphor trees, carnivorous plants, guavas, mangoes, and other exotics. Foreign countries also participated in the indoor show, testifying to the improved abilities to transport plants across the open seas. Jules LaChume of Havana, Cuba, displayed a large collection of century plants, orchids, and cacti. B. S. Williams of England brought rare hothouse plants that, while necessarily small due to transport issues, demonstrated differences in European and U.S. horticultural techniques.

Exhibitors may have quibbled about Horticulture Hall's amenities or the depth of the plant collections, but most visitors were charmed. As the contemporary author J. S. Ingram observed:

> Perhaps the gem of the whole of the big buildings as far as decoration is concerned, was the Horticultural Hall. The appearance of the exterior is very attractive, but the interior is a marvelously beautiful triumph of decorative art. The color charms without dazzling the eye, and when the building was filled with shrubs and flowers, a perfectly enchanting coup d'oeil greeted the visitor . . . Even the cultivated taste of skilled Paris artisans who visited the Exhibition was impressed with the beauty of the scene around Horticultural Hall—first, by the beautiful design of the building itself, and next with the exquisite arrangement and utilization of the landscape around it.[28]

Unlike later expositions where flower features decorated the entire landscape, only the immediate environs around the 1876 Horticultural Hall exhibited major concentrations of plantings. The report of the U.S. Centennial Commission explained: "It was early determined to make the out-door features of the Horticultural Department more extended and elaborate than had been attempted at any previous International Exhibition; and this was both difficult and uncertain of success. The ground subsequently

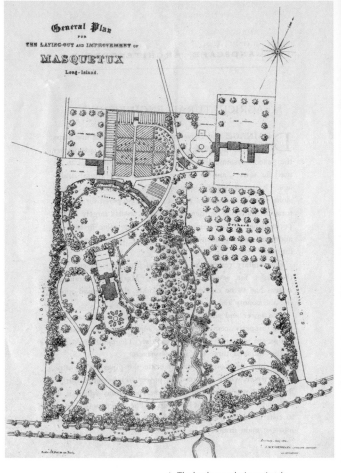

▲ The landscape designer Jacob Weidenmann exhibited a plan for the Long Island estate Masquetux showing a mix of traditional flower beds and a more refined naturalistic style. (Author's collection)

occupied by the gardens was in a rough and entirely uncultivated condition, and it seemed doubtful whether there was time to produce satisfactory results."[29] Despite a late start, the grounds near Horticultural Hall resembled a quilt appliquéd with intricately scrolled and curved designs. Intensively planted arabesques and circles of colorful blooms were assigned to exhibiting nurserymen, while unclaimed sections were landscaped by horticulture chief Charles Miller and his crew.

The eastern "backyard" of Horticultural Hall afforded a dramatic prospect on the Schuylkill River and beyond. A large, tiered fountain displayed by J. L. Mott Ironworks anchored the east garden, encircled by small shrubs, and a ring of flower-filled stars cut into the lawn. Foreign exhibits were featured as well, including with the Dutch nurserymen Krelage & Son's bed of five hundred gladioli (*G. Brenchleyensis*) which, according to George Thurber, was "brilliant" and afforded the only example of massing with bulbs of a single kind. South of Mott's fountain, France's exhibitors showed semicircular beds of tulips and, later in the season, gladioli. The Philadelphia nursery-

man Thomas Meehan pronounced this exhibit of Charles and Eugene Verdier of Paris "undoubtedly the finest thing of the kind ever seen in this country."[30]

One of the first displays of U.S. native plants was presented, ironically, by foreigners. North of Mott's fountain, a half circle of lawn was planted by Krelage & Son with masses of butterfly milkweed (*Asclepias tuberosa*). George Thurber noted that while this U.S. native plant with brilliant orange flowers should have succeeded, it was in fact a "complete failure," due perhaps to improper planting.[31] Thomas Meehan disagreed, noting that Krelage's native butterfly weed "shamed Americans" and that "thousands who saw it no doubt suppose it is from China or Japan, or some other far-away place, and no doubt orders will flow to Holland for the roots."[32]

Directly in front of Horticultural Hall, the most extensive and popular floral displays offered visitors many design ideas. Bordering the long, sunken garden that ran due west from the hall down Fountain Avenue, sinuous walking paths wound around display beds designed by some of the world's leading nurserymen. Closest to the hall

◄ The interior of Horticultural Hall featured chandeliers and Miss Foley's Fountain in the center of two transecting aisles. (Author's collection)

▲ Looking east from Horticultural Hall, a formal garden extended almost to the Schuylkill River. Note the star-shaped geometric beds of annuals, and the tiered fountain by J. L. Mott Ironworks, a typically elaborate Victorian ornamentation. (Author's collection)

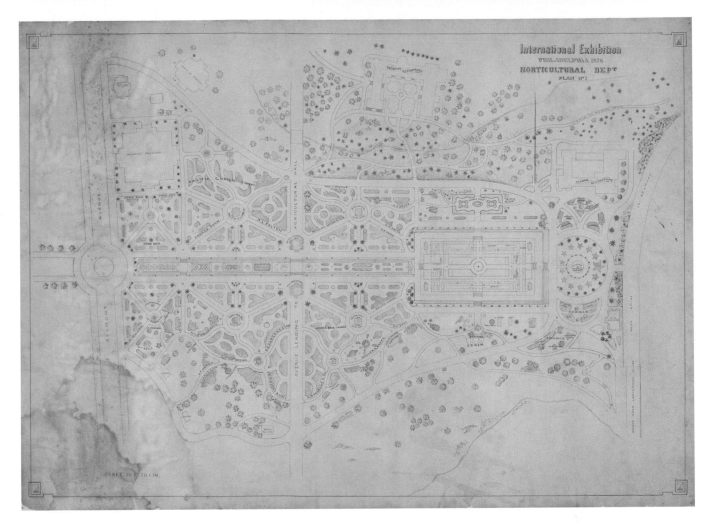

International Exhibition
PHILADELPHIA 1876
HORTICULTURAL DEPT
PLAN Nº 1

SCALE 50 FT TO 1 IN.

▲ This drawing shows the approximate locations of the planting beds assigned to various U.S. and foreign exhibitors. Unclaimed beds were filled in through the Bureau of Horticulture. (Courtesy of Fairmount Park Historic Resource Archive, Image AS-50)

itself were the gardens of the Philadelphians Henry A. Dreer, Miller & Hayes, and Robert Buist. Miller & Hayes (of which Horticulture Bureau chief Charles Miller was co-owner) offered an exhibit intended to "illustrate arrangement and taste in landscape gardening."[33] The oblong tract featured clumps of rare evergreens at either end. These shrubs bracketed a raised bed planted in concentric circles beginning with a center of devil's walking stick (*Aralia spinosa*),[34] surrounded by cannas, then circles of pampas grass and variegated giant reed (*Arundo donax*), bloodleaf (*Irisine herbstii*), and finally, after a few feet of grass, an edging of Dusty Miller (*Centaurea gymnocarpa*) on plane with ground level. Dreer's garden included an early display of named hyacinths, verbenas, petunias, and his signature gladioli.

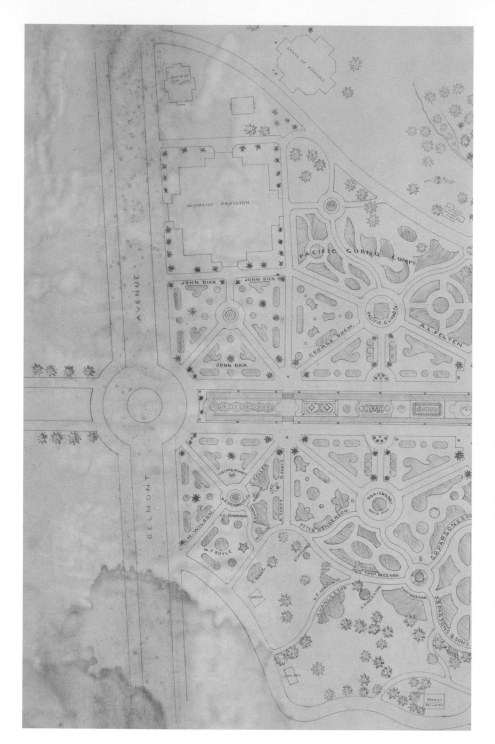

◀ This detail of the preceding illustration shows the plantings of annuals, which reigned in the horticultural gardens. Philadelphian John Dick displayed about 130 pelargonium varieties, along with *Euonymus radicans variegate, Salvia coccinea, Plumbago capensis,* and *Alternathera.* The Pennsylvanian C. H. Wilson exhibited a circle of cannas, scarlet geraniums, coleus 'Queen Victoria,' silver artemisia, and a ring of *Alternathera versicolor.*

The long, sunken parterre leading from Horticultural Hall became the Centennial's iconic floral feature, reproduced on countless postcards and other memorabilia. This low garden enabled visitors to best see the patterns and shapes of the beds from the raised walkways. Thomas Meehan noted: "Usually the forms of flower beds amount to nothing. Their real outlines can be seen on a piece of paper, but not on the grounds . . . but here the beds can be looked down on from considerable elevations, and the harmonies of color and form [can] be seen and appreciated."[35] Thurber observed that "the largest and most elaborate bed upon the grounds was a design in chain-work at the end of the parterre nearest Belmont Avenue. The chain-lines were planted in golden feather [feverfew] and centaurea, with [yellow dwarf nasturtium] (*Achyranthes lindeni*) margins; the open spaces of the links were filled with vinca rosea and petunieas [sic], with a coleus centre in each; the chain was surrounded by a parallelogram of achyranthes, with grass between this and the chain."[36]

The outdoor grounds featured garden ornament as well as plants. Exhibitors such as M. Walker and Son sponsored charming follies in the center "rotaries" of the main beds. In the northeast quadrant, Walker showcased displays of wirework, from hoop edging to a gazebo. On the south side of the parterre, O'Brian & Brothers built rustic houses in two circles, and a matching gate in a third. Siebrecht exhibited some unfortunate rockwork, which both Meehan and Thurber found inappropriate. "In many localities artificial rock-work may be appropriately introduced, but it is entirely out of place in a formal garden," Thurber sniffed. "Its first requisite is that it shall be natural; a stone-heap is not rock-work."[37] Nevertheless, he noted that Siebrecht's work was fine, if ill-placed.

North of Horticultural Hall, the "Flower Tent," a large, canvas-covered temporary structure, housed shows of seasonal flowers. The most significant show was the May display of rhododendrons by the London nurseryman Anthony Waterer. This well-known horticulturist brought from overseas an incredible 1,500 rhododendrons representing about eighty varieties. Thomas Meehan, who dedicated almost two pages to the exhibit in his *Gardener's Monthly,* declared, "We think it safe to say that nothing ever exhibited in a floral way in the United States attracted so much attention or received such unqualified admiration."[38] Yet, for all the success of the rhododendron show, perhaps due to inadequate planning and the rigors of shipping fresh flowers, no other major flower exhibition was mounted.[39]

▲ Looking toward Horticultural Hall, the ghostly images of M. Walker & Son Wireworks, including gazebo, fencing, and arch, are visible. (Author's collection)

The Pomology Department, which displayed fresh fruits and vegetables, was much more impressive in terms of seasonal displays. The "foundling" department of pomology, as Meehan dubbed it, was adrift until adopted by the Agriculture Department and its bureau chief, Burnet Landreth. The Centennial Commission then hastily built a temporary 36,000-square-foot exhibition space next to Agricultural Hall to house pomological exhibits.

Perhaps due to Landreth's influence with his peers, or perhaps reflecting the relative portability of produce over fresh flowers, the number of pomology exhibits far exceeded those of horticulture. Evaluations of pomology exhibits appeared in *Gardener's Monthly.* In late May and June, in regular exhibition, fairgoers viewed lemons from Italy, onions from Bermuda, two hundred varieties of potatoes from Bliss & Son of New York, roots for feeding cattle from Landreth and Sons, and "keeping apples" (although very late in the season) from fruit cellars of Michigan and Iowa. Visitors encountered such heretofore unknown tropical fruits as "cocoa nuts" from Jamaica, which, Meehan explained, were "boiled and used as a food for infants, also as a mild form of domestic medicine."

In all, fifteen thousand plates of fresh fruit were exhibited in the pomological section. Most of the individual entries came from nurserymen in the nearby region— New Jersey, Pennsylvania, New York, and Massachusetts.

Reviews and Legacies

While Centennial guidebooks and the popular press were enthusiastic in their praise for the exhibition grounds, some horticultural publications were less impressed. In many cases, the huge exhibition halls overshadowed immature and inappropriate plantings. Victorian carpet bedding, while a good solution for obtaining instant effects, was not scaled for the monumental structures. Probably the most satisfying landscapes were those that occurred naturally, remnants of the existing forests and ravines of Fairmount Park. Structurally, the landscape plan was effective—the major arterial roads, elegant architectural fountains, and man-made lakes—but the plantings seemed a disjointed afterthought, as might be expected of a landscape installed piecemeal without any organizing principles.

Though generally positive, Thomas Meehan's reports on the fair nonetheless concluded: "It is no secret that the [overall Centennial] plan as originally drawn out and partially acted on almost ignored Agriculture and Horticulture. At the eleventh, or more properly, near the twelfth hour, the subject was taken up. Horticulture had an early recognition from Philadelphians, and the great conservatory became a part of the original plan; but the commission never seemed to know what to do with it, and instead of its having any bearing on the great central idea of the exposition—the giving of the people an idea of how horticulture has progressed in America during the last century—it became a mere deposit for a few palms and economic plants."[40]

Most visitors, including professionals, enjoyed the display surrounding Horticulture Hall, and allowances were made for the tight time frames and unbearable weather. Centennial judge George Thurber generously noted, "It is seldom that plants are subjected to so severe a test as they were by the intense heats and long drouths of the summer of 1876; and the wonder is not that some beds failed, but that any maintained even a tolerable appearance."[41]

The impact of the Centennial's horticultural and landscape efforts on U.S. gardens was considerable. The plants themselves, more than 1,800 species from around the world,[42] and the thousands of pomological exhibits provided visitors a firsthand look at new products of the soil. Observant visitors could glean some rudimentary lessons in landscape gardening, from plans to executed designs. The carpet bedding as show-

cased in the Centennial's main sunken garden attracted a good deal of attention that probably contributed to the American public's growing enthusiasm for it. As the Centennial Commission report concluded, "Perhaps the very simplicity of arrangement added to the educational value; because it demonstrated that with comparatively few and easily-obtained plants very beautiful floral effects may be produced."[43]

The Centennial left a permanent legacy in Philadelphia's Fairmount Park. As intended from the outset, Horticultural Hall and Memorial Hall remained for public use. Thanks to Philadelphians' dedication to horticulture, Horticultural Hall became a centerpiece of culture and redevelopment activity, a symbol of fine gardening for the era. The hall itself, until it was razed following hurricane damage in the 1950s, became the host site for many flower shows and events. Today's Horticulture Center was built in 1976 on the site of the original structure. The modern building is filled with an excellent collection of plant specimens and retains a long view west down an allée of trees and gardens. Miss Foley's Fountain remains intact in an honored alcove in the rebuilt conservatory. The landscaping near the hall changed with the times—a long reflecting pool replaced Charles Miller's sunken gardens, and once spindly trees gradually acquired their mature stateliness. Nearby, the 20-acre Centennial Arboretum, dating to 1876, includes trees of Asian, European, and North American origin.

Spurred on by the Centennial horticultural fever, trees were purchased for other Philadelphian public parks and city squares, and for planting the grounds of "institutions of learning and charity." Eli K. Price, chairman of the Committee on the Michaux Fund of the American Philosophical Society, wrote, "Within the Park the Landscape Gardener will exert his skill to blend in beauty the self-sown forests there growing, with artistic planting, as the formation of new avenues and fresh grading will demand; where the new trees will be of kinds not native to our environs, and show in contrast the hand of Art; but at the same time greatly add to the variety and novelty of the trees and plants; so that the trees of the Park shall become a great Arboretum, and its flower beds become Botanic Gardens."[44]

Fairmount Park today is a grand living tribute to America's first great international exposition. A lovely Japanese garden and teahouse, much larger than the original Japanese Bazaar, remind visitors of a country that so staunchly supported America's first fair. The park retains several other structures from the exposition. The Ohio Building remains, as do two brick comfort stations near the old Horticultural Hall. Memorial Hall still stands as a tribute to its architect and to the American citizens who endorsed culture and beauty. The Catholic Total Abstinence (C.T.A.) Fountain continues to offer its waters to cool the breeze and refresh the spirit. Michaux Grove endures, too, as an arboretum of majestic and mature trees.

In addition to the physical remnants in Fairmount Park, the Centennial left a permanent mark on garden fashion in the United States. Warren Manning observed: "The general use of hardy rhododendrons, and the introduction of bedding-out designs in tender plants were direct outgrowths of this exposition. The introduction of rhododendrons was of real, permanent value. The use of bedding-out plants developed into a craze almost as bad as the tulip mania of the Dutch, and its more ardent devotees devised such astonishingly curious and ludicrous conceits that discredit was cast upon such a use of plants."[45] The carpet bedding fashion, derided by many landscape architects, would nevertheless continue to flourish in front yard gardens and U.S. world's fairs for decades to come.

Landscape Lessons from the 1876 Centennial Exhibition

As the first major world's fair in the United States, the 1876 Centennial set a precedent for the creation of landscapes for all future world's fairs. As its chief designer, Schwarzmann had faced many new questions: How many visitors would come, and how should the landscape accommodate the crowds? How should the land parcels be

PHILADELPHIA LAWN MOWERS
AT HORTICULTURAL
HALL.

apportioned among exhibitors? How could a pleasing landscape be wrought in a short time frame? What was the definition of a public park, and how should buildings be placed therein?

In his 1902 retrospective essay "Influence of American Expositions on Outdoor Arts," Warren Manning noted:

> We must not overlook, however, the Centennial at Philadelphia in 1876, and its very marked influence upon the outdoor arts. Here the design of buildings and grounds was governed very largely by the engineer. The architectural profession did not then have the influence which it has now, and landscape design was represented by only a few able men, whose public work had been confined almost wholly to public parks, the design of which had not at that time developed sufficiently in beauty for people to realize that the profession would eventually stand at the head of the arts of design.[46]

In 1876, although Frederick Law Olmsted and Andrew Jackson Downing had achieved great name recognition in the United States through writings and books, most designed landscapes were limited to estates of the wealthy. Many members of the general public were introduced to the concept of landscape design at the Centennial through the grounds displays and presentation plans by well-known landscape designers. The roles of engineer, landscape architect, florist, and gardener received scrutiny and discussion as Herman Schwarzmann assumed many responsibilities, yet coordinated with others in related disciplines.

Garden designs displayed by Schwarzmann and Centennial exhibitors reflected current trends in bedding out, and also introduced new styles such as Japanese gardening. The Centennial horticultural grounds brought the art of carpet bedding to the imaginations of the masses, if not to their actual homesteads. Urban public parks, many in the developmental stages throughout the country, would adopt the style that then was copied in surrounding front yards across major cities.

A well-manicured lawn is a necessary ingredient to carpet bedding. The smooth greenswards around Horticulture Hall became a symbol of the ideal American lawn, and ads for the Philadelphia lawn mower kept the Centennial gardens in the public eye. The post-Centennial lawns and carpet bedding that were frequently espoused in popular garden periodicals, however, best suited the practicalities of public parks and the estates of the landed wealthy. Throughout the next decades, as evidenced in later world's fairs, debate continued over the aesthetics and appropriateness of the style.

The Centennial Japanese gardens gave many Americans their first look at what would become an enduringly popular style.[47] In the late 1850s, U.S. Navy Commodore Matthew Perry opened trade relations with Japan. Japanese plants then became available to Americans, but typically only through private or institutional collections. After the Centennial, in 1878, H. H. Berger of New York and San Francisco became the first seed catalogue business specializing in Japanese plants.[48] In 1883, a writer for the popular *Vick's Illustrated Monthly* described a Japanese catalogue as a curiosity with two hundred maple species printed "on paper of the peculiar texture we are acquainted with coming from that country and China."[49]

The pragmatic *Prairie Farmer* magazine reprinted a *Scribner's* article noting the "quaint pygmies of trees" at the 1876 Japanese Building, commenting, "We doubt if gardeners of the West will emulate them [Japanese gardeners] in their mimicry of nature; but they may well emulate their pains-taking skill which makes such small successes possible."[50] The author suggested that miniature gardens may be appropriate for Japan, where "a few square rods may be all at command," but were unsuited for the vast open lands in America. A scant three years later, *Scribner's* had found a good use for Japanese gardens—in the smaller city lots of America. It was suggested, however, that if Chinese or Japanese plants were used, they should be "American grown and employed in American fashion."[51] Presumably this meant selecting naturally dwarf specimens for which Japanese pruning techniques would be unnecessary. Later expositions would intensify the interest in Japanese gardens and stimulate further experimentation in the style among American gardeners.

Like Japanese gardens, the showy flower displays in Horticultural Hall also captured public imagination and spurred interest in new plants. Prior to the Anthony Waterer display of rhododendrons, the palette of this plant had been limited largely to a few hybrids of native species. Rhododendron shows had been sponsored by U.S. horticultural societies before the Centennial, but most were hybrids developed by English nurserymen from the native American *Rhododendron catawbiense.* In 1875, the botanist Hugh Fraser published the *Handy Book of Ornamental Conifers of Rhododendrons and Other American Flowering Shrubs Suitable for the Climate and Soils of Britain.* Its title highlights the one-way traffic in hybridization between the two countries. Even as British plant collectors gathered American plants for hybridization, Americans bought back the modified plants as great novelties.

As Thomas Meehan observed, native plants received very little attention at the Centennial, save for the small planting of butterfly weed previously mentioned. Americans had not yet recognized the value of their indigenous plants, preferring foreign species from Europe or tropicals from South America. The former often reminded newly settled immigrants of home or were used as familiar plant stock by European-trained gardeners who tended American gardens. Future expositions would gradually expand the attention to native plants. Meehan himself may have helped stimulate the interest with his *Native Flowers and Ferns of the United States in Their Botanical, Horticultural, and Popular Aspects,* written two years after the Centennial.

By starting a tradition of conventions for allied horticultural trades, the Centennial paved the way for new methods of educating the public about plants. World's fairs were natural gathering places, and many societies and symposia piggybacked on the exposition fanfare. At the Centennial, the American Pomology Association hosted their national fall meeting. A newly formed conservation group, the American Forestry Association, also convened at the fair at about the same time. Many individuals belonged to both groups and were therefore doubly motivated to come to the fair. Reports of the meetings were disseminated among leading periodicals of the day.

The very display of outdoor, labeled plants at a U.S. exhibition was novel. When Thomas Meehan himself first arrived as a visitor to the horticultural grounds, security guards forbade him to examine the plants, thinking that they were intended to be appreciated from afar rather than studied closely. Meehan addressed a letter to Centennial director-general Alfred T. Goshorn, "pointing out that the exhibitors in the open ground planted *their allotments* for people to examine the varieties, and not as mere masses of flowers and foliage for the landscape adornment of the Centennial grounds."[52]

Outdoor plant displays, already well established in Europe, were just coming into vogue in the United States. Permanent tree planting at Boston's Arnold Arboretum—

which was founded in 1872 and was the oldest arboretum in North America open to the public—did not begin until 1885. Planning was initiated for many arboreta and botanic gardens in the United States during the Centennial and thereafter,[53] and while many disparate elements contributed to the developing character of U.S. public gardens, including European trends and the advancement of U.S. horticultural societies, the Centennial publicity and critical analysis were certainly among these.[54]

Along with the development of public arboreta, planning for many of the nation's major urban parks was well under way during the Centennial. This was the era of the great pleasure parks, wherein cities purchased large tracts of land and hired designers such as Olmsted to create oases of nature in the midst of encroaching industrialization. Spurred on by notions of healthy country living, proponents of the pleasure ground rejected the idea of man-made structures in the parks that would detract from the idealized images of nature. Museums, comfort stations, commercial ventures, restaurants, and entertainments that drew loud crowds were seen as intrusions by purists.[55] With its many sculptures, fountains, and concessionaires, the Centennial clearly defied this notion, while avoiding criticism by characterizing the structures as "temporary." The erection of Memorial Hall and Horticultural Hall as permanent structures could be viewed as an assault on the pleasure park ideal by means of the Trojan horse of a temporary exposition. Future exposition management teams, investors, and public reaction forced similar issues in future exposition cities.

Among other urban planning concerns addressed by the Centennial were transportation issues. By planning the fairgrounds around railroad connections, the Centennial established a long-lasting alliance between railroads and expositions. In many future U.S. expositions, horticultural and agricultural produce would be organized and categorized according to the railroads sponsoring each growing region. Railroads became invaluable to expositions in the transport of perishable fruit and flowers, as related technologies such as refrigeration and packaging continued to improve.

Transportation also affected technological achievements in landscape construction. Techniques for tree-moving at the Centennial may have surpassed those shown at European fairs. According to Meehan: "In the exhibitions of the Old World the plants were removed just as ordinary nursery trees are—with the usual result—a deplorable appearance the whole summer after. But our American exhibitors have improved on this. Many of them have had their trees growing in tubs and pots for a whole year ahead, and now that they are set out, they are leafing out and blooming as if they were 'to the manor' as well as to the 'manner' born."[56] Tree transplantation techniques would continue to evolve at U.S. world's fairs, including efforts at the next major exposition in New Orleans, where trees from Mexico were planted.

2

World's Industrial and Cotton
Centennial Exposition

One year after the Centennial, U.S. federal troops withdrew from the southern states
in a formal end to Reconstruction. It would be many years, however, before the South's
agrarian-based economy recovered. Mark Twain dubbed this period the Gilded Age
in his book of the same name, and the term came to be associated with an era of rapid
economic growth fused with political corruption and greed.

Much of this nationwide growth was driven by fortunes made in the railroad industry: more than 7,000 miles of track were laid each year in the 1880s.[1] In 1883, new
routes opened such as the Atchison, Topeka & Santa Fe running between Kansas
and New Mexico, and the Southern Pacific Railroad between New Orleans and Los
Angeles. Railroads, largely owned by northerners, helped rebuild commerce with the
South by connecting cities across the nation and with shipping ports in Latin America.

New Orleans, an important port and rail hub, figured prominently in this transformation. Serving as the capital of Louisiana from the end of the Civil War to 1880, the

city attracted legitimate investors and carpetbaggers alike. An exposition, fair boosters hoped, would catalyze development in New Orleans and showcase the progress of the South, as well as its potential to link to new Latin American markets. As a *Century Illustrated* magazine contributor observed, "The Exposition sprang from the conviction that the future growth of New Orleans depends on securing a larger share of the trade of Latin America."[2] Exhibitors from Mexico and other Central and South American countries participated in large numbers. What started as the "Cotton Centennial" became the World's Industrial and Cotton Centennial Exposition to reflect not only the international focus of the fair but also the South's evolution away from an agrarian economy and toward an industrial one.

Exposition visitors would not have seen many manicured public green spaces in New Orleans. The city had but few public parks in the postbellum era: Historic Jackson Square, near the French Quarter, and City Park, a former plantation bequeathed to the city in the 1850s, were the major public parks.

The exposition landscape, while falling short in the eyes of some contemporary reviewers, would provide opportunities for fairgoers to experience gardens and plants from other countries, particularly Mexico. These exhibits helped bolster the idea of the South, and New Orleans in particular, as a national and international hub for com-

merce. Perhaps even more successfully, the exposition made a substantial contribution
to the city's green space. The World's Industrial and Cotton Centennial Exposition led
to the development of the world-class Audubon Park, which ultimately rose from the
site of the old fairgrounds.

Creating the Fairgrounds

The World's Industrial and Cotton Centennial Exposition not only marked the one-
hundredth anniversary of America's first cotton export, but also highlighted the New
South's duality in industrial potential as well as its agrarian roots. As the first U.S. exposition held during the winter months, from December 1884 through May 1885, the
New Orleans Fair tempted cold-weary northerners with lush subtropical blooms. Yet,
hastily assembled and poorly financed, the fair struggled from its rain-soaked opening
days to its barely attended conclusion.

Although a financial disappointment, the fair offered significant horticultural
milestones. The Cotton Exposition was the second of only three American world's
fairs to endow its host city with a permanent horticulture hall.[3] It also established the
groundwork for today's Audubon Park, landscaped postfair by the Olmsted firm. The
exposition grounds, once a sugarcane plantation, then by turns a Confederate and

Union army camp, illustrated the South's trajectory in microcosm and recast its place in America's horticultural history.

In 1871, the City of New Orleans purchased the land that would ultimately become the exposition site. After a decade of inattention, and after several other potential sites were eliminated, a city ordinance in 1883 granted use of the park to the Exposition Corporation from 1883 to 1885, with the understanding that a "suitable building in the grounds of Upper City Park for use as a Horticultural Hall" would be built.[4]

The 249 acres earmarked for the exposition, west and slightly south of the Vieux Carré on the bend of the Mississippi, were essentially wilderness. Bounded on the north by St. Charles Avenue and on the south by a busy wharf and levee, the site suffered from marshy conditions. One account called the unimproved park a "combination of cattle pasture and frog-pond,"[5] and said of the ultimate transformation that "where melancholy herds browsed on the waving grasses now serpentine paths meander off beside artificial lakes and beneath live oaks with all the geometrical accuracy of surveyors' skill."[6] Within an almost impossibly restrictive time frame—barely a year—the grounds were laid out and planted. Nevertheless, while fair boosters likened the landscape to a Shangri-la, many newspapers were critical in the opening months, noting that the sparse plantings and hastily planted cactus afforded only bleak views.[7]

Unlike the 1876 Centennial, no single name appears prominently linked with the overall ground plan. Most likely the plan was driven by the exposition's engineers and its supervising architect, the Swedish immigrant G. M. Torgerson (1840–1902). Like Schwarzmann, Torgerson designed most of the exposition buildings, but it appears he did not have unilateral design authority; rather, he bowed frequently to committee demands. Working with Torgerson to meet the punishing deadlines were Samuel H. Gilman, a New Orleans inventor and engineer, and Frederick N. Ogden, the exposition's chief superintendent and a New Orleans merchant. Like many of New Orleans's leaders of the era, the latter two men had been officers in the Confederate army.[8] Accordingly, the design of the grounds appeared to be more reflective of military expediency and engineering precision than of aesthetic considerations.

Some of New Orleans's community of florists and nurserymen lent their expertise in preparing exhibits for Horticulture Hall, while others worked on the grounds. Julius Fonta, who owned a greenhouse and business on St. Charles Avenue, personally planted what would come to be known as the exposition's Magnolia Avenue with its namesake trees. But perhaps most influential in determining the plantings for the fairgrounds were officers and members of the Mississippi Valley Horticultural Society.

Included among the society's members were nurserymen, florists, seedsmen, wholesalers, academics, and other horticultural leaders from around the United States. In an era in which horticultural societies abounded as the primary networking venue for those in the trade, the Mississippi Valley Horticultural Society commanded a major following. Its roster of officers boasted vice presidents hailing from twenty-four of the thirty-eight states then making up the Union. More than seventy-five regular correspondents reported to the society, including high-profile professionals such as the pomologist Robert Manning of Salem, Massachusetts; nurserymen James Vick and Patrick Barry of Rochester, New York; nurseryman Charles Downing of Newburg, New York; and U.S. entomologist C. V. Riley of Washington, D.C. Because it was so inclusive, the society renamed itself the American Horticultural Society at its annual meeting, which was held at the exposition in February 1885.[9]

Exposition management placed the control and care of the Horticultural Department entirely under the auspices of the Mississippi Valley Horticultural Society.[10] Its remit extended not only to the displays within Horticultural Hall, but also to the ornamentation of the grounds. The society eagerly accepted the challenge: as society president Parker Earle wrote, "Thus it will be seen that an Industrial Fair Association has at last been found, able and willing to recognize the importance of Horticulture and the great fruit interests of this country and the world; and to provide for their exhibition in the most liberal spirit as one of the most important and attractive departments of a World's Exposition."[11]

Parker Earle was appointed chief of the exposition's Department of Horticulture; W. H. Ragan, the society's secretary, became the superintendent of the Division of Pomology; and society members P. J. Berkmans and S. M. Tracy were named, respectively, the Horticulture Department's commissioner of foreign exhibits, and the superintendent of the Division of Plants and Trees. While Tracy concentrated mostly on the interior exhibits, Earle supervised many of the outdoor plantings. Earle was quick to caution against excessively high expectations, noting in an October 1884 interview: "I fear that many people may expect impossible things regarding the park improvement. The public must remember that we are primarily making an exhibition for instruction and education, rather than for simple display of beauty. We do not forget the claims of beauty, and we shall study landscape effects so far as possible in all of our planting . . . I particularly desire that the people shall remember that it takes years of time, as well as large expenditures of money, to create a great park covering hundreds of acres of ground. Therefore, do not expect too much. Two months ago, when we began our park improvement, we had but a wilderness of weeds."[12]

The timetable for completing building construction seemed impossibly tight, and grounds improvement necessarily suffered. Construction of Horticultural Hall itself was not completed until September 1884, and its heating apparatus was not functional until November. That same month, the newly excavated lakes were filled with water, and walks were still being graded to the hall from the wharf—a disturbance that surely affected placement of trees and gardens.[13] As Earle had predicted, the plantings had not had a season of growth in situ and consequently appeared, with a few exceptions, temporary at best.

The fairgrounds were nearly level, and workers cut and graded the land to fill existing swamps and create artificial lakes. The Main Building, raised slightly on terraced land, dominated the grounds. Said to be the largest building ever erected, the rectangular behemoth stretched from north to south 1,378 feet and 905 feet from east to west.[14] Horticulture Hall, the Factories and Mills Building, and the Mexican Buildings occupied the southern end of the exposition site. Other minor buildings and concession stands were scattered throughout. All major buildings faced east, toward the city of New Orleans and the main land-based entrances. Noticeably missing from the fair was an agricultural hall. Although an earlier plan showed such a building and surrounding gardens,[15] time and cost constraints seem to have intervened, and agricultural exhibits instead were housed in a decentralized fashion with individual state displays.

Water features formed an integral component of the grounds, and required advanced pumping mechanisms. Both functional and attractive, the main artificial lakes were carved from the flat earth to fill the northerly swamp and other low-lying areas, and a long canal connected the north end of the Main Building to a nearby swampy area to accommodate rainfall drainage.[16] The exposition's official visitors' map highlighted an 80-foot-high "Grand Fountain," on an island in the center of the largest lake just northeast of the Main Building. Smaller fountains were scattered among other, lesser lakes and ponds. Four miles of crushed-shell or asphalt walkways and a 3-mile electric railroad—said to be the longest in the United States—circled the fair site, helping visitors navigate the grounds.[17] Several bridges crossed lakes and streams to aid circulation patterns and provide picturesque effect.

While piecemeal plantings adorned isolated areas in the overall grounds, the beds immediately surrounding Horticultural Hall were the most intensively planted with flowers and shrubs. By April 1885, most of the grounds had been planted, albeit reflecting Parker Earle's emphasis on educational display over landscape effect. According to an enthusiastic account in the *New Orleans Times-Democrat,* the display extended north and west from Horticultural Hall to and including the Mexican Barracks, and north to the outer wall of the Main Building, all of which was graced with

⌃ Rustic bridges crossed man-made lakes that drained water from the swampy site. (Author's collection)

a luxuriant growth of soft Bermuda grass, inlaid with numerous beds of beautiful flowers and studded with the grand old trees that are universally admired [presumably live oaks]. At the back of the hall [west], running clear to the out-skirts of the grounds, is a broad, shady avenue with numerous seats . . . On each side of the avenue but at some distance from it, is a pretty little lake, around which in the one case bloom hundreds of handsome rhododendra, and in the other a variety of Dutch bulbs and other charming flowers. Rose trees, huge and curious century plants, strange plants from the tropics, a large California garden, and an infinity of other objects combine to make this portion of the grounds one of exceeding attraction.[18]

➤ Although this exposition purported to showcase modern in-dustrialism, significant manual labor was needed to create the landscape. Trees were hauled by horse and wagon, and irrigation was done by hand. (*Harper's Weekly,* December 27, 1884; author's collection)

After Opening Day in December, laborers tackled the task of tree planting. The *Times-Democrat* reported on December 26 that "Prof. Tracy and Mr. Earle, with their large force of workmen, are taking advantage of the rainy weather to put out as rapidly as possible the large number of trees and shrubs that have been hauled in for some weeks."[19] Cedar trees surrounded the small lake between Horticulture Hall and the Art Gallery to the north.[20] Although the construction crew did not have to work around a winter schedule of snow and cold as did laborers for many northern fairs, work was accomplished primarily through sheer manual effort, with few mechanical laborsaving devices employed. Trees, for example, were transported by horse and cart, and watered by hand. Special arrangements had to be made for exceptionally large specimens. When three huge aloes, eight to nine thousand pounds apiece, arrived by steamship for the Mexican Garden, the ship's tackle "used for hoisting heavy weights, broke down under the extraordinary strain."[21]

Mexico sponsored many departments in the exposition, reflecting the emphasis New Orleans placed on trade from that country. The Mexican Garden was planted

MEXICAN PAGODA.

under the supervision of its own representative, and included a fountain 60 feet in circumference, a miniature "mountain" adorned with maguey (agave) and surrounded with flowers native to that region. Geometric circle and crescent shapes were planted with maguey, *Chamaedorea* palms, cactus, and ferns. A few American states also exhibited outdoors. In the southern part of exposition grounds, near the river, two orchards and a collection of four hundred ornamental and evergreen trees from the State Agricultural Collage at Columbia, Missouri, were exhibited. The State Horticulture Society of Nebraska also displayed examples of osage-orange as a hedging material on the plains, as well as Russian mulberry and catalpa.[22]

While these gardens received acclaim, the most celebrated aspects of the landscaping were the existing groves of live oaks. These arboreal curiosities of the South garnered much excitement, particularly among northerners who had never seen such broad-spreading trees draped with Spanish moss. A grove of live oaks was preserved near Horticultural Hall during construction, and another existing allée was incorporated into the avenue leading from the hall to the Main Building. The *Times-Democrat* acknowledged the awe-inspiring power of the oaks in describing the reaction of a "prominent horticulturist of New Jersey" who, upon gazing from Horticulture Hall

The allée of live oaks, a preexposition landscape feature, drew the most admiration from visitors. (Author's collection)

down the 90-foot avenue of trees, said, "This sight alone repays a Northern man for his visit to the Exposition."[23]

Inside Horticulture Hall—"A Fairy Palace"

The exposition's official *Visitors' Guide* declared Horticulture Hall, 600 feet long by 194 feet at its widest point, the largest conservatory in the world.[24] At the center of the hall's long glass wings was one of its most distinguishing features; a majestic glass tower rising to a height of nearly 90 feet. Beneath the tower, in the central atrium, a magnificent fountain delighted visitors. In its circular basin, the sprays from seventy-five evenly spaced water jets created a shimmering half globe around the central water jet whose vertical spray nearly reached the top of the tower. The fountain was surrounded by a variety of potted tropical plants and trees including date, coconut palm, and banana.

The hall was assembled using a new "puttyless glazing" system devised by Arthur Rendle of New York. Previously used in England, and patented there by Rendle's brothers, the system was said to admit 33 percent more light than conventional systems, which typically secured panes of glass to wood structures with putty.[25] The advantages of puttyless glazing were apparent to nurserymen and hobbyists alike. A scant two years after the fair, although the system had its detractors, *Gardener's Monthly* declared that "putty was of no consequence to builders as it is no longer used on the best work."[26]

Advances in lighting technology also enhanced the visitor's experience, according to the *Times-Democrat*. Nightly illumination of Horticultural Hall, outlined with hundreds of electric lights, called to mind a "fairy palace" or "iridescent iceberg," with "liquiescent luminosity not unlike that of a silver fire."[27] Evening fireworks only enhanced the spectacle.

Railroad travel proved to be an unreliable means of shipping large quantities of perishable items across country. Iowa's shipments were literally derailed. Its state exposition commissioner reported that "the plans of the Commission received a severe shock on December 1, 1884, by a railroad wreck occurring to the display then en route upon the B., C. R. & N. R'y." By this unfortunate accident "a large portion of the exhibit was totally destroyed, and much damaged beyond use grains, seeds, vegetables, and nearly every fragile article were ruined. The lateness in the season utterly precluded their re-production. They had been collected with especial reference to this display,

WORLD'S INDUSTRIAL & COTTON CENTENNIAL EXPOSITION AT NEW ORLEANS, LA.

DIMENSIONS, SIX HUNDRED BY ONE HUNDRED & NINETY FOUR FEET.   CENTRE ARRANGED TO SHOW 20,000 PLATES OF FRUIT.

HORTICULTURAL HALL.

▲ Fair boosters claimed Horticulture Hall, the exhibition's sole permanent structure, as the world's largest glass building. (Library of Congress Prints and Photographs Division, Washington, D.C., LC-DIG-pga-01657)

and were, in fact, the 'cream of the harvest.'"[28] With only two short weeks remaining before Opening Day, Iowa was hard-pressed to find suitable replacements for perishable displays.

The weather also conspired against exhibitors. Heavy rainfall just before Opening Day rendered many roads impassable, and railroad lines and even shipping lines were delayed. Unavoidably detained en route, the fruit and cut-flower shipments arrived either in poor condition or not at all for the grand opening on December 16, 1884. Parker Earle placed a notice in the local papers appealing urgently for help from New Orleans florists and nurserymen. "In view of the detention on the road of a quantity of fruits and flowers," Earle pleaded, "the Department of Horticulture in the World's Exposition respectfully invites the gardeners, florists, orchardists and citizens of New

Orleans and vicinity to make liberal contributions of flowers and fruits to decorate the tables in Horticultural Hall on the opening day . . . Bring them the offerings of your beautiful gardens, be they but one bouquet or one plate of oranges."[29]

The Mississippi Valley Horticultural Society vowed to provide a magnificent fruit display and, at least with regard to the numbers, achieved its objective. About twenty thousand plates of fruit were exhibited by twenty-three states and five foreign countries. Five 3,000-foot-long rows of tables were needed to showcase the fruit.[30] Awards for fruit displays acknowledged the extreme variation in growing conditions among exhibiting regions. Prizes for displays of pears, grapes, tropical fruits, and apples were awarded in February.

> A huge jet of water surrounded by arcs of smaller water sprays formed a focal point under the tower in Horticulture Hall. In the foreground, tables of fruit await judging. (Author's collection)

American exhibits were divided into three fruit districts—Northern, Southern, and Pacific—in which differences in regional culture requirements were again acknowledged. The Northern District, for example, offered awards for autumn and winter fruits, and for fruits "best adapted to severe winter climates."[31] The Southern District recognized "best plate from most ancient trees," and "best varieties for the extreme South." The Pacific Region granted premiums for the "best collection of the largest and handsomest apples" and "best collections" for the coastal climate, the mountain climate, and fruit varieties "grown in and adapted to the climate of the dry valleys."[32] By means of these narrowly defined categories, the exposition judges afforded U.S. regions equal footing in the competitions.

Although displays of citrus fruit were a novelty at northern expositions, they were numerous at the New Orleans fair, particularly among the exhibits from Florida and the Gulf Coast. In fact, the titles of awards were so granular that one wonders if everyone went home a winner. There was, for example, "best collection [of citrus fruits], not less than 20 varieties, grown in Florida," as well as "best collection, not less than 20 varieties grown on Gulf Coast, West of Florida."[33]

The most active foreign exhibitor, Mexico, sponsored indoor exhibits in the southwest corner of Horticultural Hall. These included specimens of agave, pineapple, alligator pear, India rubber tree, and tuna—the fruit of the prickly pear, or yucca—newly used for paper manufacture and pulque, a Mexican beverage. A hothouse near the side entrance showcased a large collection of Mexican orchids.[34] Adding to Mexico's displays, British Honduras sent a collection of orchids, and Guatemala offered twenty-four cases of coffee, cocoa, ginger, and flowering plants.[35]

On January 14, 1885, the Mississippi Valley Horticultural Society held its sixth annual meeting on the fairgrounds, the first time the society had ever met at a world's fair. Parker Earle gave the opening address, extolling the unique opportunities afforded by the fair to view fruits and forestry from different lands. Many of the lectures focused on basic cultural techniques (for example, "Pruning the Vine," "Fungoid Diseases of the Strawberry," "Cross-Fertilization of Our Popular Fruits," and "Preserving Fruits by Evaporation"). Others had a societal or cultural emphasis: "Growing Small Fruits as a Business for Women," "Who Will Own the Farms of the Mississippi Valley in the Next Generation?," "Some Hints toward Landscape Improvements of Country Homes," and "Market Value of Fruits and Vegetable."[36]

In addition to passing a resolution to rename themselves the American Horticultural Society, the group refuted persistent negative reports about the fair and issued a strong endorsement of the exposition: "*Whereas,* various rumors adverse to the best interests of said Exposition have been widely circulated throughout the country, much to the injury thereof; therefore, be it *Resolved* by the American Horticultural Society that the Exposition now in progress here is in all respects a grand one, worthy of the careful study of the American people, if not the people of the world."[37]

▲ This display of "parent and baby cactus," according to the stereoview title, was one of many curiosities on display. (Author's collection)

The End of a Fair and Start of Audubon Park

Despite the attempts to produce creditable fruit and flower shows, and despite the American Horticultural Society's important endorsement, the fair suffered ongoing losses. Many visitors eventually did arrive—more than 1 million. Yet even though the grounds, weather, and exhibits improved daily, and despite a late infusion of cash from

Congress in March 1885, the exposition was financially unable to survive. The World's Industrial and Cotton Centennial Exposition officially closed on June 1, 1885.

When all eleventh-hour efforts failed to elicit sufficient funds to sustain the fair, the fate of the exposition grounds precipitated considerable debate. Public sentiment favored continued park improvements, but complications around ownership issues and responsibility for the tract prevented quick resolution. By June 14, 1885, a charter had been created establishing the organization and mission for what was first called the New Exposition, then later renamed the North, Central, and South American Exposition, and, finally, the American Exposition. Within a month, the entire exposition property was sold at auction to this new entity for $175,000.[38] The intent of the organization, headed by the railroad magnate George Pullman (whose railroad empire naturally would benefit from exposition travel), was to reopen the fair in November 1885 and keep it open through March of the following year. There was much work to be done. Buildings and landscaping had suffered from two months of neglect, although trees planted for the original fair had taken root and were thriving. The second incarnation of the exposition posted lackluster attendance during its brief resurrection in 1885 and the early part of 1886, and subsequent improvements to the grounds were desultory. The park was renamed Audubon Park in 1886, and an Audubon Park Association was created through Louisiana state legislation in 1891 with an objective of improving the grounds. Funding constraints nonetheless continued to inhibit meaningful progress. The park, as described by the writer of one 1892 *New Orleans Daily Picayune* article, was a desolate place, featuring only a modest artichoke garden, some lonely live oaks, and a decrepit Horticulture Hall. The park's grand entrance gate was "about as handsome and picturesque as an inspired toadstool," and the remaining live oaks stood "like two lonely sentinels left over from a forest that has been cut down and turned into houses and coffins and ashes, that once settled on long dismantled hearths."

Park commissioners discovered, to their dismay, that Horticulture Hall had been built without a foundation, and "it was as rotten as the schemes of a dishonest ward politician, about to collapse and about to fall into a state of innocuous desuetude." Although a plan was commissioned, funds ran out before it could be fully implemented.[39] "At present," the *Daily Picayune*'s account concluded, "the park's chief attractions are the Horticultural Hall, the three grand avenues of oaks, the interesting experimental farming station, leased to the government for ten years, and about two and a half miles of roads that, since they are only twenty-four feet wide, are just about twenty-six feet too narrow."[40]

Park commissioners and Audubon Park Association directors pointed to other large cities such as Chicago where substantial park improvements had made national headlines. "Audubon Park has reached a period in its development which calls for a plan, and the time is come when we may do something toward obtaining the plan," park officials wrote in their 1897 *Year Book of Audubon Park*.[41] Shortly thereafter, John Charles Olmsted, nephew and stepson of Frederick Law Olmsted, was commissioned to develop a plan for the park that ultimately became one of the world's finest public parks. Horticultural Hall, the birthplace of the American Horticultural Society and New Orleans's pride, was destroyed in a hurricane in 1915, but the fair's impact on America's horticultural community was permanent.

Landscape Lessons from the 1884 World's Industrial and Cotton Centennial Exposition

The World's Industrial and Cotton Centennial Exposition achieved only some of its lofty goals. The attempt to portray New Orleans as a bustling hub of agriculture and commerce was largely thwarted by the railroad delays and cold-storage malfunctions that affected both the horticultural product displays and the gardens. Although the 1884 Exposition encompassed about the same amount of acreage as the 1876 Centennial, its attendance totals were barely one-tenth those of its northern counterpart. Nonetheless, as the South's first major foray into world's fairs,[42] the fair must be remembered as the site of some significant horticultural achievements.

New·Orleans's subtropical climate had promised to lure visitors during the cold, northern winter months. However, since many exhibits and displays remained unfinished until the summer, early reports of poorly tended fairgrounds hurt later attendance. The southern climate, a blessing in winter, turned unrelentingly hot and humid during the summer months and further deterred visitors. This extreme heat also took its toll on perishable fruits and vegetables. Cold storage, touted as a technological advantage by exposition promoters, failed to meet expectations.[43] The negative feedback on cold-storage facilities proved a costly lesson for this world's fair, and one that provided a cautionary tale for those following.

Other horticulture-related technologies at this fair found greater success. The "puttyless glazing" method of constructing Horticulture Hall, while previously used in England and New York, had not been implemented on such a scale elsewhere in the United States. In addition to promising more light, the new system offered a better environment in general for plants, with fewer drafts and maintenance issues. Today, whether glass or some form of polycarbonate, greenhouses are typically assembled without putty.

The use of lighting inside and outside of Horticulture Hall set the precedent for future fairs. Certainly gardens had been illuminated since the earliest times with candles, torches, and gas lights, and even early electric lights. But the introduction and subsequent improvement of Thomas Edison's carbon filament bulb in the 1880s brought new possibilities to both outdoor and indoor lighting. Fair visitors could now better enjoy (and pay admission for) world's fairs in the evenings, and might be inspired to envision lighting in their own gardens.

The beauty in garden design at the 1884 World's Fair did not achieve the critical acclaim accorded to the 1876 Centennial. Nevertheless, as one *Harper's Bazaar* writer commented, "If the Philadelphia Exposition could claim higher artistic or aesthetic aims, the present fair can boast of imparting information of a more practical value and the spectator can see at a glance the manufactures, fruits, grasses, grains . . . and the natural scenery of every State or Territory."[44] Despite the transportation setbacks, the exposition succeeded in displaying the horticultural wares of many states. The exhibit of citrus fruits from Florida—a large pyramid of oranges—captured much attention and became a signature Florida and California display in later fairs.

Foreign exhibitors were fewer at this exposition than in Philadelphia. Japan, while well represented in the manufactures and industry exhibits, did not create an attention-getting garden as at the Centennial. Mexico, instead, dominated the displays both inside Horticulture Hall and outside in its own regionally themed garden. Whereas rhododendrons captivated visitors at the Centennial, cacti became the plants du jour at the 1884–85 Fair. Many plants native to Mexico had enjoyed a place in U.S. gardens for years—varieties of ageratums and dahlias were staples of carpet bedding everywhere. But cacti were known only to collectors and the relatively few states or territories to which these were native. The quantity and diversity of cacti shown at the fair introduced thousands of northern visitors to the plant: "There are cacti like enormous pincushions, as big as barrels; cacti like giants' clubs standing thirty feet high; cacti with thorns a finger long; cacti with delicate gray hairs; cacti with beautiful pink tubular blossoms; cacti with big roses growing among their spikes; cacti with red, apple-shaped fruit; cacti in pods, in bulbs, in branching candelabra."[45] Cacti would continue to draw attention in later fairs, including the 1893 World's Columbian Exposition.

3

 World's Columbian Exposition

After the 1884 World's Industrial and Cotton Centennial Exposition, Europe hosted a number of large world's fairs in Antwerp (1885), Edinburgh and London (1886), and Barcelona (1888). These expositions, while drawing respectable crowds of between 3 and 6 million, were dwarfed by the more than 30 million visitors to Paris's 1889 Exposition Universelle. This fair produced the largest profit to date of any fair, and introduced a host of industrial and engineering feats, including the Eiffel Tower. Horticulture on these campus-like, 200-plus acres featured elegant walkways and fountains amid the Jardin du Trocadero, and foreign displays that included thousands of roses, Dutch tulips, and a Japanese garden. Although the United States participated in these overseas fairs, it did not sponsor any significant fairs of its own until the 1890s.

It was a time in which—although the superintendent of the Census pronounced the American frontier closed—opportunities in the United States never seemed brighter. Huge numbers of immigrants were disembarking on American soil, prompting the opening of Ellis Island immigration station in 1892. Nowhere was this optimism and growth more evident than in Chicago, a major port-of-call city where the population more than doubled between 1880 and 1890.[1]

Chicago expanded in more ways than population. The first skyscraper, built in 1885, dominated the city's skyline. Jane Addams's Hull House opened to help alleviate overcrowding and aid in the assimilation of newcomers. Civic groups established arts and culture institutions such as the University of Chicago, the Chicago Symphony Orchestra, and the Newberry Library to raise the city's national profile as well as contribute to its citizens' personal enrichment.

Both Chicago's urban park systems and its private gardens reflected changes in growth patterns as well as national trends. As the expanding railroads facilitated the development of suburbs, landscape designers hired by the development companies often produced plans for individual suburban villas within the new communities.

Created through legislative action in 1869, Chicago's parks bore the imprint of such design notables as William Le Baron Jenney, Ossian Cole Simonds, and Frederick Law Olmsted. The Chicago Fire of 1871 put a temporary hold on park and suburban development, destroying the entire central business district of Chicago and leaving more than one hundred thousand people homeless.[2] It left behind a blank canvas upon which the city could create anew both its physical structures and its reputation as the "Queen of the West." By 1873, Chicago had built a large convention hall, the Inter-State Industrial Exposition Building, to host multistate fairs and expositions. In the next two decades, the city continued its recovery, and, by the 1890s, Chicago's population had topped one million, making it the second-largest city in the nation.

The World's Columbian Exposition (WCE) of 1893 offered Chicago an opportunity to announce its recovery to the world, and catalyzed funding and enthusiasm for the city's renewed growth. With grounds encompassing more than 600 acres, the WCE was more than twice the size of the Philadelphia Centennial, the previous record holder for fairgrounds scale. With an attendance of more than twenty-seven million, the WCE boasted more than triple the gate count of the Centennial.

⌃ Horace Greeley's exhortation to "go west, young man" captured the World's Columbian Exposition's spirit of innovation in this Enterprise Sprinkler ad. (Author's collection)

This bird's-eye view of the WCE shows how water was integral to the design, as was its centerpiece, the Wooded Island. (Library of Congress Prints and Photographs Collection, LC-DIG-pga-00735)

The WCE came to be known as the "Great American Fair," a sobriquet it retains to this day. Although held during one of the country's greatest financial downturns, the fair turned a profit. More importantly, it influenced future fairs through its harmonious combination of architecture and landscape, and left a permanent legacy in the park planning for Chicago and the nation.

Prevailing 1890s stereotypes portrayed Chicago as a frontier town lacking refinement and culture. Newspaper editorials voiced concern that, left to their own devices, Chicago planners would create in the WCE nothing more than a glorified county fair, an agriculture and livestock exhibition for a meatpacking city. Debates in the U.S. Congress, fostered by competing cities, centered on whether Chicago possessed the sophistication necessary to host an international show.

The concern proved unwarranted. Chicago had achieved amazing technical and architectural feats in its rebirth after the 1871 fire. As new structural ideas permitted the first skyscraper, balloon-frame construction allowed small homes to be built quickly and cheaply. The nascent Chicago School of Architecture—with Louis Sullivan and, later, Frank Lloyd Wright among its leaders—attracted worldwide attention. Yet despite the innovations of Chicago's own leading architects, the WCE architectural committee chose the safely neoclassical Beaux-Arts style for the fair. In the interest of unity, the massive exposition buildings shared a traditional theme and were uniformly painted a blinding white. Landscape design for the fair by Frederick Law Olmsted followed a holistic plan to complement the exposition as a whole.

In Chicago, landscaping as a hallmark of culture predated architectural advances. The city's 1837 charter incorporated the motto *Urbs in Horto* (City in a Garden). This was much more than a catchphrase: civic pride routinely translated to extensive plantings of greenery in parks and private residences. The Chicago Horticultural Society dated to 1847 and included both wealthy citizens and working nurserymen. The city's elite expended great effort in landscaping their homes. On the prairie, a house's landscaping made a very visible display of the owner's wealth and taste.[3]

In the late 1860s, Chicagoans embraced the national trend for creating public parks, and Frederick Law Olmsted received a number of major commissions in the Chicago area. In 1868, he and his partner, Calvert Vaux, were engaged to develop the General Plan for the Chicago suburb of Riverside, Illinois. This community, a National Historic Landmark village today, became a national model for urban planning. In 1869, Chicago established its Parks Commissions, and Olmsted and Vaux were again chosen, this time to design two large pleasure grounds, Washington Park and Jackson Park, known as the South Parks. Meanwhile, Olmsted's contacts with members of Chicago's elite, many of whom were transplants from the East Coast, led to private estate commissions.

WCE officials next chose Olmsted to design the grounds of the Columbian Exposition. Working with him on this project were Henry Codman, an associate from Olmsted's firm; Warren Manning, also a one-time associate who would later design the 1907 Jamestown Exposition; and the designer Rudolph Ulrich, whom Olmsted probably met through his work in California. Ulrich would later design the grounds for the Omaha (1898) and Buffalo (1901) World's Fairs.

Olmsted's Choice and Vision

Many Chicagoans had great respect and admiration for Olmsted's talents, but he was unimpressed with the city's landscape. Disdainful of Chicago's flat, prairie terrain, Olmsted found it bereft of any redeeming landscape qualities. As late as November 1889, he contributed toward New York's bid for the world's fair.[4] Voicing a typical East Coast hauteur, he dismissed all potential Chicago fairground locations, saying, "Of the seven [Chicago] sites to which our attention was called there was not one the scenery of which could recommend it if it had been near Boston, New York or Philadelphia."[5]

Olmsted also took a dim view of the average Chicagoan's sophistication level. On a fact-gathering trip to England in 1892, for example, he observed, "The standard of an English laborer, hack driver or cad in respect to neatness, smugness and elegance of gardens and grounds and paths and ways is infinitely higher than that of a Chicago merchant prince or virtuoso."[6] Nonetheless, Olmsted would not turn down the opportunity to landscape a great American world's fair, nor ignore the chance to implement his vision for Jackson Park. In August 1890, after Chicago won the U.S. Congress's approval to host the fair, the World's Columbian Exposition Commission hired the Olmsted firm, including Olmsted himself, stepson John Charles Olmsted, and long-time associate Codman to work as the consulting landscape architects for the fair.

Site selection became one of the firm's first jobs. This task, fraught with business risk and political quagmires, was controversial in any world's fair. In Chicago, where people lived and breathed real estate speculation, the stakes were even higher. Ease of transportation to and from the fair site typically dictated site selection. Chicago at that time was the railroad capital of the world, and railroad barons often made deals to modify the fairgrounds in accordance with their interests. Amid all these competing concerns, Olmsted had to ensure the suitability of the site for horticultural and aesthetic purposes.

Seven possible sites were offered for Olmsted's consideration—three on Lake Michigan and four inland. Ultimately recommending Jackson Park, then a swampy wasteland of low sand dunes and scrubby oaks, Olmsted sniffed: "There is at Chicago, but one natural object at all distinctively local, which can be regarded as an object of much grandeur, beauty or interest. This is the Lake."[7] Visitors from Europe, Canada, and Mexico, he believed, would never have seen such a large body of freshwater bordering a major city. He acknowledged Chicago's reputation for resourcefulness, noting: "It is to be considered also, that Chicago itself, is, in its history and in its commerce, to be a most interesting, perhaps the most interesting, of all the exhibits of the Exposition. What would have been its history, what its commerce, what its interest to the world, if Chicago were without this Lake?"[8]

To win over those who disliked his site recommendation, Olmsted used a fine mix of flattery and subtle chastisement. Appealing to WCE Board members who might otherwise succumb to local lobbying, Olmsted suggested: "It is to be desired also, let us say, that it should be better understood than it yet seems to be by some of your fellow citizens, that the Fair is not to be a Chicago Fair. It is a World's Fair, and Chicago is to stand before the world as the chosen standard bearer for the Occasion of the United States of America. All Chicago can afford to take nothing less than the very best site that can be found for the Fair, regardless of the special local interests of one quarter of the City or another."[9]

With Olmsted's benediction, Jackson Park thus became the accepted site of the world's fair. More than 630 acres of wasteland were destined to become fairgrounds for millions of visitors. The transformation of this unpromising domain into a grand and glorious exposition relied largely on Olmsted's boldness and vision.

Olmsted's WCE design emphasized the total composition of buildings and landscapes over individual planting designs for garden beds. Explaining his site choice, Olmsted observed:

> The one thing that I think instructive to the public in our course is that we have not cared a straw for advantages for gardening or decorative display, which many would suppose to be our only care as Landscape Architects; have urged a site as bare as possible of such advantages—a desert place of drifting sand and water—simply out of respect for the one feature of natural—purely natural—beauty, in which there can be no display of our professional skill, the Lake.[10]

Shaped roughly like a right triangle, the fair site's base lay at Sixty-Seventh Street, another leg aligned on a north-south axis with Stony Island Avenue, and the hypotenuse was formed by the irregular shoreline of Lake Michigan. Capitalizing on Lake Michigan as a backdrop, the plan called for significant dredging and excavation to create a system of canals surrounding the buildings. Raised on taller sand dunes created through excavation, most exposition buildings enjoyed water frontage (either on Lake Michigan or on the lagoons and canals). Ringed by impressive structures designed by the exposition's team of architects, a great formal water basin reflected the sky and was in constant motion, stirred by the cascading water from majestic water fountains.[11] Known as the Court of Honor, the basin created a grand entrance to the fair on the lakefront, and connected through the lagoons to the interior buildings.

Olmsted hoped that the reflective waterways would inspire fairgoers with a sense of wonder and a greater appreciation for nature. Indeed, Warren Manning declared, "Surely the Court of Honor at the Chicago Exposition was a dream of beauty that could not fail to lift all thoughts and aspirations to a higher plane."[12] The lagoons, designed to look like natural bayous, offered relief from the formality of the rest of the exposition. They were to be given a "rich, affluent picturesque aspect, in striking contrast alike with that of the present ground, the shores of the great lake, the margins of the Basin in the great Court."[13]

The appropriate use of water as a design element was very important to Olmsted. In a letter to chief architect Daniel H. Burnham, Olmsted asked rhetorically:

> Why was the Great Basin, why were the Lagoons and the Canals, brought into the plan to cut up and complicate the site of the Fair . . . Why were they laid out on

➤ Lake Michigan bounded the triangular-shaped fairgrounds on the east, while railroads and the city bordered the fair on the west. (Author's collection)

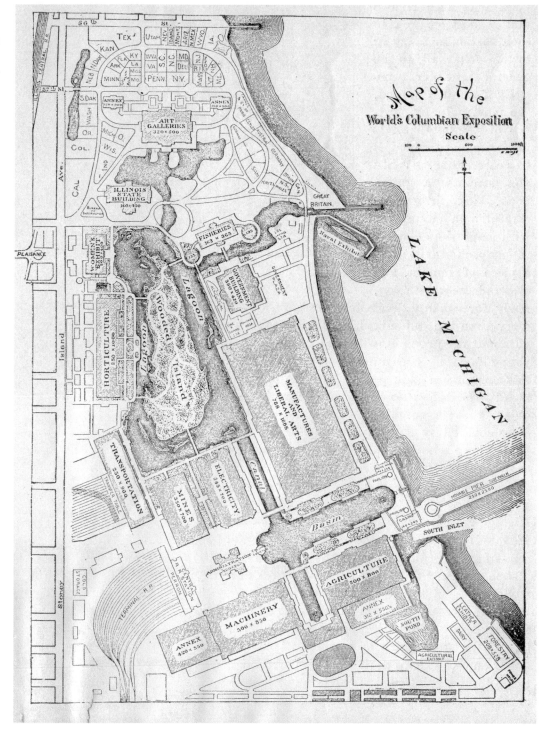

such eccentric courses as they are, with shores sometimes formal and rectilinear, sometimes picturesque or gracefully meandering? . . . Was it to save time and expense to visitors in moving from one point to another? . . . You are as alive to it as I am. You know that it was a poetic object, and you know that if boats are to be introduced on these waters it would be perfect nonsense to have them of a kind that would antagonize this poetic object.[14]

He proposed to Burnham in 1891 that the boating feature should be a "gay and lively one in spectacular effect."[15]
Olmsted achieved this effect through the interplay of waterways and shorelines. Against this backdrop of Lake Michigan views and interior waterways, Olmsted created his trademark naturalistic vistas of greenery. He explained:

The general design assumes that contribution is to be made not alone by the waters, but by their shores; by the display of foliage and verdure of many descriptions on these shores; by the bridges across the waters; by the

terraces overhanging them; . . . to be reflected in them or to be seen in direct association with them . . . All these elements of design have, accordingly, been studied
with great care to adapt them to contribute to the desired general scenic effect of
the Exposition as a whole.[16]

Central to the design was a tract of land surrounded by lagoons and known as the
Wooded Island. In a design memo dated 1891, Olmsted identified three key objectives
for the island. It was to provide a low foreground against which the exposition buildings would rise, "gaining in grandeur of effect upon the imagination."[17] There would
be a broad expanse of natural scenery that would be "counteractive to the effect of the
artificial grandeur and the crowds, pomp, splendor and bustle of the rest of the Exposition."[18] The third objective perhaps captured the essence of the Olmsted vision for the
World's Columbian Exposition:

Without losing a general unity and continuity of character in the shores . . . [the
design] will allow of mysterious poetic effect, through the mingling intricately
together of many forms of foliage, the alternation and complicated crossing of
salient leaves and stalks of varying green tints in highlights with other leaves and
stalks behind and under them, and therefore less defined and more shaded, yet
partly illumined by light reflected from the water.[19]

Spectacle and mystery met at the shorelines, and here the Olmsted team expended
considerable effort and attention. Railroad carloads of aquatic plants indigenous to
northern Illinois riverbanks and swamps were situated around the shoreline to soften
the edges and create a naturalistic border. Olmsted railed constantly against the use
of contrived floral arrangements, contending: "It is not desired that there should anywhere appear to be a display of flowers demanding attention as such. Rather the flowers to be used for the purpose should have the effect of flecks and glimmers of bright
color imperfectly breaking through the general greenery. Anything approaching a gorgeous, garish or gaudy display of flowers is to be avoided."[20]

Protective of his design intent for the Wooded Island, Olmsted fought off many
attempts to corrupt the island's use. In a letter to Henry Codman, he complained, "I
am vexed that the Advertising Committee should have sent out a general publication
in which the Island is promised to be made a little Eden. It is still a question in my
mind whether it would not be better to regard it simply as an element of landscape,
to be looked upon from a distance across the water."[21] Others had different ideas, and
wanted the island for outdoor concerts, displays, and concessions. Even Theodore
Roosevelt wrote a letter requesting a spot to erect a demonstration hunting camp.

Olmsted finally lost part of this battle, and ceded 10 acres of the interior space to horticultural displays and a Japanese garden. He often went on record against this usage, noting grumpily, "We consider that these introductions have much injured the island for the purpose which in our primary design it was intended to serve."[22]

Olmsted wanted a landscape design that would both complement the architecture of the exposition and offer relief from its assault upon the senses. In implementing his design, he hoped to catalyze efforts to create long-term, lasting improvements in Jackson Park, improvements he had initiated over two decades. Nevertheless, he knew that the landscaping for the fair would be temporary, writing, "The work is thus to be in some degree of the character of a theatrical scene, to occupy the Exposition stage for a single Summer."[23]

Building the Landscape

The task of implementing Olmsted's vision fell largely to Codman and Rudolph Ulrich. Codman frequently visited the site and served as a liaison with the larger exposition construction team. German-trained Ulrich, a New York City landscape architect, had designed large properties in Europe, along with West Coast projects at Stanford University. He would rely on his WCE experience when he designed the landscape for the 1898 Trans-Mississippi Exposition and the Pan-American Exposition of 1901. Warren H. Manning was particularly instrumental in making horticultural and planting decisions. Frederick Law Olmsted Jr., Olmsted's college-age son, apprenticed at the exposition site while on break from Harvard. While Olmsted Sr. juggled his other client work—including the creation of Biltmore, the Vanderbilt estate—he was kept apprised of activity through daily and weekly missives from the WCE team.

Except for about 90 improved acres in the northern part of Jackson Park, the balance of the 645 acres was, in Ulrich's words, "a morass," about a third of which was underwater. Existing native flora, by Ulrich's survey, included bur, white, pin, and swamp oaks with undergrowth of elder, wild plum, wild cherry, and willow bushes. Native wildflowers included *coreopsis, achilles, helianthus,* iris, solidago, and water plants such as *carex, acerus, typha, scirpus, and eragrostis.*[24] These plants were the botanical foundation of Olmsted's design for the Wooded Island.

In 1891, workers began excavating and grading the land to establish the outlines of the canals and create the necessary elevations for the buildings. This was backbreaking work, and, as Ulrich recounted, "many accidents happened, and we often had to dig out teams sunk down to their bodies and wagons to their axles."[25] The crew had to contend with quicksand, and in hot weather, Ulrich reported, "a south wind would blind the eyes of man and beast."[26]

A de facto village was established on the grounds during the construction period. A makeshift hospital, restaurant, offices, boardinghouses, storerooms, and more were hastily constructed. Eleven greenhouses for plant propagation were built and dispersed among the Wooded Island, the Midway Plaisance, and off-site locations. As early as March 1891, Ulrich was prompted to complain, "The island is literally covered with small buildings, I am sorry to say, it resembling a mining camp."[27] By June 1891, Ulrich himself, working around the clock, slept in a room in the landscape department office on the island.

Lake Michigan's naturally fluctuating water levels, which likewise affected the connecting lagoons, created one of the most vexing landscape challenges. The water level could vary significantly in a single day, and much more from season to season. Bare shorelines exposed during times of low water could ruin Olmsted's idealized vision of nature. The solution seemed to lie in shoreline plantings of hardy aquatic and semi-aquatic plants. The entire 1891 planting season thus became a period of experimentation. Each day, water level and temperature measurements were taken morning, noon, and evening. In the summer of 1891, efforts intensified to acquire plants for experimentation and permanent planting. Expeditions into the nearby countryside were conducted to find suitable aquatics, and local property owners were tapped for plant contributions.

George Pullman, the railroad car magnate, offered the use of his property around the nearby Calumet Lake for the collection of rushes, *Acorus,* and wild iris. Plant-hunting expeditions were conducted along the right-of-way on the Illinois Central Railroad and the outlying prairie. Olmsted Jr., a frequent participant in these expeditions, wrote to his father of one trip to the nearby Waukegan countryside: "We found an unlimited supply of *nymphia* [*sic*] a great deal of *sagittaria* which was growing along the banks of a little stream and was very fine, exactly the effect you want to produce on the lagoons. We also found mandrakes, *hepatica, dolicathium, arisema, trillium, Symlocarpus fortidus, Caltha palustris* and *Aquilegia canadensis* in sufficient quantities to warrant collecting them."[28]

The technology of plant shipping and packing remained imperfect, and Ulrich struggled with damaged shipments. Excessively tight packaging caused overheating, sogginess, and rot. Sometimes transportation delays wreaked havoc with shipments. Ulrich groused about a carload of *Eleagnus, Cornus* and *Clethra* specimens from Parsons nursery: "The trees were packed in the car without any packing whatever, just as they were taken out of the ground and thrown in the car . . . They arrived here nearly all dried up, and only severe pruning will help them to break forth again."[29]

Excavations and planting continued throughout the summer of 1892. Olmsted, however, was having second thoughts about the plants they had propagated and acquired.

While on a European trip, he had toured local public and private gardens and characterized the "floral or modern style of decorative gardening" as "childish, vulgar, flaunting, or impertinent." Concerned about the potentially gaudy effect in the Grand Basin, he mused, "I distrust even our intended gay trimmings along the parallel ground of the grand court."[30] Thus, even though Ulrich and his crew had already spent considerable time propagating annuals, these types of displays were significantly scaled back, with lawns substituting for floral effect.

Throughout 1892, mature trees were transplanted from improved sections of the park or relocated from building site areas. Sod was laid around newly completed buildings, and, with the installation of irrigation pipes, grass seed was sown. In the spring of 1893, just before the exposition opened, Olmsted uneasily observed in a letter to Ulrich that "White City" had become the fair's popular name and that he feared the brilliant buildings would be overpowering. He urged Ulrich to soften the effect with dark-green foliage and subtle hints of red and yellow to intensify the greens. In the letter, Olmsted expressed concern that the grounds might create a carnival-like atmosphere:

> I did feel at one time that there was danger that some of our ground might have a bare and unfinished aspect unless masses of foliage and flowers should be introduced upon it. But as I see the constantly increasing numbers of small structures for which concessions are making, and which are to be scattered everywhere to supply visitors with water, cigars, newspapers, lemonade, tea, chocolate, parched corn, peanuts, fruit, medals and other souvenirs, and as I realize the number of seats, awnings, flags and streamers which the architects are planning to use at innumerable points, I have begun to feel that instead of being unfurnished, the spaces between the buildings are in great danger of being crowded with incidents, and I now have much more fear that they will have a vulgar, fussy, over-decorated aspect than that they will be too plain and simple.[31]

This letter is especially poignant in that Olmsted was now relying on Ulrich to see this part of the project through.[32] Olmsted himself was in poor health, and with Codman's untimely death, it fell to Ulrich to see to all the innumerable details before Opening Day in May. Olmsted worried that although Ulrich had proved to be a tireless worker, he tended to focus on flower details rather than the total composition.[33] He cautioned Ulrich: "Never lose sight of the fact that our special responsibility as *landscape* artists applies primarily to the broad, comprehensive *scenery* of the Exposition. This duty is not to make a garden, or to produce garden effects, but relates to the scenery of the Exposition as a whole."[34]

The Wooded Island Conflicts

As was often the case in world's fairs, the goals and membership of the Department of Horticulture differed from those of the Building and Grounds Committee, so conflict was inevitable. The former focused on individual fruit and flower exhibits, whereas the latter supervised the total landscape scheme. Typical for world's fairs in this era, the Horticulture Department was organized and operated by individuals in the florist and seed trades, or from within the pomological or horticultural societies. The aims of such groups were sometimes at odds with those of Olmsted's landscape architecture ideals. In the United States and Europe, gardening styles were slowly undergoing a shift from garish Victorian "carpet bedding" to more naturalistic styles. The latter designs, which often employed native plants that could be obtained in undisturbed countryside, received little support from most nurserymen, for whom sales of carpet bedding plants were profitable.

Kentucky native John M. Samuels, appointed chief of horticulture in 1891, was an officer or member of several horticultural organizations, including the American Pomological Society, the Society of American Florists, and the American Horticultural Society. Samuels was supported by John Thorpe, Charles Wright, and H. M. La Rue, superintendents of the Bureaus of Floriculture, Pomology, and Viticulture respectively, and also prominent in allied societies. Experienced professionals, these men needed to work out compromises with the exhibitors whose plans did not conform to Olmsted's design vision. L. H. Bailey, a prominent horticulturist from Cornell University, commented on how aesthetic and commercial interests, represented respectively by Olmsted and the nurserymen, often landed on opposite sides of the style debates:

> There has arisen nothing more important during the year than the debates concerning the place of flowers in land-

▶ Fanciful decorations such as the "Globe" adorned many Chicago parks—contrasting with Olmsted's naturalistic style. (Author's collection)

scape ornamentation. The subject was opened in 1889 by a powerful invective against formalism and carpet bedding in landscape gardening, by William Mac-Millan, of the Buffalo Parks. Since this time, the florists have thrown themselves into the aggressive in the endeavor to save the florist business one of its most profitable outlets. The discussion has been largely a mistaken one, for the florists have seemed to understand that the landscape gardeners of the naturalistic school attack the use of flowers in general, while they have only endeavored to reform the popular taste for gross designs.[35]

Ultimately, Olmsted reluctantly relinquished much of the naturalistic interior of the Wooded Island to floral displays implemented by the Horticulture Department.

In designing gardens for the Horticulture Palace and the immediate surrounding grounds, Samuels and his team worked to satisfy the public's appetite for extravagant displays. Chicagoans, for example, remained enchanted by elaborate floral concoctions. Fanciful creations such as the "Floral Gates Ajar" and the "Globe" decorated nearby Washington Park, which connected to the Midway Plaisance.[36] Olmsted, in a letter to Rudolph Ulrich, wrote: "Let all our decoration be a protest, challenge and defiance against the taste that calls for such decoration as has been exhibited in Washington Park. Let us manifest the taste of gentlemen."[37]

The interior of the Wooded Island thus devolved into a patchwork of floral exhibits. Formal plantings like the rose garden and stiff exhibits of "show" flowers were inconsistent with his ideal of naturalistic plantings. Only the outer borders and curved walkways remained true to his plans.

With its overall contemplative spirit, the Japanese Ho-o-den Temple and Garden on the northern part of the island was more in sympathy with Olmsted's design and won his tacit approval. The garden disappointed many Victorian visitors who considered themselves well-versed in all things Japanesque since it lacked the miniature trees or ex-

Wooded Island became a florist's showplace of patchwork displays that ran counter to Olmsted's vision of a naturalistic landscape. (Chicago Public Library, Special Collections and Preservation Division, WCE/CDA IX/16)

otic plants that amateur gardeners expected. Contemporary garden writers were more charitable in their assessment: "Mr. Isawa [the professional Japanese gardener] has had much to contend with in the construction of his garden, for want of the right kind of trees and rocks, proper to be used in a real Japanese garden. It is not to be doubted that Mr. Isawa is a thoroughly experienced man in his profession, and the shortcomings are to be charged up to paucity of proper material to work with."[38]

Poor soil conditions and a mix-up in space allocations for the Japanese exhibit caused further problems. L. H. Bailey complained: "The garden is simply a succession of low, smooth, grass-covered mounds with a few narrow walks winding about, and a hapless dearth of anything Japanesque in its planting . . . [T]he Japanese gardener, Izawa [sic], freely declares that it in no sense represents Japanese garden-art."[39] Still, Bailey appreciated the nursery portion of this garden where several varieties of Japanese maple, tree peonies, and hundreds of *Iris kaempferi* made a handsome display.

Foreign and U.S. nurserymen exhibited several acres of perennial and annual beds south of the Japanese gardens. The 1-acre formal rose garden comprised forty individual beds.

Even though the general public raved about the Wooded Island, professional horticulturists longed for displays with greater educational value. Illegible or inadequate flower labeling hampered plant study. Hodgepodge collections distracted from the overall landscape effect. Typical was this opinion from a regular garden columnist: "The comments heard on numerous trips through the Island prove that the exhibits would have made a greater impression on the public had each exhibitor shown a succession of masses of flowers composed of but one variety . . . In short it would have supplied the old reliable flowers with credentials that would have given them a new standing, and a fresh send-off for the new century."[40]

Plantings on the Wooded Island and other fair sites also suffered from nineteenth-century urban pollutants, the inevitable by-product of industrialization. One fair visitor noted: "What struck me particularly was the blackness of the tree trunks, so that in some instances I thought they were painted with coal-tar to preserve them from insects, until I discovered the same peculiarity in Lincoln Park, and in the trees in Chicago. I finally concluded that it must be a combination of moisture from the lake with the smoke of bituminous coal which gives them this melancholy hue."[41]

▲ The Japanese Gardens drew mixed reviews: Visitors liked the exoticism, but professional horticulturists found it lacked authenticity. (Chicago Public Library, Special Collections and Preservation Division, WCE/CDA IX/21)

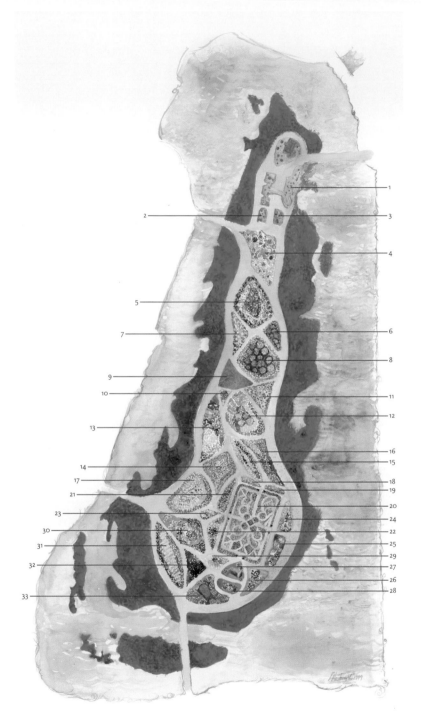

◄ This artist's rendering of the garden plots on Wooded Island hints at the riotous color that Olmsted decried. (Watercolor by Liita Forsyth, based on 1893 sketch by L. H. Bailey; author's collection)

PLOT	MAJOR PLANTINGS
1–4	Japanese garden plots
5	German exhibit: roses, stocks, dahlia, tuberous begonia, zinnia
6	Hydrangea bordered by clematis
7	Tamarisk bordered by hydrangea, edged by carnations and dianthus
8	Hydrangea and *Rosa ruqosa* bordered by *Lobelia syphilitica* and pinks
9	Open greensward
10	Single and double dahlias
11	Sunflowers
12	*Oenothera fruiticosa* 'Youngii,' *Eryngium amethstinum, Pyrethrum uliginosum, Zauschneria californica,* hydrangea, *Prunus pissardi*
13	Annual and perennial mixture
14–16	200 species and varieties, including pyrethrums, native sunflowers, *Boltonia glastifolia, Gaillardia grandiflora, Coreopsis lanceolata, Hibiscus moscheutos,* datura, zinna, pinks
17	*Sedum spectabile, Monarda didyma,* dahlias, peonies, delphinium, phlox, sunflowers
18–19	*Helenium autumnale, Aster novae-angliae, Veronica spicata, Coreopsis lanceolata, Boltonia latisquama*
20	Rose garden
21	German exhibit: tea roses, dahlia, canna, climbing Japanese cucumber
22–23	New York exhibits
24	*Hibiscus californicus* and peonies
25	Azalea and rhododendron
26	Waterer azaleas: *A. mollis, A. sinensis, A. occidentalis*
27–28	Garden tool house, sodded lawn and rhododendron display
29	Rhododendron, lilies, gladiolus, tigridia
30	Azalea
31	Azalea and bulbs
32	Dahlias
33	"Harp of Erin" floral motif with house leeks (*Cotyledon secunda* and *C. sempervivum*) and *Alternathera paronychoides*

The Horticulture Palace

Across the lagoon from the Wooded Island, the crystal dome of the Horticulture Palace glimmered, a Venetian Renaissance-style confection designed by William Le Baron Jenney. Jenney and Olmsted had collaborated before, notably on the Chicago suburb of Riverside. Although better known for his architectural works,[42] Jenney was also a leading landscape designer and had created plans for a number of public and private properties in Chicago. With a footprint of 1,000 x 250 feet and at a cost of about $300,000, the WCE Horticulture Palace was one of the largest conservatories in the world. It was topped by a 113-foot-high glass dome, which was flanked by a pair of glass-roofed galleries. The palace radiated romance and glamour, and became a popular meeting spot.

HORTICULTURAL HALL.

⌃ Separated by a lagoon from the Wooded Island, the Horticulture Palace featured galleries of conservatory plants and preserved specimens. (Author's collection)

➤ The so-called "floral mound" under the Horticulture Palace dome covered the Crystal Cave—modeled after its recently explored namesake in Deadwood, South Dakota. Professionals questioned its aesthetic and educational value. (Author's collection)

Exhibits inside the hall ranged from novelties to exotics. The most controversial attraction, an artificial floral mound in the center of the main dome, supposedly represented a mountain with a cave beneath. This 70-foot-high lump of plants invoked sharp criticism from L. H. Bailey: "The structure is full of ugly gaps, many of the plants are dry and sere, and the whole object is a most unhappy and crest-fallen spectacle . . . [I]ts design is without purpose and is bad; it accomplishes nothing more than a rude filling of the space; it represents no mountain vegetation, nor the flora of any land, nor has it any artistic value."[43]

Underneath the mound was a private concession, the "Crystal Cave," an attempted facsimile of the original in South Dakota's Black Hills, complete with stalactites and stalagmites.[44] Yet, notwithstanding Bailey's critique and a hefty admission charge, the

mound, cave, and entire palace were popular with the general public, as typified by this description from an East Coast traveler, Johanna Wisthaler:

On entering the Palace of Horticulture north of the Transportation Building, our organs of sight and olfactory nerves were equally affected by the dazzling and odoriferous display of exuberant flowers and fruitage . . . Fruits of every form and description, sent from all zones, climes, and countries were represented here. Many of the exhibits were maintained at a high standard by being constantly replenished with fresh fruits at great expense, particularly the Californian citrus pyramid, comprising 31,150 oranges.

The richly decorated court planted with ornamental shrubs and flowers, led to the center pavilion which was roofed by a huge crystal dome. This translucent cover transmitted the light and sunshine necessary for the floricultural display beneath. Stately palms, tall tree ferns in great variety, and gorgeous specimens from the flora of almost every section, formed an immense pyramid of shrubbery. The luxuriously growing vines entwined their tendrils around the iron-work of the building, adding greatly to the beauty of the panorama.[45]

The promenade gallery on the second floor of the dome displayed herbaria, models of villa gardens, pressed plants, and photographs of showcase gardens. It also provided a fine vantage point from which to see plant exhibits in the north and south gallery wings below. In the southeast gallery, plants were staged in a progression by height; smaller plants in the foreground, tall ferns and palms in the rear.[46] Exotics including orchids, begonias, cycads, and gardenias provided visual interest midway through the gallery. The northeast gallery, with its foreign exhibits, had a greater variety of plants. A middle island of staghorn and tree ferns (some of the latter nearly 60 feet high) separated plantings along the east and west walls of the gallery.

Apples, pears, peaches, plums, and other pomological items were elegantly displayed west of the ornamental plant galleries, separated by interior courts. A California orange orchard, reproduced on a small scale, perfumed the north court, while a German wine display and lily tanks adorned the south court. Viticultural products from around the world were displayed in the south court, and seed displays and gardening implements were shown in the north pavilion.

Flowers and nursery exhibits surrounded the Horticulture Palace. Outside the main entrance, exhibits of cactus and desert gardening coexisted happily with a display of aquatics. A masonry lily tank with forty species of water plants from the nurseryman William Tricker, then of New York, had been installed near the front entrance of the palace. Outlined by extensive plantings of pansies in spring and cannas in fall, the lily tank marked a transition from the Horticulture Palace to the lagoon and Wooded Island to the east.

A greenhouse display west of the Horticulture Palace served a dual function: it was an exhibition of working greenhouses but also provided a succession of plantings around the fairgrounds. Exhibits such as New York's "Old Fashioned Garden" surrounded the greenhouses.

At the entrance to the Horticulture Palace, a ground-level masonry tank contained labeled aquatic plants (*right foreground*) and a display of cactus (*far left*). (Chicago Public Library, Special Collections and Preservation Division, WCE/CDA V/59)

Foreign Exhibits and Influence

Twenty-three foreign exhibitors mounted displays of fruit, grain, and plants native to their countries. Orchids arrived from Liberia, bedding plants from Russia, figs and olives from Greece. Switzerland installed a full-scale greenhouse, and Mexico built a miniature replica of the Horticulture Palace that incorporated 110 pounds of delicate silver filigree. While many displays were of nonperishable items, several countries brought fresh fruits or live plants. Transportation of these inevitably involved uncertainty and risk. The apples from New South Wales, for example, arrived after fifty-two days in transit by land and sea.

Foreign horticultural efforts extended to the landscaping around each country's own buildings. The writer M. C. Robbins noted: "In front of the French Building is a pretty parterre, carefully tended and full of flowers which makes a fitting accessory to the construction itself, which, like everything from France, is in excellent taste. A fountain plays in the grassy curve half-enclosed by the building, and here is a gay French parterre brilliant with blossoms, and skillfully tended and renewed like the beds in the Champs Elysees, so that as one set of flowers fades another takes its place."[47]

European landscaping concepts also influenced the overall fairground design. Olmsted and members of his firm often took trips abroad to exchange ideas with leading landscape designers. They also had visited the 1889 Exposition Universelle, and in April 1892, Olmsted returned to the old fairgrounds accompanied by the preeminent French landscape designer Edouard André. Olmsted found inspiration for details such as iron edgings for walkways, plantings for terrace vases, and even more ideas in the grand basins and fountains near the Trocadero, once part of the 1889 exposition site. In turn, André was enthusiastic about Olmsted's overall design for the exposition, particularly the plans for the Wooded Island, and requested permission to print a copy in the prestigious *Revue horticole*.[48]

In contemporary Parisian landscaping in general, however, Olmsted was disappointed. He disparaged the Tuileries to his team, noting: "We should do better to disregard it entirely and trust to our own invention. The shrub planting is poor, confused, undesigned. [Warren H.] Manning would do much better without special instructions." He was equally disenchanted with Versailles and Chantilly, the latter of which he termed "mechanical" and devoid of invention. He summed up his experiences with the complaint: "We have seen no landscape architecture in natural style of modern design. It is all designed bit by bit, theatrically and without connection or breadth or unity."[49]

▲ Today, Jackson Park includes this reinterpreted Japanese garden and, in another area, naturalistic plantings. (Photo by the author)

the flowering shrubs and green trees of the island form an agreeable mass of color, behind which rise distant domes and towers . . . The yellow light plays softly on the white buildings, under the bridges glide the graceful gondolas, distant bells are softly chiming, flowers are blooming, the summer throng comes and goes, idly lingering to gaze. All is light, color, perfume, melody, the realization of the most fanciful dream of those old masters. The sense of beauty is so intense, so gratifying, that the eyes fill with tears, and for a moment the work-a-day world vanishes, and we, too, are in Arcadia. And this enchanted scene seems to belong not to the America of to-day, but to some far-off hour to come in its millennium.[61]

Landscape Lessons from World's Columbian Exposition

The creation of the WCE fairgrounds constituted the largest effort up until its time—in the United States or elsewhere—to mold exposition landscapes from undeveloped land. The notion of installing specimens so that they would have at least a year to take root (as with the Wooded Island plantings) helped render the trees at Chicago's World's Fair as permanent additions to park landscapes. Although few world's fair landscape designers have ever enjoyed the luxury of an unhurried schedule, the lead time for the WCE was extremely generous compared to, for example, that for the 1884 World's Cotton and Industrial Centennial Exposition. Future exposition landscape designers would argue forcefully for more time.

The World's Columbian Exposition is often credited with being the catalyst for the City Beautiful movement in the United States, a widespread effort to improve the social and aesthetic aspects of industrialized cities. The integration in city planning of landscaping and architectural and infrastructure elements became a pillar of the movement thanks to the success of the WCE fairgrounds. The highly touted 1909 Plan of Chicago, authored largely by Daniel Burnham, emphasized integrated beltways of greenery thanks to advice from the landscape architect Jens Jensen and others. City Beautiful movements spread to many cities including Cleveland, Columbus, Des

Moines, Denver, New York City, and San Francisco. According to the world's fair historian Robert Rydell, "the triumph of the World's Columbian Exposition revivified the American world's fair movement and set a standard against which every subsequent exposition would be measured."[62]

The success of the Wooded Island inspired more naturalistic designs not only in future world's fairs (especially the 1907 "Canoe Trail" by Warren Manning and 1915 Palace of Fine Arts landscape by John McLaren) but also in public and private landscapes. The movement away from Victorian bedding-out styles and toward naturalistic design gained momentum. In Chicago, Jens Jensen, along with contemporaries O. C. Simonds and Walter Burley Griffin, dramatically influenced the new style of gardening in the Midwest and the nation as a whole. In a *Garden and Forest* article, J. G. Jack, of the Arnold Arboretum, praised the heretofore overlooked value of native plants as seen at the WCE, citing knotweed (*Polygonum pennsylvanicum*) and pigweeds (*Chenopodium* and *Amarantus*) as excellent wild plants that handily filled in landscape gaps.[63]

The WCE redefined the use of water in landscapes. In the 1876 Centennial and 1884 Cotton Centennial, small lakes became part of the landscape as a by-product of cut-and-fill grading. In addition to traditional reflecting pools and fountains, Olmsted's design incorporated water as transportation through the use of canals. The integration of a variety of water elements became a technique that influenced the fairgrounds design of the future world's fairs.

WCE officials increased the visibility of the landscape architect in America by hiring Frederick Law Olmsted. Just six years after the WCE, ten men and one woman, many with direct connections to Olmsted, joined together to form the American Society of Landscape Architects, thus formalizing the young profession. The notion of planning a landscape rather than settling for piecemeal gardening efforts became increasingly influential in both public and home landscape design across the nation.

The WCE also saw a significant increase in the elements of national character in foreign exhibitors' gardens, and customized gardens commissioned by and for individual building sponsors. Bertha Palmer, for example, the grande dame of Chicago society and a devoted Francophile, commissioned Edouard André to design the grounds

▲ Like many nurserymen, J. C. Vaughan, a major participant in several expositions, parlayed his involvement at the fair into sales materials. Through catalogues like these, the images of the fair and its gardens persisted. (Author's collection)

around the Women's Building. State buildings displayed more regionalism in their surrounding landscapes, and Japan, as usual, demonstrated the most effort in landscaping.

In the years between the 1876 Centennial and the WCE, Japanese gardens had taken hold in the United States—first on both coasts and later in the Midwest. The New York Horticultural Society hosted a major chrysanthemum show in 1886 that included a Japanese garden, and a Japanese Horticulture Society was formed in New Jersey to create a garden near South Orange, New Jersey.[64] After the fair, the Japanese government gave its Wooded Island garden to Chicago as a permanent exhibit. Similarly, after the 1894 Midwinter World's Fair in San Francisco, the Japanese Tea Garden was preserved for the public in Golden Gate Park. Also influential were books such as Josiah Conders's 1891 *The Flowers of Japan and the Art of Floral Arrangement* and his 1893 *Landscape Gardening in Japan*.[65]

The advances in horticultural technology and landscape design shown at the WCE had lasting impact. More than six hundred new plant introductions were made to the American trade in 1893. Award winners in the horticultural exhibitions parlayed their success into sales and found buyers in backyards across America. Leading tastemakers such as the art historian Mariana Griswold (Mrs. Schuyler) Van Rensselaer wrote extensively of Olmstedian designs in *Garden and Forest* magazine and, later, in her book *Art Out-Of-Doors: Hints on Good Taste in Gardening*. Between 1888 and 1897, *Garden and Forest*, founded by Charles Sprague Sargent, an Olmsted colleague and director of the Arnold Arboretum, ran many articles on the WCE and on or by Olmsted or his contemporaries. Such opinions of the vanguards of style found their way into popular periodicals and ultimately, gardens across the United States.

▲ The WCE floral exhibits, in contrast to the naturalistic plantings on Wooded Island, were a metaphor for the crossroads of design styles. (Author's collection)

LANDING OF THE TROOPS.

OUR COUNTRY'S CALL.

4

 Pan-American Exposition

BUFFALO, 1901

Electric Rainbows of Colorful Flowers

Economic and political turmoil marked the years immediately following the World's Columbian Exposition. The financial panics of 1893 and 1897 dealt severe blows to the U.S. economy and slowed the galloping railroad speculation. Workers' strikes, notably the Pullman Strike of 1894, sometimes became violent. The Klondike Gold Rush of 1897 brought hordes of prospectors to the Yukon Territory. In 1898, simmering hostilities erupted into the Spanish-American War. U.S. President William McKinley and Congress responded to the sinking of the USS *Maine* with the full force of the U.S. Navy. The six-month-long Spanish-American War ended in 1898 with a U.S. victory, and the United States continued its ascent as a world power.

The fin de siècle brought with it the first international Olympics of the modern era, held in the summer of 1896 in Greece, and the death of Queen Victoria in 1901. Major innovations such as the automobile and movie projectors were introduced in the 1890s, as well as such everyday products as the zipper, aspirin, and Jell-O.

At the turn of the twentieth century, Buffalo, New York, lobbied for and secured the privilege of hosting the Pan-American Exposition of 1901. With 40 million people living within an easily traveled 500-mile radius of the city (more than double the comparable density ratio of Chicago), and as the locus for twenty-six railroad lines, Buffalo seemed likely to attract a great number of visitors.[1] As the fourth-largest commercial center in the world at the time, Buffalo had few rivals in shipping, rail, and automotive transportation.

Roadways were exquisitely landscaped by Olmsted and Vaux in what would become Buffalo's nationally renowned parks and parkway system. In 1869, Olmsted and his successor firm began a long relationship with Buffalo that was to include the design of

▲ The Spanish-American War of 1898 showcased U.S. military strength, but also provided a historical backdrop that influenced the planning of the Pan-American Exposition. (Library of Congress Prints and Photographs Division, Washington, D.C., LC-DIG-pga-01623)

This bird's-eye view of the Pan-American grounds shows the connection with existing Delaware Park on the south, and the long, formal north-south axis culminating in the Electric Tower, which, when lit at night, sparkled with the electricity of the era. (Library of Congress Prints and Photographs Division Washington, D.C., LC-DIG-ppmsca.07832)

Niagara Falls State Park, the oldest state park in the United States. Three decades after that auspicious beginning, Olmsted's influence would be seen again in the city, through his protégé Rudolph Ulrich, this time for the Pan-American Exposition of 1901.

The Pan-American Exposition of 1901, while confined to exhibitors from the Western Hemisphere, ushered in both the twentieth century and the era of electricity, and, after the success of Chicago's brilliant white buildings, it reintroduced color to U.S. expositions. It also launched America's most prolific decade of world's fairs, and marketed itself as a truly American exposition. The fair began in optimism but ended in financial ruin and with the tragedy of President McKinley's assassination.

Landscaping and architecture at the Pan-American Exposition was markedly different from that at the World's Columbian Exposition. Whereas Chicago's fair had been dubbed the White City because of its gleaming white Beaux-Arts buildings, Buffalo's fair became known as the Rainbow City. Public sentiment for expansive shows of color in flower beds—fueled perhaps by the rising enthusiasm for chromolithography and hybridization—reversed the subdued, naturalistic ideals of the 1893 World's Fair. The Pan-Am Fair's loose interpretation of Spanish Renaissance architecture suggested the influence of mission settlements and the peace following the Spanish-American War. The color consultant and artist Charles Yardley Turner used a progression of colors on the buildings to symbolize, according to the Pan-Am's *Official Catalogue and Guide,* "the fierce struggle of 'man to overcome the elements.'" Turner had served as assistant director of decoration at the World's Columbian Exposition, and his use of color at a fair would set a precedent for fairs to come. As one walked toward the fair's central iconic Electric Tower, the buildings appeared in ever-paler colors, purportedly emphasizing a more sophisticated sensibility, until one reached the tower itself, painted a light cream color, symbolizing the pinnacle of man's mastery over the elements.

Ulrich and Scott Design the Grounds

The Pan-American Exposition was to have been a glorious fin de siècle extravaganza. Originally the fair was scheduled to open in 1899, and planning was well under way in 1897. The outbreak of the Spanish-American War in April 1898 necessitated a temporary pause during which new members were added to the Exposition Company, and a desire arose to secure a site closer to the city of Buffalo than the original location of Cuyuga Island in the middle of the Niagara River. In March 1899, the exposition's Joint Committee of Architects and Engineers produced a list of fifty-three architects, landscape architects, and engineers to recommend the best site and plot plan for the fair.[2] The Executive Committee selected the Olmsted firm and D. H. Burnham for advice on site selection, with assistance from Warren Manning.[3]

The trio (with John C. Olmsted substituting for his stepbrother, Frederick) quickly whittled the list of twenty prospective sites down to three.[4] The so-called Rumsey parcel was ultimately chosen for its convenient transportation options and potential for expansion after the fair. Once a farm owned by a family of the same name, the Rumsey site lay between the city of Buffalo and its prized Delaware Park. Said to be one of the most compact exposition sites to date, the land was largely featureless except for a country club, destined to become the exposition's Women's Building, and a row of Lombardy poplar trees lining Amherst Street, which traversed the site.

Rudolph Ulrich and Frederic W. Taylor were charged with transforming the site with landscaping and horticulture exhibits. Ulrich and Taylor had previously collaborated on the 1898 Trans-Mississippi World's Fair in Omaha.[5] Ulrich, Olmsted's superintendent for the World's Columbian Exposition, was appointed chief landscape architect on August 1, 1899, at a salary of ten dollars per day.[6]

Ulrich was immediately faced with a formidable task: only two planting seasons (spring and fall 1900) remained for preparing the grounds, and virtually no landscaping had yet begun. With the experience of two expositions behind him, Ulrich went immediately to work. According to one newspaper account:

> When Rudolf [sic] Ulrich, the gray-haired superintendent of the landscape effects, arrived in this city and assumed control in his department, he decided that when the Exposition opened, the floral and horticultural effects of the ground would be in readiness and that each day of the six months during which the Exposition is in progress should see an abundance of grass and a succession of flowers. Mr. Ulrich met with little encouragement from his associates, who were inclined to scoff at his idea, but nevertheless he began his efforts.[7]

Ulrich was assisted in designing the Rainbow City's extensive flower beds by the local gardener William Scott. Scott's nearby florist business in Corfu, New York, provided local connections, and he was known nationally for his writings in *Garden and Forest* and elsewhere.[8] Scott, while attuned to popular taste for brilliant gardens, also shared with Ulrich an understanding of the broader goals of landscape architecture. In his 1906 book *The Florist's Manual,* Scott wrote of the pitfalls of strict adherence to naturalistic principles when they ran contrary to popular taste:

> The landscape architect, especially of the most approved style, would, I feel sure, declaim against this bed [a colorful bed of annuals] on the lawn and say it was bad taste, not in harmony with the grass and the shade of elm and maple and linden. The up-to-date landscape artist doesn't want you to plant a golden elder or variegated cornus or *Prunus [p]issardii* in shrubbery groupings because the coloring is abnormal and not in accordance with nature. What does the proprietor care about such things? He wants to be cheerful. This sticking to nature is carried to excess. To be true to nature we would have to undergo a great change. We would not cut our hair or pare our finger nails or use knives and forks and would retrograde to the days of the fig leaf . . . It is the mission of the florist to suggest the most appropriate style of bedding to his customers where advice is asked for, and poor policy to crowd in more than is discreet when it is left to his judgment.[9]

Scott, with his commonsense approach to balancing loftier aesthetic ideals with customer demand, designed the extravagant flower beds for which the Pan-American Exposition is remembered.

As he did at the World's Columbian Exposition, Ulrich lived upon the grounds in order to closely supervise the work. A service building was hastily erected to house Ulrich and other men supervising engineering and construction.[10] To enclose the grounds, the workers built an 8-foot-tall fence using hemlock boards and cedar posts. Trees and shrubs were planted alongside this utilitarian structure to disguise it. Two greenhouses were also quickly built so that the cultivation of plants could begin.

The site was essentially a plateau, bounded on the north by railroad lines and on the south by Delaware Park. The venerable, Olmsted-designed Delaware Park was considered a valuable feature of the extended site, and public outcry prohibited exposition planners from disrupting any aspect of it. Instead, its borrowed views offered an elegant entryway to the grounds, where visitors could stroll along the meandering pathways and to the fair's main approach on the south. The Delaware Park entrance was planned as the official approach, but many more visitors arrived via railroad at the north entrance or by streetcar at the southwest gate.

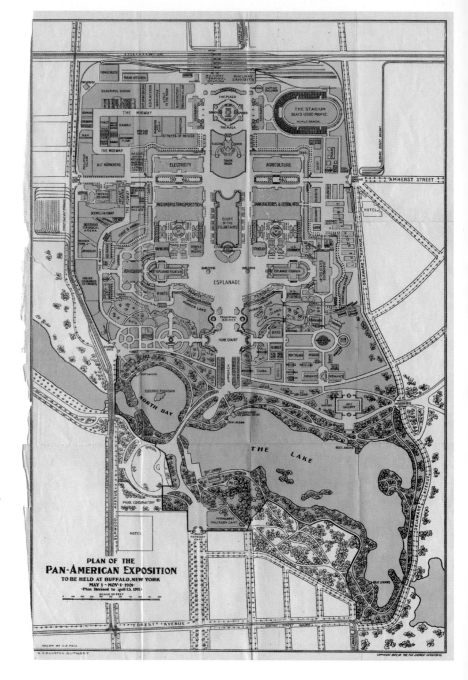

The fairgrounds were oriented along a north-south axis that led from the formal "Approach," across the Triumphal Bridge, through the Court of the Fountains, and culminating in the Electric Tower, a 375-foot monument to electricity and the signature architectural feature of the fair.

Landscaping complemented the Rainbow City theme, but did not attempt a strict adherence to the buildings' graduated progression of hues. In contrast to Olmsted's conscious decision to tone down the World's Columbian landscaping, designers of the Pan-American Expo celebrated a cacophony of color. One Buffalo newspaper offered this interpretation:

Visitors to the World's Fair in Chicago seven years ago will recall that all the flowers on the grounds were confined to a small patch in front of the Horticultural Building and on the wooded Island . . . At the [1893] World's Fair, the management, for some reason, barred flowers from the larger part of the grounds. It was supposed to be on account of the white buildings, unrelieved by other colors. The aim was to confine the colors to white and green—the white of the buildings and the green of the grass and trees. The effect was pleasing, but Pan-American officials believe that they will improve on it by a more general distribution of flowers brought here from all over the world. The colors will blend agreeably with the tinted staff [cement-like exterior] of the buildings.[11]

Although a student of Olmsted, Ulrich did not imitate the master's refinement of floral display, perhaps adhering to the dictates of the Pan-American architectural committee, or possibly following his own preference for mosaiculture.[12]

The Board of Architects strongly influenced the formal landscape design. The chief architect, John M. Carrere, is credited with the overall site plan, with its T shape and strong axial lines. The architect and board member William Welles Bosworth had studied at the École des Beaux-Arts and was much taken with French formal gardens, later even working to restore Versailles. He reported, "It was the desire of the architects in charge of the landscape work that some of the Pan-American gardening should be done in this spirit [formal French landscapes], a type of gardening evolved especially to harmonize with formal lines of fountains and balustrades and to be used in the immediate proximity to buildings."[13]

In the first few months of the fall of 1899, old fences crisscrossing the Rumsey farm were cleared, and fast-growing trees—including 2,400 small poplars, 1,200 willows, and 700 other shrubs—were planted around the perimeter of the fairgrounds. Seventy-five mature trees were relocated from within the grounds to avenues along its border.[14] By November, Ulrich had inspected local nurseries and purchased 200 large (at least 14–feet-high) cedar trees at six dollars each from Albert Wadley of New Jersey. Ellwanger & Barry won the contract for 200 large maple trees at $7.50 each, along with poplar trees. Trees, shrubs, and vines were ordered from other nurseries.[15]

As at the World's Columbian Exposition, water was a prominent feature of the fair's landscape. Excavation began on a series of canals and lagoons that would circumscribe the main buildings. The Grand Canal wrapped from the west to the east side of the fairgrounds. Mirror Lake, bisected by the Triumphal Bridge on the south, formed a symmetrical reflecting pool. Water was also an integrating element between Delaware Park and its lake on the south and the Niagara River and Falls. Because the fairgrounds occupied a slightly higher elevation than Delaware Park, elaborate pumping mechanisms, housed in the Machinery Building, were used to draw water from the river into the canals, basins, fountains, and artificial cataracts. According to *Harper's Weekly,* "The profuse use of water, quiescent and in motion, brings up the suggestion of the great lakes and the frontier river with its mighty cataracts nearby and links the [fair] grounds with the park."[16]

With only a few weeks to go until Opening Day, visitors were skeptical that the grounds and buildings would be ready. Wooden planks covered the walkways, and except for plantings near the canals, the flower beds were barren. The April 12 *Courier* offered hope: "The work on the grounds has progressed so materially in the past three or four days that the visitors of last Sunday would fail to recognize the place today . . . Along the banks of the canals, in front of the buildings, in fact everywhere that the workmen have not covered the ground with sidewalks and streets, grass and flowers are sprouting in profusion." Before the crowds descended, protective straw was removed from the beds around the southern side of the Horticulture Building, where 75,000 bulbs including hyacinth, narcissus, and crocus were arranged for a progression of bloom from May through fall.

Horticulture Building and Grounds

Unlike the other Spanish-influenced buildings, the Horticulture Building, designed by the Boston architects Peabody and Stearns, had an Italian flavor. Boasting 64,000 square feet of floor space, it soared more than 240 feet high to a glass lantern-topped roof. This deviation from the prevailing architectural style at the fair was only one of several oddities about the structure. Square-shaped with octagonal towers at each corner, it was connected to the Graphic Arts and Mines Buildings by curving glass-roofed arcades.[17] The connection to these two buildings may have served a symbolic purpose, but it did not grant any superior status to horticulture.

Frederic Taylor, who supervised the Horticulture Department, predicted optimisti-

▲ The Fountain of Abundance sparkled with lights at night and was surrounded by uplit plants. (Library of Congress Prints and Photographs Division, Washington, D.C., www.loc.gov/pictures/item/99472509/resource/#)

declared aquatic garden areas to be effective examples of French "embroidery gardening." He also highlighted the architectural nature of the beds: "The essential difference between these formal flower beds and the treatment usually employed in our public parks and gardens is not only in the severe architectural border lines, with vases, steps and balustrades, but in the design of the beds themselves within these borders. The various edges of box or pivot [sic—probably privet] outline sweeping curves or ornament which are in turn expressed in brilliant colored flowers. The pattern thus formed is set off on a ground of clear-colored sand, separating it from the border-beds, which follow the architectural outlines of the curbings."[29]

Parterres of flowers accented open spaces such as the Forecourt, Esplanade, and Court of Fountains. Hundreds of vases added not only architectural elements but also flowers in tight spaces where ground-level beds were not possible. There were six styles of vases, differentiated by their bas-relief ornamentation.[30]

The fountain gardens were greatly enhanced with the much-touted use of electricity at the Pan-American Fair. Earlier fairs had only dabbled with outdoor lighting.[31] According to Luther Stieringer, an exposition lighting engineer who had consulted on previous world's fairs: "The incandescent light has now disclosed its adaptability beyond any other light for exposition purposes. This broad statement is justified by the results finally attained at the present Pan-American Exposition."[32] Thanks to the power of the Niagara, Pan-American buildings were completely outlined with 8-candlepower incandescent lights. Thomas Edison, who visited the Pan-American grounds in July 1901, reportedly said: "It is a wonder. As for the illumination, it is a record breaker."[33]

This exposition was arguably the first to attempt artistic lighting of the landscape. While both the Pan-American and the World's Columbian Expositions boasted electricity, the Pan-American highlighted gardens. Late in the season, the exposition's Electrical and Mechanical Bureau placed 3,000 incandescent lamps in the flowerbeds.

As the *Buffalo Express* reported: "About the Fountain of Abundance at the southern end of the Grand Basin, there are rows and rows of beautiful flowers arranged in semicircular beds, bordering the walks of the Esplanade. At night the form of these beds and their contents are visible . . . but the color of the flowers, their chief beauty, is lost."[34] The paper reported that while this method had been attempted on a trial basis at the Trans-Mississippi Fair, "this is the first time flower-bed lighting has been attempted in just this way."

Legacies

While greeting visitors at the fair on September 6, 1901, President William McKinley was shot by the anarchist Leon Czolgosz and died eight days later. Theodore Roosevelt took the oath of office in Buffalo on September 14. The tragedy cast a pall on the fair, and attendance in the final months declined dramatically. Civic promotion, rather than extensive park development, was the original intent of the fair. One editorial proclaimed: "The Pan-American Exposition was intended to advertise Pan-America and her resources and her products. It has done so. Buffalo has had the largest share of the advertising. The United States as a whole has been benefited from this advertising, and the whole of North and South America has been benefited."[35]

Promoters of the Pan-American Exposition had originally intended to retain only the New York State Building. Enamored of the fair, however, Buffalo citizens made several proposals to retain some of the fair buildings and preserve the fairgrounds as parkland, and aldermen lobbied accordingly. Detractors of the proposal said that Buffalo's existing parks "were rich men's parks rather than playgrounds for the poor people."[36] At a meeting of the South Park District Taxpayers Association on December 11, officials concluded that "no more parks should be acquired until the city could properly care for what it has."[37] This ambivalence toward large parks anticipated the Progressive Era movement to create smaller, neighborhood parks instead.

Today, the former New York State Building, now home of the Buffalo and Erie County Historical Society, is the only structure remaining on its original site from the Pan-American Exposition. Situated at what was once the southwest quadrant of the exposition, its view across Hoyt Lake of Delaware Park is preserved. The remainder of the fairgrounds, however, was subdivided and is now given over to expressways and residential communities.

Landscape Lessons from the Pan-American Exposition

While it may seem an unsophisticated regression from the World's Columbian Exposition's naturalistic design, the Pan-American Exposition's generous use of bright, familiar annuals planted in patterns appealed to public taste and suited the fair's rainbow-colored buildings. With the return to elaborate multihued flower beds that recalled those of the 1876 Centennial, the Pan-American Exposition showed a latter-day sophistication of placement and scale in buildings and sculpture. The use of color as a thematic element in the exposition buildings would be a trend followed in many future fairs, as would harmonizing plantings with building color.

The first hydroelectric plant having been built near Niagara Falls, it is no wonder that innovative lighting effects marked the 1901 World's Fair. Whereas previous world's fair lighting emphasized the architectural components, an effort was made at the Pan-American Exposition to showcase the plantings at night. Landscape lighting would become a key element of future fairs, notably the Century of Progress Exposition in 1933.

Underground cold storage in the Horticulture Building improved the freshness of the fruit and vegetable displays throughout the season. The idea of presenting a working cold-storage system as an exhibit in itself introduced the world's fair practice of portraying the business side of horticulture—a practice that would become more common in the future.

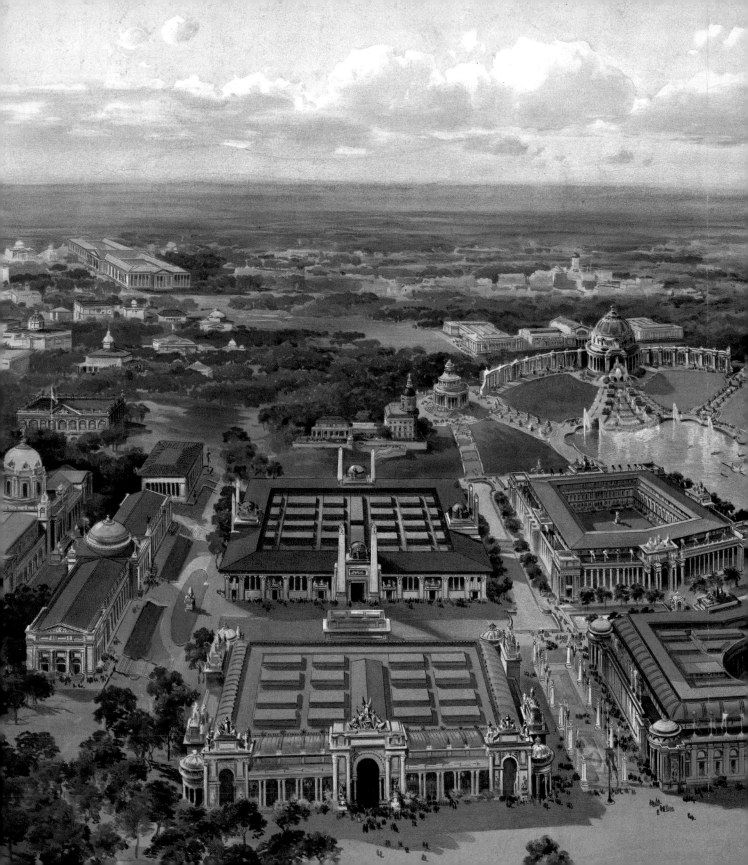

5

Louisiana Purchase Exposition

A Fair in the Forest City

In March 1901, just as the Pan-American Exposition planners were preparing for Opening Day, the U.S. Congress authorized another world's fair to be held in St. Louis, Missouri. During Theodore Roosevelt's presidency (1901–9), no fewer than five world's fairs brought visitors from around the globe to the United States.

These fairs reflected the optimism of the Progressive Era, but could there really have been enough innovation in the intervening years to warrant a new exposition? Consider these landmarks. Between 1901 and 1904, the Wright brothers made history at Kitty Hawk, the twelve-minute film *The Great Train Robbery* thrilled audiences with its realism, work began on the Panama Canal, and popular toys such as the Teddy Bear and crayons made their debut. Certainly other significant events occurred, but shortened periods between fairs meant host cities needed to increase the size and scope of their fairs in order to justify them.

St. Louis met the challenge in hosting what was, and remains, the largest world's fair in terms of acreage. St. Louis, a busy commercial center with rail and Mississippi River connections, processed much of the heartland's grain. In addition to commerce, the city boasted a thriving cultural scene. The ragtime musician Scott Joplin lived there in the early 1900s and wrote "Cascades" in the new rag style for the fair. The city had a long tradition of civic beautification; its parks dated to the 1850s. Horticulture thrived in St. Louis, with the philanthropist/botanist Henry Shaw opening his personal garden (later to become the world-famous Missouri Botanical Garden) to the public in 1859.

Foreign-influenced gardens on private U.S. estates flourished at the turn of the twentieth century, and the Louisiana Purchase Exposition (LPE) offered the masses an opportunity to see facsimiles of these in person. Coincident with the interest in foreign gardens, Edith Wharton published her *Italian Villas and Their Gardens* in 1904. In *The Golden Age of American Gardens,* Mac Griswold and Eleanor Weller note, "Like other cultivated Americans of her day, Wharton was eager to import European garden elements to compensate for the artifice she found lacking in her native landscape."[1] English garden influences also thrived, with the noted British garden designer Gertrude Jekyll publishing seven of her thirteen books in the four years between 1900 and 1904. Both Italian and English gardens enjoyed a heyday in the United States during this era.

Reflecting this interest, the Louisiana Purchase Exposition of 1904 boasted the most extensive list of foreign-designed gardens of any previous U.S. fair. The variety of landscape features reflected the massive acreage included in the fairgrounds. The postfair efforts by local citizens to preserve the host location, Forest Park, signaled a renewed value placed on city parks.

▲ The prominent feature of the Louisiana Purchase Exposition— the Cascades—was memorialized in Scott Joplin's rag of the same name. (Courtesy Lilly Library Indiana University, Bloomington, DeVincent Collection, Lilly Library ID: LL-SDV-042058)

Just as the 1803 Louisiana Purchase exponentially increased America's territory, the LPE, with more than 1,200 acres, nearly doubled the acreage of Chicago's World's Columbian Exposition and easily exceeded the site of any previous international fair. St. Louis had earned its moniker as the Forest City largely through its urban parks. At the time of its selection as the site of the 1904 World's Fair, Forest Park had served the city's populace for nearly thirty years. Whereas other world's fair landscape designers were charged with creating landscapes that could evolve into new parklands, the LPE landscape architect, George E. Kessler, needed to design a public playground that would, after the fair, disappear back into the original parkland.

Forest Park officially opened in 1876. Its landscape designer, German-trained Maximillian G. Kern, developed an ambitious plan that included artificial lakes, winding driving roads, zoological and botanical gardens, and a hippodrome. In May 1901, the city approved use of the western half of Forest Park, comprising 657 acres, for the exposition.[2] The site was expanded through the purchase or lease of land from Washington University or private owners nearby to a total of 1,270 acres—almost as large as the combined total acreage of the Centennial, World's Columbian, Trans-Mississippi, and Pan-American Expositions.

The LPE Commission of Architects determined that fair architecture should be of a "classic and academic" style. While color would be important to the exposition, "the scheme as a whole shall not depend upon color decoration."[3] The commissioners also decided on a fan-shaped arrangement of the main palaces, thus providing multiple radiating vistas. Landscaping was to complement this architectural design.

The so-called "Main Picture" of the exposition contained eight major palaces and was situated in a plateau that would accommodate large structures. The wooded portion of Forest Park dominated the southern half of the fairgrounds, and here most of the smaller states' buildings were located. The ground rose about 65 feet from the Main Picture to the forested area, offering a picturesque overlook from the Fine Arts Palace strategically sited on the hill.

In a departure from previous expositions, no natural water features bordered the LPE fairgrounds. (The River des Peres bisecting Forest Park was actually covered over in preparation for the fair). Nevertheless, the site itself was attractive. As George Kessler noted: "Other expositions were built on flats with only slight differences in elevation. St. Louis' site trends up-hill and down-dale. There is wooded upland and brushy lowland, smooth lawn and dense forest. Except on the flattened area of about 500 acres where will be built the 'main picture' the land rolls in the most picturesque way."[4] The hill also provided the topography for the fair's signature water feature: the Cascade Gardens, featuring jets of water that flowed from the hill in front of the Fine Arts

WORLD'S FAIR, ST. LOUIS, 1904.
CELEBRATING THE CENTENNIAL OF ACQUISITION OF LOUISIANA TERRITORY.
OPENS APRIL 30, 1904.   CLOSES DEC. 1, 1904.

Palace to the Grand Basin below. A series of man-made canals outlined the two build-ings that flanked the Grand Basin—the Education and Social Economy Palace and the Electricity and Machinery Palace.

In contrast to the World's Columbian Exposition, where the Wooded Island and Horticulture Palace were central to both the overall design concept and the physical fairgrounds themselves, the LPE's so-called Agriculture Hill was entirely removed from the main fairgrounds. Skinker Road formed the western boundary of For-est Park, and both the Horticulture and Agriculture Buildings lay just to the west of

▲ This birds-eye view of the fair shows how topography influenced the layout—with the Cascade Gardens dramatically falling into the Main Picture of the Exhibit Palaces. (Library of Congress Prints and Photographs Division, Washington, D.C., Digital ID: g4164s pm004473)

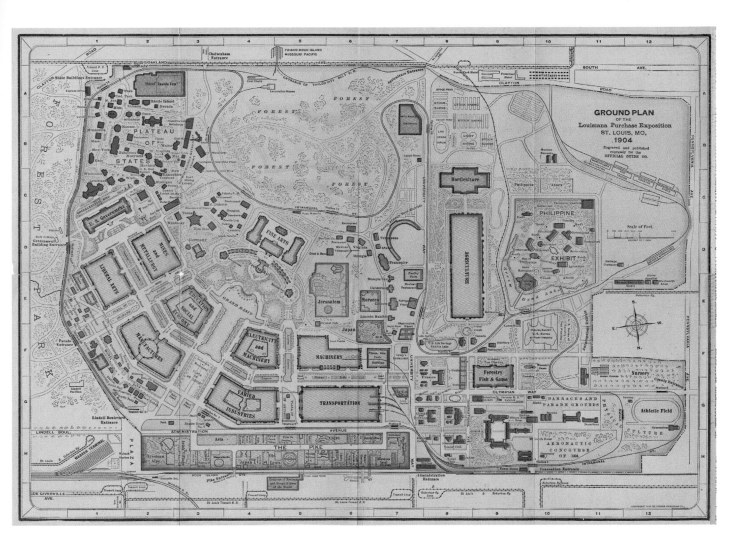

▲ In this plan view, the isolation of the Agriculture and Horticulture Buildings (*right*) from the Main Picture is apparent. (Author's collection)

Skinker Road. Thus separate from the other main exhibition palaces, Agriculture Hill was often described as a mini-exposition in itself. As a result of Agriculture Hill's isolated setting, Kessler did not have to contend with the competing demands of nurserymen and florists when he designed the landscape for the rest of the fair.

With its long axis running north and south, Agriculture Hill consumed about 80 acres, of which the rectangular Agriculture Building occupied 20 acres and the Horticulture Building 6. This left more than 50 acres for exhibitor displays of flowers and gardens around both buildings.

Creating the Landscape's Main Picture and Agriculture Hill

George Kessler envisioned a three-part division of the grounds, based on the natural features of Forest Park. According to one official account of the fair, "The topography [of Forest Park] led naturally to the use of the lower plain on the north as the site of a comparatively compact city of exposition palaces tied together by great formal avenues and crowned on the contiguous hills by the beautiful structures overlooking the lower levels, the slopes between being so shaped as to give the opportunity for the Cascades and their surrounding gardens."[5] The natural topography of the park lent itself to this ideal, but countless hours were required in order to transform the vision into reality.

Kessler reported to Isaac Taylor in the Department of Works—a relationship that began inauspiciously. At the start, Kessler proposed a six-thousand-dollar annual salary. Taylor countered with a per diem of twenty-five dollars, with Kessler's services used on an as-needed basis. Kessler felt that the scope of the job: "place[d] this work on the footing on which the landscape department of the Columbian Exposition was handled by Mr. Olmstead [sic], and the compensation, should be the same . . . although the problem is a considerably more difficult one."[6]

Kessler, aided by his foreman, D. C. Perry, began work in the fall of 1901, just as the Pan-American Exposition in Buffalo was closing. On December 20, 1901, ground was broken with much ceremony. Large trees posed one of the first landscaping problems. Trees had to be removed from construction sites and added to barren spots. In a recycling effort, Isaac Taylor queried Kessler about using the plants from the 1901 World's Fair in Buffalo, New York: "There are a lot of trees and shrubs for sale at the Pan-American Exposition grounds. I believe that it would be very good to look over same, and see what would be to our advantage to buy."[7] While some of these leftover trees may have been used, the vast majority of mature trees were transplanted from within Forest Park and neighboring tracts of land.

Work began in January of 1902, and despite poor weather and underqualified subcontractors, hundreds of trees were moved. More than two hundred silver maples ranging from 10 to 16 inches in diameter were installed along the avenues between the exhibit buildings. Kessler noted that "as a result of the rough condition of the ground at that time some of the trees were placed where the surrounding ground was five or six feet above the final grade surface, at other points as much below."[8] With subsequent rearrangement and careful maintenance, most of the trees survived.

Kessler became concerned about the limited time available for growing other plants. As of March 1902, plans still called for the exposition to open in 1903. Kessler grew increasingly worried, and urged fair officials to accelerate the timetable for obtaining plants. "With the Fair in 1903," he wrote to Taylor, "we cannot rely on the growth of plants to make the proper showing but must plant very closely and use large plants, and the enormous quantities needed will surprise your Committee . . . If you wish to provide for summer plants in the gardens an adequate green house plant will have to be ready for service September 1st, otherwise contracts will have to be made with florists to provide them at the proper time in the spring."[9]

Although officials ultimately rescheduled the fair to 1904, Kessler's appeals for expedited purchase and culture of plants worked. Existing greenhouses from the neighboring Tesson tract were acquired for early plant propagation. The Tesson property also became the site for a 15-acre nursery, and "several hundred Iris and Yucca plants have been taken from the Skinker property, subdivided and planted in this nursery."[10] A larger nursery was established near the southeast entrance to the grounds for trees and shrubs including arborvitaes, cedars, maples, Japanese cherries, and 2,400 willow cuttings. Ultimately, about 520 trees were planted along the avenues, and more than 200 specimen trees planted in the lawns. About 900,000 annuals and bedding plants were installed in the gardens, and 13,000 vines clambered up buildings and trailed along the grounds. Counting additional trees, shrubs, perennials, and bedding plants situated around the buildings, Kessler reported that a total of more than 2.6 million plants had been used in the exposition.[11]

▼ South and east of the Agriculture Building, floral motifs, including the American flag and the years 1803 and 1903, decorated the terrace. The Horticulture Building is at the left. (Missouri History Museum, Image 826)

It soon became apparent to Kessler and the Landscape Department that landscaping the Main Picture alone would require a Herculean effort. In an attempt to avoid the sort of battles Olmsted had had with exhibiting nurserymen, it was decided that the Department of Horticulture would assume responsibility for the area around the Horticulture and Agriculture Buildings. Prospective horticulture exhibitors were then contacted to see if they would commit to landscaping portions of Agriculture Hill. The response was enthusiastic, with nurserymen and florists from around the world offering to mount displays.

This approach differed markedly from Olmsted's for the Columbian fairgrounds. The Wooded Island at the World's Columbian Exposition was designed by one man with a single vision of a naturalistic oasis where the "hand of man" could not be seen. LPE's Agriculture Hill was designed by a committee with an eye toward showcasing the wares of individual exhibitors. The LPE Horticulture Department report explains the design philosophy as one of compromise:

> In placing exhibits there are to be considered always, three elements: the exhibitor, the Exposition and the visitor. An exhibitor has a right to expect his material to be so placed as to meet the eyes of a reasonable number of visitors, among whom it is expected will be purchasers. The Exposition Management desires that with the least possible expense, results in landscaping be produced to harmonize with the structures erected to receive the exhibits of merchandise. The visitors expect . . . that exhibits not only appeal to the eye as beautiful but should teach how . . . results may be reached by anyone with a little perseverance.[12]

In laying out the grounds around Agriculture Hill, Frederic Taylor, Horticulture Department chief, used his experience in the 1901 and 1898 expositions to ensure that each exhibitor had a favorable display location. "With the intention of making it an object lesson as well as a pleasure to the visitor, this great outdoor exhibit or model horticultural park was laid out as simply as possible," Taylor explained. "Its sections and beds were so arranged and so penetrated and bordered by paths as to be of easy and effective access and also to permit of direct passage through any part of the reservation to other sections of the exposition grounds."[13]

Plans for Agriculture Hill were finalized in January 1903, and planting began that spring. Considerable grading and filling was required to prepare the grounds around the hill. According to the LPE report: "The north slope of the hill, where the great clock was afterward placed, . . . was rough, washed into ditches, almost entirely without soil, the stiff clay subsoil cropping out almost everywhere and a very uninviting subject for the gardener's skill. Between the Palace of Agriculture and Skinker Road . . . it was necessary to do much filling in order to bring the surface into conformity with the plains. This left very little of the ground in such condition that it could be utilized as it was found."[14]

Horticulture Building and Agriculture Hill

The 400 x 800 foot Horticulture Building designed by E. L. Macqueray, chief designer of the exposition, was plain and unremarkable compared to the palaces in the Main Picture. The central square of the structure housed the pomology section, the west

The plain LPE Horticulture Building contrasted with the exuberant architecture of previous world's fair horticulture palaces. (Author's collection)

wing held cut flower and implement exhibits, and the east wing displayed conservatory plants.

All exhibits in the Horticulture Department were organized according to the producing state. Thirty-eight states and territories participated with the largest displays submitted by (in order of square feet) Missouri, California, Illinois, New York, and Washington.[15]

With more than 160,000 square feet dedicated to pomology—more than one and one-half times the combined square footage of the Conservatory and Implement Section—fruits clearly took center stage. St. Louis exhibitors wanted to show the great advances made in just over a decade since the World's Columbian Exposition. Mindful of the problems Chicago had had with storing perishables—not to mention the fire of the Cold Storage Building—Chief of Horticulture Taylor conducted exhaustive research into current methods of keeping fruit. Circulars sent to the secretaries of each state's horticultural society asked for the recommendations of those experienced with storage and packing. Choosing the best practices, the committee then advised participants as to best methods for picking fruit, wrapping, packing, and display. For apple exhibits, nearly all states kept from 100 to 1,200 barrels of fruit—some dating back to the harvest of 1901—in cold storage on or near the fairgrounds.[16] Because of their excellent keeping properties, apples were by far the largest display category. A list of the best "keeping" varieties was then compiled and published in horticultural societies' reports.

Not all improvements in the pomological exhibit were of scientific significance; some were merely aesthetic. Exposition planners gave considerable thought to how the fruit would be displayed. Fair managers rejected the traditional white china plates, and fruit was shown on a custom-designed 8-inch green display plate with a 4-inch cream-colored central circle stamped with the LPE monogram. Use of the official display plate was mandatory, and other regulations dictated the size and height of the exhibit itself. Because Exposition officials were preoccupied with constant comparisons with the World's Columbian Exposition, President David Francis was pleased to note

in his final report that "in improvement of horticultural methods and in magnitude and variety of products, progress since 1893 was shown."[17]

While there was much to see inside the Horticulture Building, many exhibitors saved their best displays for the outdoors. The armchair tour below begins on the east side of Agriculture Hill and proceeds counterclockwise to the Great Floral Clock on the north.

East Terrace: The steep slopes of the east embankment were sodded and terraced to prevent erosion. The terraces were embellished with floral tableaux depicting significant events or personages of St. Louis. Bracketed by two flower beds in the shape of fleurs-de-lis, the names Napoleon, Jefferson, McKinley, and Roosevelt were spelled out in floral scrolls, as were the names of prominent horticulturists. A floral version of the Louisiana Purchase Exposition flag—red, yellow, and white stripes and a fleur-de-lis atop a blue field—was on display as well. Most of these beds incorporated hyacinths, tulips, and crocus for an early display and annuals for a later one.

Rose Garden: Planted in the spring of 1903, the 7-acre Rose Garden, touted by LPE guidebooks as the largest in the world, displayed a year's growth. Boasting well over a thousand bushes, the garden contained many new varieties. The most plentiful roses on display included 'Magna Carta,' 'Paul Neyron,' and 'Clothilde Soupert.'

South of the Rose Garden, the aquatics display offered the use of rowboats so visi-

⌃ Missouri had the largest pomological exhibit, shown in precise displays of fruit pyramids on a green-and-white plate. LPE lore has it that the phrase "An apple a day keeps the doctor away" was coined by the Missouri horticulturist J. T. Stinson at an exposition lecture. (Author's collection)

▲ The aquatics display in the lily pond near Agriculture Hall featured giant *Victoria regia* and other popular plants. (Author's collection)

tors could enjoy close-up views of plants. Two small lakes of 2 acres had been sited atop the slope. Named after the children of Frederic Taylor, Lake Marion and Lake William teemed with aquatics by Henry A. Dreer of Philadelphia. Lake Marion was further accented with a rustic bridge and such water lilies as *Zanzibariensis rosea,* 'Mrs. Ward.'

West Side: In accordance with the nation's newfound interest in conservation, the 2–acre Wildflower Garden, planted west of the Agriculture Building, was a favorite spot on Agriculture Hill. Planted with 18 varieties of indigenous shrubs and more than 150 varieties of herbaceous plants, the display was designed to remind visitors of their own dooryard gardens. Trees such as *Acer rubrum, Cercis canadensis,* and *Prunus serotina* sheltered mixed plantings of asters, helianthus, hibiscus, liatris, wild phlox, aquilegia, and monarda. A brook ran through the garden, creating miniature waterfalls along its way to a small lake filled with aquatics.

North: Space was allocated to the U.S. Life Savings Exhibit with its small lake surrounded by shrubbery and coleus. But the greatest attraction of this area was the great Floral Clock. The mechanics of the clock, provided by the Johnson Service Company of Milwaukee, operated a dial 100 feet in diameter. The numerals on the dial, nearly 15 feet long, were made entirely of flowers, and a 5,000-pound bell sounded on the hour and half hour. A rustic fence had to be built around the clock to protect it from curious visitors. The clock's floral composition included: 1,500 'Golden Bedder' Coleus, 1,500 *Coleus verschaffeltii,* 3,000 *Centaursa gymnocarper,* 4,000 *Cineraria maritma candidissima,* 4,500 verbenas (in center), 1,000 *Coleus verschaffeltii* (border around verbenas), and 2,500 Coleus 'Hero' (clock numerals).

Controversy surrounded the building of the clock. Kessler derided it on aesthetic grounds, writing to Isaac Taylor: "You doubtless remember the rules we got up last week for surroundings of the state and foreign government buildings, which contained something like this: 'Eccentric or incongruous flower beds will not be permitted.' My position would always be that floral designs of this kind would be classified under that prohibited list and while they may prove attractive to a large number of people, I do not think we want to be responsible for exhibition of this sort."[18]

▲ The Floral Clock on the north end of Agriculture Hall measured 100 feet in diameter. (Missouri History Museum)

Main Picture and Foreign Exhibitor Gardens

The Main Picture of the fair featured eight palaces interconnected by a series of lagoons. Sited atop a hill, the Fine Arts Palace overlooked Festival Hall and the Grand Basin, a long, formal reflecting pool. The Cascades, a series of three terraced waterfalls running from Festival Hall to the Grand Basin, pumped 90,000 gallons of water per minute. Surrounded by statuary and brilliantly illuminated at night, the Cascades must have been a dramatic sight. Extensive flower beds bordered the waterfalls and terraces.

On the east side of the fan-shaped Main Picture, the popular Sunken Gardens, between the Palace of Mines and Palace of Liberal Arts, featured formal plantings along a longitudinal axis. The gardens were sited about 5 feet below the level of the surrounding promenades. They were traversed by red gravel walkways and reached by a series

⌃ Twenty thousand incandescent lights featuring three different hues bathed the Cascades and Festival Hall. (Author's collection)

➤ The Sunken Gardens exemplified the formal gardens in the plazas of the Main Picture. Geraniums and salvia were favored for their constant color. This view faces southeast, with the Palace of Liberal Arts on the left, and the Government Building at the end. (Author's collection)

of stone steps. While this design harkened back to the sunken gardens of the 1876 Centennial, Kessler described his design philosophy as follows:

> As a rule most landscape gardeners, I as well, detest the formal carpet bedding, especially when introduced in informal surroundings, but this entire exposition scheme is one of the highest types of decorative uses, both in architecture and gardening, and the formal gardens introduced here are certainly justified in uniting the two into one harmonious picture. This is especially true in the floral display in Cascade gardens, and in the more formal area of the sunken Gardens, between the Manufacturers Bldg. and Liberal Arts Bldg., and again between the Machinery and Transportation Bldgs. In the Sunken Gardens the lines are sharp and clear and purely formal. The Cascade gardens are partly formal, merging into the informal and natural scenes.[19]

Eighteen foreign countries participated in the Horticulture Department, either through exhibits in the Horticulture Building and grounds or at their own pavilion. Whereas only Japan had a significant outdoor display at the World's Columbian Exposition, many more foreign countries at the LPE planted their pavilions with gardens representative of their nation. The LPE exhibits of some countries were particularly impressive, as noted in the *Official Guide to the World's Fair:*

> French Garden: . . . The French Government reservation covers fifteen acres. The center driveway is flanked on both sides by raised terraces of sward, and shaded by parallel rows of parked Carolina poplars. The slopes along the driveways and table and of the terraces are done in the finest example of French floral embroidery. Statuary intersperses the arcade of trees. To the south of the drive, across the terrace gardens, the ground falls away to lower levels in a series of terraces, solidly banked with French horticulture. Outspread on a great level, running away from the foot of the terraces, is the gem of the French display, a beautifully fashioned landscaping set in bas-relief . . .
>
> Chinese Garden: The use of Prince Pu Lun's country seat for the Chinese National Pavilion furnishes a royal excuse for pilfering from the Imperial Gardens at Pekin. The garden effect was designed by Madame Wong Kai Kah, wife of the Imperial Chinese Vice Commissioner of the Exposition. An open court in the center of the Chinese Pavilion is a feature . . .
>
> English Garden: A replica of the Orangery of the Kensington Palace, is surrounded by an English country seat garden of 200 years ago. Hedges are a prominent feature, and the borders give the gardens a distinctly English appearance. The hollyhock, preeminent two centuries ago, is one of the flowers prominent in this garden of old England. There are old-fashioned roses, the juniper and yew, and other shrubs, some so pruned that they take on the forms of lions and peacocks and other birds and animals. Perhaps the most English of any of the features of this old garden is the pleached alley [sic] extending along the east side of the Orangery tract.[20]

Germany's pavilion, with its elevated position atop a hill overlooking the Cascades, was surrounded by a replica of Berlin's Charlottenburg Gardens. The gardens of Sweden, Cuba, and Mexico were also highlighted in the guide. But once again it was the garden of Japan, on the western boundary of the Cascade area, that captured popular fancy.

Said to include copies of gardens surrounding the emperor's palace, the Japanese display covered nearly 150,000 square feet. The garden surrounded a complex of several buildings including a reception hall, the Formosa teahouse, the Kinkaku teahouse, and several smaller structures. According to one contemporary report: "Hills and waterfalls, ponds and bridges were presented in miniature scale. In the verdant lawns flowers of different colors were all harmonized into an artistic unit in unique landscape gardening. Beautifully trained dwarf trees, centuries old, were brought from Japan for the special purpose of

ornamenting the garden. There were also the drooping wisteria and gay peony, the scented lily and blushing maple."[21]

> Japan created its traditional gardens, with appropriately scaled shrubs and water features. (Author's collection)

Like other world's fairs, the LPE provided a variety of professional groups who chose to present lectures and flower-related shows an opportunity to convene. The St. Louis Florist's Club hosted the twentieth annual meeting of the Society of American Florists and Ornamental Horticulturists from August 16 through August 19 at the fair. Later, despite inclement weather, the World's Fair Flower Show Association produced a very successful juried competition between November 7 and 12. One hundred leading florists and affiliated businesses posted a guarantee to provide premiums and make the Flower Show self-sustaining. The first day was devoted to chrysanthemums and orchids, the second to roses, the third to floral arrangements and carnations. The final days showcased floral arrangements as well.

Legacies

Although the St. Louis public had been promised that Forest Park would be returned to its prefair state in two years, the undertaking actually required nine years. George Kessler supervised the work, complaining in his private papers, "When all these buildings are removed, and there remains nothing but a plain sixty feet below the general level of the upper surface on which the Art Buildings stand . . . a sluice way of the River Des Peres, the empty lagoons, the whole will be a picture of desolation."[22]

Fortunately, park officials chose to do otherwise. Officials agreed fairly quickly that it would be impractical to attempt to restore the park to its prefair state. Too many changes had been implemented, and furthermore, as with many previous fairs, the general public had grown fond of the fairgrounds and was loath to see them disappear. Kessler instead redesigned the park to include both passive and active recreational areas, work that continued until April 30, 1913.[23]Conflicting visions for the park's use hampered the work schedule. Kessler wanted a return to "the sylvan beauties of Forest Park, its restfulness and opportunity for quiet enjoyment."[24] However, some St. Louis citizens and public officials coveted space for more vigorous recreation such as skating, tobogganing, and bicycling. Others expressed a desire for a permanent art museum, the funding of which would have required state legislation. These and other legal entanglements pitted St. Louis and the LPE management against each other until, just shy of the expiration date of the commission's charter, the city agreed that the LPE corporation had fulfilled its duty.[25]

Today, in the Main Picture area, the Grand Basin remains, along with Art Hill—the elevated site of the Palace of Fine Arts, now the St. Louis Art Museum—and remnants of the lagoons. Tennis courts, golf courses, and a zoo now are interspersed amid pastoral views. Although Agriculture Hill has been replaced with contemporary buildings, many other vestiges of the fair remain in Forest Park.

Landscape Lessons from the LPE

With its enormous size and preexisting park landscape, the LPE offered new lessons to landscape designers charged with hosting a temporary exhibition in an established park. No other U.S. fair to date had required that the fairgrounds be returned to its undisturbed original state. Although some fairs had adjoined existing parks (for example, the 1876 Centennial in Philadelphia's Fairmount Park and the Pan-American Exposition near Buffalo's Delaware Park), those fairgrounds themselves were created on undeveloped land. George Kessler was faced with the significant challenges of creating an exposition landscape theoretically destined for complete restoration into the preexisting landscape.

Eventually, George Kessler's influence extended well beyond the boundaries of Forest Park. Not only did his work expand to properties throughout the nation, but he also designed more than thirty-five private and public landscapes in the St. Louis area between the close of the fair and the start of World War I.[26]

The LPE exhibitor list included more foreign participants than any previous U.S. exposition. Foreign involvement extended not only to displays of machinery or arts in the allied exposition palaces, but also to much more nationally distinctive landscapes surrounding each nation's pavilion.

The LPE Japanese Garden, far more elaborate and complete than that at the 1893 World's Fair, fully reflected the American public's newfound enthusiasm for this style. As noted in a 1903 issue of *Town and Country* magazine: "Now that the Italian garden fad has spent its force, the Japanese garden is in vogue . . . Just at present the English and Italian gardens are being overdone, and it is probable that Japanese landscape gardening will now be much studied in America."[27]

Even as foreign gardens beguiled LPE fairgoers, the expansive Wildflower Garden on Agriculture Hill put the beauty of America's native plants on display. Compare this dedicated space to the lonely display of butterfly weed at the 1876 Centennial. The steadily growing conservation movement in the United States found a powerful supporter in Theodore Roosevelt. From increased preservation efforts in national parks and territories to the 1902 founding of the Wildflower Preservation Society of America, U.S. gardeners became more aware of the benefits and uses of indigenous plants.

More typically, endless colorful beds of annuals covered most of the LPE in both the formal sunken gardens and Agriculture Hill. The sunken garden made a reappearance at this world's fair after a hiatus since the 1876 Philadelphia Centennial. The Floral Clock, perhaps the most extravagant use of gaudy flowers at the fair, became an icon of the LPE, one of the first times a horticultural construction achieved this status. The concept of flower clocks dated at least to the time of Linnaeus, who proposed a "Horologium Florae" that used the daily bloom times of various flowers to coincide with the hours on a clock. The LPE Floral Clock was the first such clock with mechanical movements in the United States, and possibly the world.[28] At 100 feet in diameter, it eclipsed its nearest competitor in Edinburgh, Scotland, by almost five times. Today, floral clocks grace many American public parks, notably, the 49-foot flower clock in Niagara Parks.

6

 Jamestown Exposition

JAMESTOWN, 1907

Native Plantings Frame City Planning

Only three years passed between the Louisiana Purchase Exposition and the Jamestown Exposition of 1907, yet five additional world's fairs had been celebrated or were under way around the globe. The 1906 Milan Exposition, with 400 acres, was the largest of the four overseas fairs. In the United States, Portland, Oregon, hosted the Lewis and Clark Exposition of 1905. Horticulture exhibits were subsumed by the overwhelming presence of the Forestry Building and industry at this latter fair. With a landscape design by the Olmsted firm, the grounds captured beautiful views of Mount St. Helens, yet all vestiges of the exquisite lake and site were subsequently lost to development.

At about the same time, on the eastern seaboard, laborers began clearing a swampy site for the Jamestown Exposition, held during the tercentennial celebration of the founding of the Jamestown colony. The exposition originated with a 1901 proposal from the Association for the Preservation of Virginia Antiquities (now Preservation Virginia). Such a historically tethered fair was appropriate for the Commonwealth of Virginia, a state blessed with many heritage landmark sites and supported by groups such as the Mount Vernon Ladies' Association, which spearheaded estate-preservation efforts as early as 1860. With its proximity to the historic James River plantations, the Hampton Roads exposition site in Norfolk, Virginia, offered visitors exquisite landscapes against which the fair's marvels could be viewed. The 1907 Jamestown Exposition is an interesting landscape in a state filled with historic properties. Only a few buildings remain from the fair, and the Naval Station Norfolk now occupies the site.

The Jamestown Exposition was beset by severe monetary deficits, delayed construction, indifferent exhibitor representation, and low visitor attendance. Whether because of world's fair fatigue,[1] inefficient management, unpopular military and historical themes, or simple bad luck, the Jamestown Exposition never really captured the nation's attention and is often treated as a footnote in world's fair literature. Nonetheless, it offers a fine example of urban planning by the noted landscape architect Warren H. Manning.

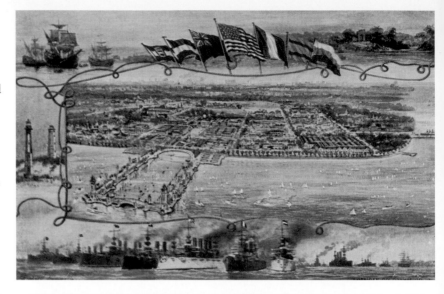

BIRD'S-EYE VIEW OF THE JAMESTOWN EXPOSITION

⌃ ⌃ The Jamestown Exposition celebrated America's history under many flags, as well as its burgeoning imperialism, marked by the launch of the Great White Fleet. (Author's collection)

⌃ This birds-eye view shows the orientation of the exposition grounds toward the sea and military themes. (Author's collection)

The Boston-based Manning (1860–1938) was the son of the Massachusetts nurseryman Jacob Manning and apprenticed for several years with Frederick Law Olmsted. An exceptional plantsman, Manning had served as one of Olmsted's key designers at the 1893 World Columbian Exposition. He was a cofounder of the American Park and Outdoor Art Association (1897), and an early proponent of wild, or natural, gardens.[2] Manning's world's fair experience, passion for civic planning, and naturalistic design was exceptionally suited to the Jamestown Exposition. His urban planning experience was important in Jamestown because it was the first (and only) U.S. exposition at which the postfair site was destined to become a residential development. To accommodate this future use, more permanent buildings were specified than was typical for world's fairs, and Manning needed to plan both "instant-effect" plantings for the exposition and the long-term landscapes for its aftermath. In effect, the Jamestown Exposition would become a small town that required an interesting combination of scaled-down architecture coupled with circulation patterns that could accommodate a one-time influx of crowds and, later, a less trafficked street network suitable for a suburban community.

During the City Beautiful era, Manning was an outspoken proponent of civic planning and enhancement through green space. His American Park and Outdoor Art Association united many towns' civic improvement groups in beautifying cities through effective landscapes. Writing in 1901, Manning identified the many organizations working to improve city planning, from Women's Clubs to the AIA, the ASLA, and the Outdoor Art Association he helped to found. Manning felt that education of the public was critical to success, and thought an exposition would be an excellent opportunity to draw attention to the importance of city planning.

Real estate speculation, often the catalyst for U.S. world's fairs that transformed undeveloped land to prime parcels, shaped much of the Jamestown Exposition. Prior to construction, the area near the fairgrounds consisted of isolated farms and a single hotel, the Pine Beach Ocean Resort Hotel. Inadequate public transportation and swampy environs had inhibited previous real estate investment. Responding to the problem, the Exposition Landscape Department drained 1,000 acres, half of which would be allocated to the fairgrounds.[3] When the *Virginian Pilot* headlined "$1,325,000 for Exposition Finally Voted by Congress," on June 30, 1906, Abbott Morris & Co. Real Estate Investments of Norfolk was quick to take out a half-page ad in the same newspaper, proclaiming, "Jamestown Exposition a Certainty." The ad coaxed: "Have you been postponing your expected investment? Why Wait Longer? Next Week May be too Late . . . Ocean View: Lots on Exposition avenue are sure profit bringers."[4] Investors knew that the fairgrounds would ultimately be given over to a housing development, and thus outlying areas near the fairgrounds received infrastructure upgrades as well.

Designing the Maritime and Land-Based Fair
The Jamestown Exposition posed a unique landscape design challenge in that it was to focus upon water features instead of land forms. In the imperialistic McKinley/ Roosevelt era, this exposition was to be a celebration of military strength, with a special focus on marine and naval capabilities. According to one promotional booklet,

"Never in the history of the world has there been such an array of battleships as can be seen on the historic waters of Hampton Roads."[5] Naval fleets from the major countries of the world performed military maneuvers and displays. While the grounds were important, the harbor front was deemed the focal point of the fair, and in a visually striking development that must have pleased fair organizers, the renowned Great White Fleet of navy battleships departed Hampton Roads harbor on December 16, 1907, for its multiyear voyage around the world.

The land-based centerpiece of the Jamestown Exposition, a greensward called Lee's Parade that dominated the fairgrounds, served as a setting for military drills. The amusement and concessions area (the equivalent of the World Columbian Exposition's Midway and the Louisiana Purchase Exposition's Pike), dubbed the "War Path" at President Roosevelt's suggestion, was surrounded by huge military encampments. Not everyone was enamored of this military emphasis—the exposition's Advisory Board issued a protest, noting: "The extravagant militarism of the program of the coming Jamestown exposition . . . is a profound shock to a great body of the American people . . . [The current plan] is utterly different from that given when the plan of the Jamestown exposition first was submitted to the public."[6]

Manning and his team thus faced conflicting design objectives. They had to create a beautiful wild garden in the midst of a military zone and prepare for a permanent small suburban village, while accommodating huge exposition crowds all within a severely constrained and constantly dwindling budget. Despite these formidable challenges, Manning developed one of the most charming exposition sites of the new century.

Extensive draining operations went on throughout 1905, not only to render the land buildable, but also to eliminate "breeding places for the malarial mosquito which had practically depopulated the region."[7] The marshy character of the land—the storied Great Dismal Swamp was a nearby attraction—had resisted previous attempts at drainage.[8]

Manning was adept at creating beauty from the mundane. He designed and installed a "living fence" that would become an unlikely favorite feature of the fair. Fences were essential but generally uninspired elements of world's fairs, necessary both to keep sightseers out during the construction phase and to ensure that fair visitors entered through the sanctioned, paid-admission gates. Two years before the exposition's opening, Manning's crew built an 8-foot-high woven wire fence topped with 2 feet of barbed wire. Disguising the wire were thick plantings of Japanese evergreen honeysuckle interspersed with thousands of crimson rambler roses. Trumpet vines adorned each fence post. The fence, both practical and beautiful, became a surprise attraction, touted by a typical promotional brochure as "a beautiful wire trellis heavily covered with flowering vines, suggestive of the semi-tropical climate of this spot which, for all-the-year-round comfort, has no equal anywhere on the Atlantic seaboard."[9]

Despite the fair's limited budget, Manning seized his chance to implement the outdoor art principles he espoused. One of his major precepts, as he explained in his talk at the exposition's Congress of Horticulture, was the importance of using indigenous plants and preserving natural features. "The broadest aspect of the civic improvement movement, however, lies in permanently preserving and improving the natural beauty of a region and securing convenient and attractive access thereto for all citizens," Manning advised.[10] Nearly all of the 1 million plants used on the Jamestown grounds were obtained either from the exposition site itself or from the land nearby.

As much as possible, natural features were protected and incorporated into the ground plan. The exposition-sponsored *Jamestown Magazine* reported: "The tree growth had an important influence on the building of the Exposition and the arrangement of the grounds and buildings. The roads and walks were planned to conform to the natural conditions, in such a way that the trees might be saved and impart to the buildings an agreeable landscape setting . . . Everywhere in the reserve spaces in nooks and corners of the grounds the native tree and shrub growth has been retained with pleasing effect, special care having been given to very little detail by the landscape designer in charge of the work."[11]

During the winter of 1905–6, crews of laborers began removing undergrowth from the grounds. Director of Works William Dixon wrote: "For one who only saw the completed exposition it would be difficult to realize the density of the vines and shrubs which burdened the property. In many places the growth was impenetrable by anything larger than a rabbit."[12] Dixon noted that attempts were made to protect the wildlife—except snakes, which were abundant—but most animals disappeared with the onset of construction and human activity. Healthy and desirable native trees and shrubs were saved, and Isaac Hicks & Sons of New York, "probably the best known tree-moving contractors in the United States,"[13] moved more than three thousand large trees, some more than 30 inches in diameter.

Building construction began in January 1906. Dixon reported that there were constant changes to the plan, "and finally it was very evident that there was no fixed plan," but that the building of this exposition "unlike its predecessors was an evolution . . . It was impossible one day to tell what the plan would be the next."[14] Manning claimed credit for the original siting of buildings, and pointed out that his plan for a double pier extending into the harbor had won out over the architects' curved pier design.[15]

Directly across the main land entrance from the north, Manning's Grand Basin, with its parallel piers, embraced maritime visitors. The future town square of the planned postexposition city was to be located between these two entrances on the highest ground of the site. As one early bulletin reported: "When the Exposition is over 'The Square' will be the public square of the city that is expected to rise on the Exposition site . . . The temporary parts are to be removed when the Exposition is over, the permanent parts left for the purposes of the projected city as it grows up on the Exposition site."[16]

Manning grouped the main exposition buildings around Lee's Parade and another important green space, Raleigh Square. The Auditorium, Machinery and Transportation Building and the Manufacturers and Liberal Arts Building dominated this core area. These structures, while elegantly designed, were more human-scaled than the grand palaces of the World's Columbian or the Louisiana Purchase Expositions. State buildings, clustered along the waterfront in the northwest section of the fairgrounds, resembled a row of elegant residences. (Today, several of the state buildings remain as homes for navy officers.) Manning said that the "first work in this line [of grounds planning] was the preparation of a roads and lots plan for a town sub-division."[17]

Manning did not impose artificial curves in street design but endorsed the grid system where practical, and incorporated more sinuous roadways where suggested by nature. As he explained, "The principal streets of this plan were made to lead straight away from and parallel to an eighty-foot shore boulevard, to conform to some already graded and because there was nothing in the topography to justify curving lines until the street system encountered the arms of Boush Creek."[18]

Expositions and City Planning

In his 1907 essay entitled "Civic Horticulture and Improvement," given at the exposition's Horticultural Congress, Manning proffered several suggestions for employing horticultural material in an urban design. Knowing that the site was destined to become a city, he adhered to all of these points in the Jamestown site. Specifically:[19]

1. *In developing street plans, use "trees best suited to each street and an arrangement of trees that will give desirable uniformity."* Manning attempted to give each major street its own character by planting a signature tree species, noting: "[The civic horticulturist would be especially interested in] suggestions regarding the use of enough of one plant in these private plantations to give each street a special distinction. One street for example having lilacs at intervals throughout its length, another magnolias, another hydrangeas, etc."[20] Large red bay trees lined Powhatan Avenue, and Commonwealth Avenue was bordered on both sides with yucca trees.[21]

The *Jamestown Magazine* reported: "The same [tree] varieties are used in the zones throughout the length of the streets, in order that there may be long lines of color to greet the eye . . . In the center of many planting spaces have been used flowering dogwood, wild plum and calli carpa for the summer, and violet colored fruit for the autumn."[22] Manning extended his harmonious composition in the shrub and herbaceous layers of the street planting. He explained, "Each street had also its special shrub through the center of the planting spaces, with hardy herbs outside and a groundcover instead of grass, of such annuals as petunias, zinnias, calliopsis, planted in the spring of the opening year. Thus were long lines of color provided in each street during the flowering season—at one time a street full of roses; again, full of marshmallows, petunias, zinnias and the like. During all the season there was something in bloom."[23]

2. *Create open front lawns and private backyards.* To give residential streets a "distinctly American" sense of openness,[24] Manning advocated broad lawns. This democratic style of contiguous front lawns was favored by Manning's mentor, Frederick Law Olmsted, an example being the 1869 plan for Riverside, Illinois. With the passage of time, Manning recognized that homeowners needed privacy screens in the front yard and a personal haven in the back. He suggested "screening plantations" in the front to provide some privacy, yet still maintain an open look. Designs for the individual state buildings, although influenced by the states themselves, generally adhered to this principle. Sited along the waterfront on Willoughby Boulevard, which would ultimately become a residential street, most state buildings featured foundation plantings near the house and uninterrupted lawns in front. To accommodate the needs of public buildings, the ratio of building footprint to front lawn was generally greater than would be seen in a residential neighborhood, but the democratic effect of continuous green lawns was not marred by individualistic plantings.

3. *Emphasize indigenous plantings.* The use of native plants was the hallmark of this exposition. In his 1907 essay, Manning advised horticulturists to pay attention to "the treatment of natural vegetation to develop its greatest beauty and usefulness and the treatment of artificial plantations. Upon such details would be indicated roads, trails, vistas, thinning, the selection of trees and shrubs and the additional plantations of exotic trees, shrubs and herbs."[25] Manning preserved many existing stands of trees: groves of native pine trees, some 70–80 feet tall, towered over holly trees, themselves 30–40 feet high. The *Jamestown Magazine* reported, "Many species of oaks have been left standing where the hand of nature planted the tiny acorns long years ago . . . [and] will serve to shelter multitudes from the summer sun during the Exposition period."[26]

"Distinctly American" Landscape Effects

Manning embraced the Colonial architecture mandated for exposition buildings as perfectly suited to the naturalistic landscapes he planned.[27] "The idea of the Exposition management to create a permanent memorial and to utilize as an architectural theme designs based upon the Colonial type of building led naturally to a kindred scheme of landscape decoration. Lending itself admirably to this adaptation, an exceedingly varied and interesting natural growth abounded."[28] For major buildings such as the Auditorium, Manning provided a complementary formal garden style with fountains and circular plantings. For more modest buildings, such as the cottages in the Arts and Crafts Village, he devised an informal design, with the ambiance of a small town.

Manning designed the marine-based entrance on the north to blend seamlessly with the exposition buildings. What could have been an abrupt transition between exposition grandeur and military regimentation instead presented as a graceful segue from sea to land. In Raleigh Square, he mirrored the shape of the Grand Basin piers with two U-shaped reflecting pools embracing a paved rectangular peninsula centered with a fountain. The waterfront design resembled a formal plaza with sculptured rectangles of lawn ringed by low hedges and bordered by wide sidewalks. This welcoming entry from sea to land mitigated the strident patriotic fanfare on the water. The plaza would comfortably accommodate crowds

AUDITORIUM, JAMESTOWN EXPOSITION, 1907.

▼ The grounds were designed in the style of a village square with a formal fountain and gardens at the center. (Author's collection)

▼▼ Manning's naturalistic designs surrounded the model school and other smaller structures. (Author's collection)

GARDENS NEAR MODEL SCHOOL, JAMESTOWN EXPOSITION, 1907.

The venerable Powhatan Oak, spared by Manning, likely graced the grounds when the original settlers landed in Jamestown. (Author's collection)

Beloved by visitors was the naturalistic "Lover's Lane," which followed an existing stream. (Author's collection)

during the naval displays on the water, and would revert without problems to a seaport waterfront after the fair.

Manning enhanced the space around Lee's Parade greensward with old apple trees transplanted from onetime farm orchards on and near the site. He reported: "Eighty-eight apple trees were thus treated [root pruned the previous season] and placed in position as a boundary for Lee's Parade. They proved to be a most attractive feature, especially in the spring when they were covered with blooms."[29] This open green space of about 30 acres was destined to become the postexposition town square.

Manning saved the celebrated Powhatan Oak, a historic live oak 4–5 feet in diameter. With its canopy spread of more than 70 feet, the tree was reputed to be nearly one thousand years old, and "according to authentic reports, Indian war talks were made under [its] shade."[30] In keeping with the exposition's historical theme, the Powhatan Oak served as a living reminder of the original Jamestown era.

The Powhatan Oak, near the Arts and Crafts Village, was an impressive sight for any visitor strolling along "Flirtation Walk." This 2-mile footpath bordering the "Canoe Trail" became one of the exposition's most popular features. A handsome example of Manning's naturalistic landscape principles, Flirtation Walk—or "Lover's Lane" as it was sometimes called—made an inviting route through the natural vegetation that surrounded the curving shore of Boush Creek. This natural waterway bordered the east side of the exposition site, where the grid pattern of the city streets gave way to more curved roadways.

Manning carved the romantic Canoe Trail, 16 feet wide and 2 miles long, out of the existing marshland so that visitors could paddle through the stands of native trees and woodland flowers. Flirtation Walk enticed many strollers with its rustic bridges, natural spring, and the cool shade provided by flowering dogwood, sourwood, locust, red maple, persimmon, sassafras, willow, mulberry, and other native trees.

In his final report to the exposition's director of works, Manning frequently emphasized the savings accrued through use of native plants. Few nursery plants were used except around the main buildings with some last-minute foundation plantings of rhododendrons from Pennsylvania. In his final report, Manning asserted that "altogether, about a million plants were secured and planted at a lower cost than has ever been the experience at an exposition, many of the herbs having been secured in the beginning at a cost of thirty cents per thousand and the shrubs from three to four feet high as low as two dollars per hundred planted in place."[31] Whereas previous fairs highlighted the allure of exotic plants and cultivars from around the country, Manning's native plants were touted as a beautiful and economical way to landscape.

Local news accounts and promotional brochures extolled the virtues of Manning's landscapes. The *Virginia Gazette,* for example, declared the grounds an "object lesson" in design for farmers and property owners.[32] Others, such as the Illinois nurseryman H. Augustine, gave less favorable reviews: "Our first impression upon entering the Exhibition grounds was a very poor one, so far as the ornamentation of the grounds was concerned. The adornment of the grounds did not compare with the standards set by our past expositions. So far as display was concerned the exposition was generally considered a failure."[33] It is possible that the reception of Manning's efforts was soured by the overall negative press attention given to the exposition. With mounting financial difficulties and buildings still under construction a month before the fair closed, it seems likely criticism was both sharp and vigorous.

Certainly the size of Jamestown's grounds in no way compared to the St. Louis campus, nor was it allocated as much funding as previous fairs. Still, it is likely that Manning's more simple designs, in concert with naturalistic plantings, fell short of the expectations of nurserymen, who, perhaps self-servingly, wanted garish floral extravaganzas. The exposition landscape did not at all hurt Manning's career, however. Informed and wealthy clients who appreciated naturalistic style and concepts for civic horticulture continued to request his services. In nearby Virginia towns, Manning received commissions for many private estates and important public spaces such as Jamestown Island, the University of Virginia, and Randolph-Macon Woman's College.

Horticulture Displays

Unlike previous world's fairs, the Jamestown Exposition did not boast a horticulture palace. For purposes of economy, separate buildings were not built for agriculture, horticulture, or forestry. Instead, the exposition featured a single States Exhibit Building to display items from all of these fields in addition to an overflow from the Mines and Metallurgy Building. The States Palace, a U-shaped building on the east side of Lee's Parade, comprised about 2.5 acres and was surrounded by the charming and intimate structures planned for the Arts and Crafts Village on Spottswood Circle.

There were award-winning displays of fresh fruits, vegetables, and cut flowers, but most horticultural exhibits in the States Palace featured preserved specimens in glass jars. The eight-man Judges Committee for the Horticulture Exhibit was chaired by former 1884 Exposition official Prosper J. Berkmans, the so-called "Father of Peach Culture."[34] This relatively small judging committee lacked national and international representation: most were from the South, or from the USDA in nearby Washington, D.C.

Predictably, Virginia claimed the most space in the States Exhibit Building, with more than 9,500 square feet.[35] Consistent with previous expositions, the railroad companies demonstrated the value of land along their routes with displays of grain, fruit, and other produce. Maryland devoted most of its allocated 3,500 square feet to horticulture rather than fish and forestry. Live trees or shrubs marked the entrances to the exhibits of fruit and vegetables. However, the lack of adequate cold-storage facilities hampered exhibitors from having continuous fresh displays.

> Since the Jamestown Exposition lacked a horticulture building, West Virginia and other states exhibited pomological items in the States Exhibit Palace. (Author's collection)

In contrast to previous expositions, there were no elaborate outdoor displays of flowers sponsored by private businesses. Only a few stalwart nurserymen, consistent exhibitors in nearly every world's fair, maintained a presence. One such participant was Peter Henderson & Co., which seeded various exposition green spaces including the lawn in front of the New Jersey Building, which also featured outdoor beds of Henderson asters and other flowers.

Consistent with the Progressive Era's emphasis on outdoor education, the exposition did feature a popular children's garden. A year before the exposition opening, selected students from nearby towns climbed aboard special trolleys to the fairgrounds. There, under the tutelage of their schoolteachers and Warren Manning himself, they planted vegetables such as beans, peas, parsnips, and carrots. Throughout the spring and summer of 1906, the children were instructed in horticultural principles. Not only would this garden inspire the children, but, as the *Virginia Gazette* prophesized: "The landscape gardening which has transformed a wild woods into one of the most scenic parks will also serve as an object lesson to farmers and all who have grounds to beautify . . . The arrangement of trees, flowers, and plants of all kinds in various parts of the Exposition grounds can be studied to great advantage by all landscape gardeners . . . It will not be an exposition of commercialism, but one showing the beauties of nature and the value of science in peace as well as in war."[36]

The exposition featured both a Rose Carnival and a Chrysanthemum Show. Timed to coincide with the American Pomological Society's meeting, a Congress of Horticulture convened on September 23, 1907, that included professionals from throughout the nation. Warren Manning had lobbied for this meeting, prevailing upon exposition management to issue an invitation to the group. The Congress was conducted by the National Council of Horticulture, the newly formed lobbying and networking group headed by Chicago's J. C. Vaughan. Representatives from the Society of American Florists, American Association of Nurserymen, American Seed Trade Association, National Nut Growers' Association, and various seed and nursery companies such as Ellwanger & Barry, Henry A. Dreer, and W. Atlee Burpee attended along with a number of university professors. Speakers included Warren Manning, John C. Olmsted, and J. C. Vaughan: they focused on contemporary concerns such as insect control, plant disease, forest conservation, landscape gardening, horticultural schools, and experimental stations.

Legacies

The great naval shows held during the exposition convinced the U.S. Navy that the exposition site was ideally suited as a training ground. However, it wasn't until after 1917 that the navy purchased what is now Naval Station Norfolk, currently the largest naval base in the world. As can be expected, the landscape of the exposition has been markedly changed to reflect the needs of a modern naval base. Some of the individual state buildings, however, have been preserved and are on the National Historic Register. The Georgia, Maryland, Missouri, North Dakota, Ohio, Pennsylvania, Virginia, and West Virginia structures have remained on their original sites and now overlook the naval golf course leading to the harbor. The Powhatan Oak, which had presided over the fairgrounds long before English settlers arrived, finally succumbed to disease and was felled.

Landscape Lessons from the Jamestown Exposition

The Jamestown Exposition eludes classification among the horticulturally significant world's fairs. It was a unique fair with its maritime focus, decentralized horticulture exhibits, and lack of outdoor foreign gardens. Because of its importance as a model of city planning and of uniquely American garden design, however, it merits consideration.

The seeds of the City Beautiful movement planted at the World's Columbian Exposition took root at the Jamestown Exposition. Manning's effort to design exposition grounds that would ultimately become a suburban village included many elements of City Beautiful design theories, especially the integration of landscape with buildings. By the turn of the twentieth century, City Beautiful precepts had been absorbed by and were influencing architecture, landscape design, and city planning. A 1900 issue of the *Chautauquan* reported: "The impulse given by the World's Fair [of 1893] to all forms of art in America but especially to the arts of architecture, sculpture and landscape gardening is scarcely understood . . . The illustrated magazines have kept the impulse alive, until today sanitation and public beauty are two of the topics most widely discussed."[37] Underscoring the popularity of the movement, the *Chautauquan* inventoried hundreds of articles in periodicals ranging from the *Atlantic* to *Scientific American* written since the World's Columbian Exposition and addressing village improvement associations, architecture, sculpture, and landscape gardening. The last-named category included more than thirty articles on children's gardens and playgrounds alone.

Children's gardens became popular during the Progressive Era, and Manning's personal attention to the exposition's children's garden received much publicity. Although the St. Louis Exposition had boasted a small children's garden, it did not compare to that of the Jamestown Exposition. By involving local children in the actual planning and planting of gardens at the fair, Manning made exposition gardens accessible to gardeners of all skill levels.

Perhaps the most significant aspect of the Jamestown Exposition was, as Manning contended, its "distinctly American" character. In all previous fairs, European gardens had served as models in many aspects of landscaping. Even as the Jamestown Exposition hoped to capture all the lavishness of a great world's fair, Manning and exposition management endeavored to instill the spirit of small-town America. By adopting the simpler Colonial architecture found in the earliest American settlements over grander Beaux-Arts schemes, architects set the stage for Manning's landscapes of native plants. His thoroughfares and "village green" included broad lawns and street trees as might be found in any contemporary small town.

Manning's efforts to preserve existing native plants and use them as adornment for utilitarian structures such as the wire fence or pedestrian walkways further emphasized the American flavor of the fair. Like the Wooded Island at the World's Columbian Exposition, Manning's naturalistic treatment of the Flirtation Walk became a public favorite. Future exposition planners would discover, as Manning proved, that native plantings could reduce the overall cost of the landscape department.

The marine emphasis of the Jamestown Exposition also factored into future plans of City Beautiful proponents who needed to incorporate major water features. Designing the waterfront with as much or more emphasis than that given the land features brought a new facet to American landscape architecture. Most cities' harbors were utilitarian, with a focus on loading and unloading cargo. Coincident with the City Beautiful movement, city planners began to investigate ways to make the waterfront a pleasure ground as well as an efficient port of commerce. This would become evident even in the major world's fair at the Panama-Pacific International Exposition at San Francisco.

7

Panama-Pacific International Exposition

East Meets West in the Garden

In the two decades since San Francisco hosted its first fair, the Midwinter Exposition of 1894, the city and country saw dramatic changes. San Francisco rebuilt after the devastating earthquake of 1906 and even hosted the 1909 Portola Festival, a major pageant with participation from the navies of the world. As at the Jamestown Exposition, maritime development featured prominently in San Francisco's Panama-Pacific International Exposition (PPIE) of 1915.

U.S. world's fairs were maturing. After the multiple expositions between 1900 and 1910, the PPIE evidenced greater sophistication in its horticulture exhibits and reflected advances in the technology geared to producing a world's fair. Henry Ford developed the modern assembly line in 1913, and automobiles became common sights. The Panama Canal, an arduous decade-long engineering feat, was finally completed in 1914, giving the PPIE a suitable reason for celebration.

San Francisco enjoyed a reputation as a sophisticated multiethnic city, well removed from the frontier image of its gold-rush days. The 1894 Midwinter Exposition in San Francisco, though a minor fair, nonetheless had added the exquisite Japanese Tea Garden to Golden Gate Park. Frederick Law Olmsted and his successor firm had a long history in California, having consulted on Golden Gate Park, the Stanford University campus, Yosemite, and other regional landscapes. Wealthy ranch and mission-estate owners hired landscape architects such as Olmsted, Rudolph Ulrich, John McLaren, and others.

A cosmopolitan city, San Francisco welcomed garden trends from European and Asian countries. Japanese gardening in the United States had developed considerably since its beginnings at the 1876 Centennial. Numerous Japanese gardens had been established along the Atlantic seaboard, many the handiwork of the landscape designer Takeo Shiota. In 1915, even as the PPIE showcased Japanese garden styles, the Shiota-designed Japanese garden at the Brooklyn Botanic Garden was opened to the public.[1]

Shortly after the Louisiana Purchase Exposition, the Japanese American scientist Dr. Jokichi Takamine purchased two of the Japanese buildings from that exposition and incorporated them in his downstate New York garden at Merriewold Park.[2] The PPIE Japanese garden would be the largest at a major U.S. fair since the Louisiana Purchase Exposition, and would carry the fashion to the West Coast. With the increased visibility of Japanese gardens since 1907, expectations would be high for the foreign exhibits at the PPIE.

Despite the 1914 outbreak of World War I and the sinking of the *Lusitania* in 1915, the U.S. Congress did not vote to enter the war until 1917. Thus, during the years of the PPIE, the United States was not officially involved in the conflict and could host a world's fair with apparent neutrality. With its theme of the Panama Canal linking East and West, the PPIE offered the illusion of an idealized society where world powers could meet and mingle in peace.

The 1914 opening of the Panama Canal offered enormous possibilities for world commerce and cultural exchange. Held in San Francisco from February 1915 through December 1915, the PPIE similarly joined East and West in a landscape that melded Asian architecture, Western landscapes, traditional gardens, and horticultural advances.

A dramatically new form of United States exposition garden debuted at the PPIE, one that celebrated small space gardens intimately connected to the adjacent architecture. Even as the fair continued the tradition of the large public garden, the courtyard grounds plan offered opportunities for small-scale work.

⌃ Hinting at pre–World War I tensions before the PPIE, this cartoon shows a San Francisco woman asking a British official and German military officer, "Are you quite sure you won't come to my party?" (Cartoon by W. A. Rogers, ca. 1913. Library of Congress Prints and Photographs Division, Call Number CAI—Rogers, no. 161)

Main Exhibit Palaces- Pan. Pac. Int. Expo- San Francisco.

X-149

⌃ This bird's-eye view of the fair from the San Francisco hills shows why the Panama-Pacific International Exposition was sometimes called the "City of Domes." (Author's collection)

Groundbreaking and Construction

On October 14, 1911, President William Taft officiated at the groundbreaking ceremony at Golden Gate Park, although it was not ultimately part of the fairgrounds. Three days before the groundbreaking, Edward H. Bennett, a Chicago architect who worked with Daniel H. Burnham, was commissioned to draw multiple schemes for a combined three-site plan. The multisite plan was desirable for its postfair potential as a continuous green space connecting popular parks. Bennett was quite familiar with San Francisco; he and Burnham were closely tied to the City Beautiful concept and had been hired in 1904 to prepare a plan for the City of San Francisco.[3] Bennett leveraged not only this background but also his research of exposition designs, drawing from a reading list that included many books on European and other foreign gardens.[4]

Although Bennett gamely prepared many alternatives, he disliked the multisite concept and preferred a single site on San Francisco Bay. Of the so-called Harbor

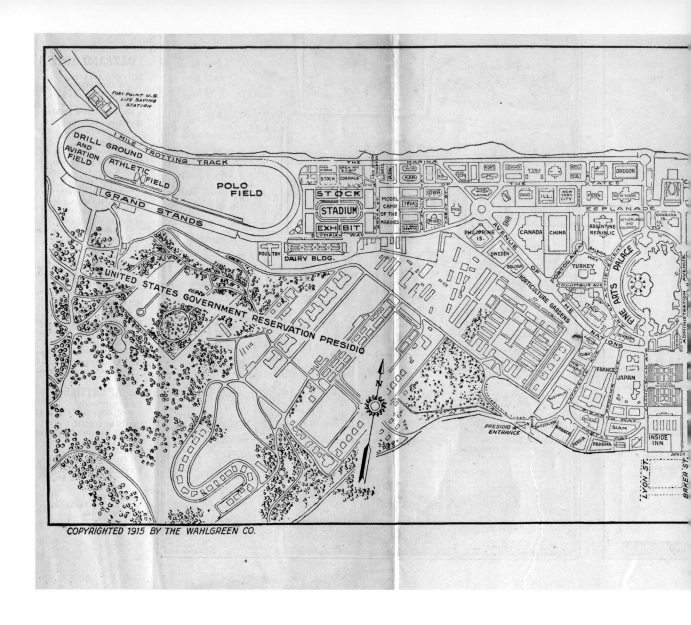

COPYRIGHTED 1915 BY THE WAHLGREEN CO.

View site, he wrote, "This site is at present bare and uninviting and will require the transplanting of many trees from the Park, Presidio, etc., but it has many advantages to offer."[5] Among those advantages, Bennett cited the bay itself as a scenic feature that "lends itself easily to the development of permanent improvements to the City."[6] Bennett envisioned lawns, fountains, and floral displays along a great esplanade next to the bay. He observed that the site, located at the base of the hilly portions of San Francisco, would offer a fine view from the city heights. Recognizing that the Harbor View site

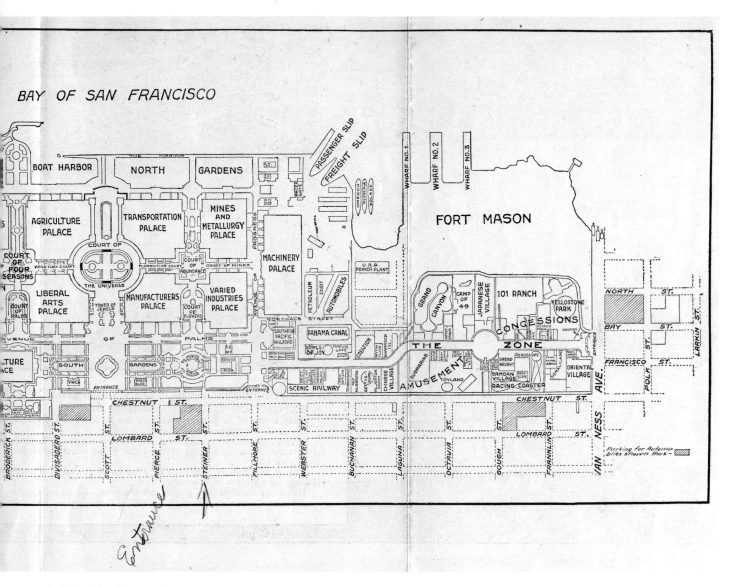

BAY OF SAN FRANCISCO

▲ The block plan of the exposition
consolidated exhibits in a small space
but also posed unique landscape
challenges. (Author's collection)

was insufficient, he suggested adding the adjacent Presidio and Fort Mason, both of
which included scenic wooded tracts. Consensus was finally reached a few months
later, with Harbor View—now the San Francisco Marina District—ultimately selected
as the primary site with acreage from the nearby Presidio and Fort Mason included.
The real work of constructing the exposition began.

Creating the fairgrounds on the Harbor View site required substantial engineering
feats and technological prowess. The mightiest suction dredge of the day, the "John

McMullen," was commandeered in the spring of 1912 to extract more than 1.3 million cubic yards of fill from the bay in a project lasting more than 140 days. The contemporary writer Frank Morton Todd observed, "One of the best exhibits at San Francisco was one that few visitors took into account . . . 70 acres of the solid ground under their feet, and under some of the largest of the palaces, where there had lately been from 12 to 20 feet of water."[7]

Among many other monikers given to this fair, it became known as the "Walled City." Bennett's "block plan" with buildings tightly clustered around open courtyards, permitted dense concentrations of exhibits that relieved visitors of the need to traverse great distances among buildings. Todd said the courtyard plan "made it [the whole exposition] a thing of outdoors."[8] The courtyards interspersed among the buildings were exquisitely landscaped and became themed garden destinations in themselves.

Bennett continued to work on the overall plan but resigned in December 1912, concerned that aesthetics were being sacrificed to economics. He wrote that he wanted to "put myself on record, once and for all, as utterly deprecating the control and direction of the Department of Works"—presumably his boss, Harris D. H. Connick. Bennett accused Connick, San Francisco's assistant city engineer, of exerting "constant and pernicious" influence on the design. In Bennett's view, the "fineness has already been eliminated from the work—it is doubtful if it can be restored; even by the efforts of the architects and designers of the Department this cannot be done unless the control is in the hands of a man trained in the work which this Department represents—architecture!"[9]

McLaren's Design and Plants

More harmonious was the relationship between Bennett and the chief of the Department of Landscape Gardening, John McLaren, who was appointed to the exposition's Architectural Commission in February 1912. He designed or consulted on three world's fair landscapes, all in San Francisco: the Midwinter Exposition of 1894, the PPIE, and the 1939–40 Golden Gate International Exposition.

Together with his son Donald, who in May 1913 became the PPIE's assistant chief of the Department of Landscape Gardening, John McLaren secured plants from his own nursery and also nearby counties. He imported 70,000 rhododendrons from Holland, 2,000 azaleas from Japan, cineraria from Brazil, and agapanthus from Africa.[10] Locally, the elder McLaren began collecting plants and raising seedlings for the fair in the spring of 1912. He dispatched scouts throughout the San Francisco area to identify and appropriate large trees and other mature plants for the fair. Morton reported: "Gardens were levied on for orange trees and great palms, and other ornaments of lawns . . . Even abandoned cemeteries were levied on for their venerable cypresses."[11]

Cypress was among the three types of trees McLaren favored in his landscape design, along with eucalyptus and acacia. He felt that cypress, particularly Monterey cypress, had character and individuality, and he found eucalyptus useful, albeit invasive in more permanent landscapes.[12] McLaren praised the continuous bloom period available through combinations of different species of acacia.

In November 1912, a permanent nursery was built in the Presidio to house seedlings for the exposition. Thousands of flats of acacia seedlings, 6–12 inches high, were grown: two years later they were transplanted as trees 12–15 feet high. Fast-growing eucalyptus seedlings attained heights of 25–30 feet in the same time period.[13] Most trees were evergreen, to provide for continuous color from February through December of the exposition year.

▲ Planting mature crated palm trees hoisted by crane achieved the scale needed in the landscape for the tall, clustered buildings. (San Francisco History Center, San Francisco Public Library PPIE Collection AAE-0826)

Tall trees were important to this exposition, not only to provide the sense of a mature landscape, but also to relieve the stark building facades. The court plan compressed the space among massive exposition buildings, and the planting of tall cypress and other trees flush against the walls softened the facades. As with previous expositions, transporting and planting mature trees became a proving ground for the latest methodology, which included trenching and boxing specimens in situ.[14] When a tree was needed for the fairgrounds, its tap root was undercut, (the side roots by then having filled in), and the tree loaded by derrick onto a railroad car.[15]

McLaren attempted to unify the exposition scheme through his planting—a tall order given the variety of architectural styles—Mediterranean, Roman, French and Italian Renaissance, and Gothic—situated in the relatively small space. He successfully integrated these styles by landscaping the transitional courts, which served as passageways among the buildings and reflected the ambience the architect was trying to create. Working with Jules Guerin, the exposition's "colorist," McLaren attempted to harmonize his plantings with the natural color scheme emphasizing hues of the sky and bay envisioned by Guerin.

The rectangular site stretched roughly 2.5 miles lengthwise from east to west, with the north and south ends bounded respectively by the bay and the city itself. A birds-eye view from the elevated overlook showcased the domes of the palaces, most of which were designed to suggest Byzantine architecture. From the west, automobiles could enter through the wooded Presidio to the Post Road entrance on the southwest end of the fairgrounds. From the north or bay side of the exposition, the Ferry Station and the Laguna Street entrance—reached respectively by boat or rail—offered fabulous views of the bay and the exposition's Esplanade. Visitors alighting from the United Railroads or Municipal Railroads entered the amusement area of the fair, "the Zone," at Van Ness Avenue.

A Tour of the Grounds

Horticulture made a spectacular first impression at the fair's main entrance at Scott Street on the city side. The entire south wall of the exposition, extending more than 1,000 feet (between Filmore and Divisadero Streets) and rising more than 20 feet high, was densely planted with ice plant (*Mesembryanthemum spectabilis*), a groundcover with tiny pink flowers. John McLaren's creation, this living wall created the illusion of an aged, moss-covered enclosure. To achieve the effect, McLaren built 8,700 mesh-covered wooden frames, 2 x 6 feet.[16] Ice plant seedlings were grown in 2 inches of soil within the frames, and then the boxes nailed together. A built-in irrigation system within the hedge provided constant watering and added sparkling water droplets to the wall of green. It was a horticultural achievement never before seen, and it became a chief attraction of the fair.

While all expositions required "instant" landscapes, McLaren could not justify a huge budget for plants with the rationale that they must adorn a future park, since the Marina District was predestined to become an urban center.[17] Instead, he creatively used native plants and experiments such as the ice plant hedge to achieve design objectives at a lower cost.

The South Gardens stretched across the front of the main palaces, bracketed by the Horticulture Palace on the west and Festival Hall on the east. Reminiscent of French-styled gardens, the formal space included two lozenge-shaped reflecting pools on either side of the *Fountain of Energy* sculpture by A. Stirling Calder. Smaller fountains punctuated the east and west ends of the pools. Flanking the water features were panels of flowers bordered by walkways and enclosed by ornate balustrades. Elaborate "electroliers" (lighting standards) and urns atop pedestals added color and light to the gardens. The basins served to reflect the lighting and outlines of plants and buildings at night, and the sky during the day.

▲ The South Gardens featured a large basin and fountain, surrounded by panels of lawn and flowers. (Author's collection)

◄ ▲ Donald McLaren, son of John, inspects the ice plant (*Mesembryanthemum spectabilis*) hedge shown assembled in its vertical interlocking position. (San Francisco History Center, San Francisco Public Library PPIE Collection AAE-0565)

◄ McLaren's ice plant hedge covers the walls of the main Scott Street land entrance, achieving an Old World look with minimal expense. (Author's collection)

Four of the main palaces faced the South Gardens, separated by the Avenue of Palms. Bordered on both sides by a double row of alternately planted Canary Island date palms and California fan palms, the Avenue of Palms lent grandeur to the composition and helped to transition from the low-lying South Gardens to the towering palaces. The palms averaged 18–25 feet in height and were among the largest transplanted specimen trees in the fair. To soften the trunks at eye level, within the crevices of the palm trunks, McLaren planted hardy ferns, ivy leaf geraniums, and mesembryanthemum: passion vines scrambled at the base of the trees, seeming to anchor them to the earth.[18] This broad avenue with its double rows of plantings gave the first hint of McLaren's progressively massed groupings, which softened and brought human scale to the sheer walls of the palaces.

Several minor courtyards among these palaces integrated the architecture and offered visual relief among the tall structures. The Court of Palms, between the Education and Liberal Arts Palaces, was an oval-shaped green space encircled by a colonnade of Roman Ionic columns, reflecting Italian Renaissance architecture. McLaren planted Italian cypress to accentuate the portals of both palaces within the courtyard. Reminiscent of the terraces of grand Italian villas, the court was built with different levels, with a sunken garden and the doorways to the palaces reached by stone stairways. Echoing classic gardens of Italy, potted standards (probably balled acacias) were showcased between columns of the colonnade. Reflecting pools visually enlarged the courtyard and provided a water element. Rows of different varieties of palms gave the court its name. Fair visitor Juliet James described the court: "Muhlenbeckia borders the pool, producing a most fernlike effect. At the side, in front of the flanking Italian Towers, are erica and epacris, in lavenders and pinks, accented by deep lavender pansies. The tiny border to the beds is *myrtus ugni*. The wallflowers, interspersed with Spanish and English iris, are massed throughout this court, with rhododendrons in the corners. Against the foundations is pink-and-cream lantana."[19]

Similar to the Court of Palms in its Italianate elements and size, the Court of Flowers' landscape nevertheless evoked an entirely different mood. The two courts demonstrated how landscaping could be used like interior decoration to create an ambience—perhaps the first example of "garden rooms" at a world's fair. The exposition architect, Louis Christian Mullgardt, wrote: "The note of emphasis and the temperamental appeal are entirely distinct. The Court of Palms is simpler, more dignified, more conventional. The Court of Flowers is richer in ornament and suggestion, more softly brilliant in atmosphere. The prevailing color is yellow relieved by pink."[20]

▼ In the Court of Flowers, lophantha are pruned as flat-topped, single-trunk specimens, and round orange trees flank the colonnade, providing sculptural counterpoint to the elaborate central fountain. (Author's collection)

Blossoms predominated in the Court of Flowers, with 80,000 daffodils and 120,000 yellow pansies echoing Guerin's color choice for the buildings. The beds were outlined in low-lying evergreen *Juniperus prostrata,* with a spread of 2–4 feet.[21] Successive plantings of begonias and other annuals ensured continuous bloom. The contemporary scholar Horace Cotton noted how McLaren integrated landscaping and architecture: "Surrounding the interior, and placed against the colonnade, are sixteen round headed orange trees, ten to fifteen feet in height, which reflect and duplicate the arches of the columned passages in a naturalistic manner."[22] Groups of evergreen brush cherry (*Eugenia myrtifolia*), a small sculptural bush that can be trained as bonsai, added vertical interest to the flower beds. A central pathway lined with benches neatly divided panels of lawn. At the end of this axis, the allegorical *Beauty and the Beast* sculpture adorned a classically styled fountain. Flat-topped lophantha trees (*Albizia lophantha*) pruned as standards with widespread crowns atop 4-foot-tall, single-stem trunks added an espaliered elegance to the walkway.

Another major thoroughfare, the Avenue of Progress offered a clear long view to the marina and was flanked on the east by the Palace of Machinery, and on the west by the Palace of Mines and Metallurgy and the Palace of Varied Industries. With such large building facades in a small space, the avenue could have felt like a long, narrow canyon. But with Guerin's color variations breaking up the monotony of the buildings, and McLaren's strategic use of planting materials, the avenue offered an inviting, visually interesting promenade.

Cotton explained that "the great problem here, as elsewhere, has been the covering of the immense, blank, wall surfaces with material which would be tall enough to produce a desirable effect."[23] By staggering the heights of trees along the walls, McLaren not only broke up the monotony of the latter, but also achieved a perspective view toward the bay, reaching from the tall buildings down to the human scale of the avenue. Graduated groups of Monterey cypress (*C. macrocarpa*, 12–55 feet); cedar (*Chamaecyparis lawsoniana*, 9–16 feet); incense cedar (*Libocedrus decurrens*, 10–16 feet); and arborvitae (*Thuja occidentalis*, 12–14 feet) sloped down to shrubs and groundcover including rhododendron, the evergreen parrot's bill (*Clianthus puniceus*), cinerarias, and nasturtium.[24]

While tall evergreens and palms predominated to offset the solid building walls along the Avenues of Palms and Progress, many other shrubs and flowers were used for accents and variety on exposition thoroughfares. Slow-growing incense cedar (*Libocedrus decurrens*), albeit smaller, provided pungent fragrance and contrasting color and foliage. Shrubby acacia (*A. floribunda* and *A. latifolia*) and rhododendron introduced a midlayer in the landscape and various shades of flowers. Vines were used to soften building foundations including Australian mattress vine (*Muhlenbeckia*) against

the base of Machinery Palace and honeysuckle around the Varied Industries Palace. Ferns were effective in those spots where tall shadows admitted no sunlight.[25]

The Court of the Universe marked the epicenter of the exposition and symbolically represented a meeting of the Eastern and Western Hemispheres, the theme of the exposition. A large oval aligned east to west on its long axis, the court was encircled by a colonnade running the length of four palaces; Agriculture, Transportation, Manufacturers, and Liberal Arts. Adorning grand fountains, the *Rising Sun* and *Setting Sun* sculptures by Adolph A. Weinman punctuated the east and west. The flower beds surrounding the fountains featured massed rhododendrons whose blooms were followed by pink hydrangeas in summer. McLaren solved the problem of poor brackish soil here by planting these shrubs in boxes, with graduated heights to hide the containers.[26] The entire plaza within the colonnades was sunken, accessed by broad, tiered grassy steps that formed seating areas in an outdoor amphitheater.

Two significant courts bookmarked the Court of the Universe along this north-south chain of courts. In the east, in the 340-square-foot Court of Abundance (sometimes called the Court of Ages), Gothic architecture predominated, with elements of English, Spanish, Portuguese, French, and Moorish design. This square court, outlined by an arcade with portals into the palaces, featured a fountain and water basin, bracketed by L-shaped flower beds. Juliet James described the mélange of garden plants used to complement this composition:

The Italian cypresses, tall and slender, stand like sentinels in front of the arches. Orange trees, ten feet in height, heavy with fruit, stand in opulence before the cypresses. Balled acacias, with repeated regularity of shape, produce in this charming cloister a delightful formalism. Solid beds of pink hyacinths add a glowing touch of color in this beauteous garden. The creeping juniper is the border used. The cistus is the border used around the other beds. Under the trees are planted calceolarias, gebara, Shasta daisies, potentilla, columbine, and many other showy flowers.[27]

Replete with statuary and special-effect lighting, the Court of Abundance imparted a sense of timelessness. At night especially, all the senses were engaged. As Cotton described the scene: "Immense, elliptical, flattened urns, placed above the level of the eye and containing red lights produce the effect at night, of being retainers of smoldering embers. Jets of steam issue from interior sources, and reflecting the red light, increase doubly the weird and picturesque imitation of smoldering fires . . . The burning fumes made a hissing sound in their escape from the tongue-like jets and add to the uncanny effect of the fire-spitting serpents."[28] The statuary, embellished with raised images of cobras and other exotic creatures, complemented the visual, auditory, and imaginative elements of the landscape.

▲ A mix of massed foliage against the columns and deep-green plantings around the fountain offered quiet elegance. (Author's collection)

In the octagonal Court of Four Seasons, plantings were subdued in contrast to the jubilant colors of the Court of Ages. Louis Mullgardt wrote, "The planting of the court [of the Four Seasons] is quiet and stately, and notably carries out its spirit with the gray-green of foliage plants and eucalyptus trees and the gnarled stems of gray old olive trees."[29] Here is an example of a restrained landscape harmonizing with the architecture. The contemporary writer John D. Barry observed: "One could get refreshment here and rest. Much was due to the graceful planting by John McLaren. His masses of deep green around the emerald pool in the center were particularly successful. He had used many kinds of trees including the olive, the acacia, the eucalyptus, the cypress, and the English laurel."[30] A smooth green lawn between the colonnade and pool offered a serene contrast to the massed foliage.

These three major courts of the exposition, Four Seasons, Flowers, and Universe, were connected to the waterfront's Esplanade by formally landscaped promenades, each with rectilinear beds and walkways. The plantings here included clusters of California poppies and anemones in spring, and banks of varied evergreens throughout the year. Many varieties of yews, junipers, pines, firs, spruces, cypresses, holly, and thuja appeared in various groupings, small to large.

These passageways, along with the outer Avenues of Palms, Progress, and Administration, could have been indifferently landscaped in the hands of a lesser artist. McLaren realized not only the utilitarian purpose of handling pedestrian and vehicular traffic, but also the aesthetic experience of a transitional passageway. He created alternating experiences of tranquility, excitement, and even adventure through his use of tropical plants, pleasing color combinations, and plant groupings thematically reflective of the surrounding architecture.

Of all the palaces and their gardens, perhaps the most memorable was the Palace of Fine Arts. The *Official Guide* reported: "The general effect of the building from a distance is that of an ancient ruin overgrown with vegetation that has sprung up in the course of centuries. This idea has been carried out with success by the landscape department in the treatment of the borders of the lagoon and the building itself."[31] Located on the west edge of the main fair site, the Palace of Fine Arts presided over an irregularly shaped natural lagoon, one of the site's few preexposition features that remained. Designed by the architect Bernard R. Maybeck, the palace, with its signature domed rotunda, cradled the lagoon in a wide arc—with a 1,110-foot curving peristyle of Corinthian columns. The structures were in simulated states of disrepair, as if left to nature's devices within an overgrown landscape.

▲ Landscaping around the Palace of Fine Arts included a lagoon and informal plantings. (Author's collection)

As with the Wooded Island in the Columbian Exposition, visitors flocked to this naturalistic landscape element, perhaps in relief from the overpowering spectacle of the main palaces. The lagoon featured a variety of aquatics including five hundred each of papyrus plants and Japanese water lilies. Catalina cherry (*Prunus ilicifolia*) added height and contrasting shapes.[32]

Apparently incongruous in this naturalistic scene was the tall manicured hedge of mesembryanthemum that flanked the rotunda. McLaren worked in concert with Maybeck to design the hedge as a foil for the loosely shaped plants. Barry reported: "People had wondered what McLaren had meant to indicate by the high hedges he had made over there with his dew plant . . . Maybeck had intended the hedge to be used as a background for the willow trees that were to run up as high as the frieze, in this way gaining depth. Through those trees the rotunda was to be glimpsed. Willow trees, with overhanging boughs, were also to be planted along the edge of the lagoon, the water running under the leaves and disappearing."[33] With trailing vines and "crumbling" columns, the landscape and architecture melded into a vision of natural age.

The Horticulture Palace

The PPIE's Horticulture Palace and gardens showcased a new direction for horticulture at U.S. world fairs. Since many of the officers of the Exposition Company were high-profile industrialists, a business focus predominated. The original chief of the Department of Horticulture, the nurseryman George C. Roeding, resigned in early

> The Palace of Horticulture showcased an opalescent dome, the last instance of palace-style horticulture buildings at a U.S. world's fair. (Author's collection)

1914 and was replaced by George A. Dennison, a businessman at heart.

Todd explained the shift toward commercialization for horticultural exhibits:

> Down to the time of the Panama-Pacific International Exposition, horticultural exhibits had been . . . exhibits of fruit, not demonstrations of the industries of growing and marketing fruit . . . Five perfect apples on a plate tell you little or nothing at all about the rest of the apples in the orchard. If you are a very logical sort of reasoner they don't even convince you of the existence of an orchard . . . Such an exhibit shows nothing about horticulture in its economic aspects, commercially . . . and hence it is a matter of very limited interest, and no public importance.[34]

⌃ The exhibit of the Hawaiian Pine-apple Packers Association included a café as well as demonstrating the manufacturing process. (Author's collection)

According to Todd, the exposition "resolved to get as far away from the five-on-a-plate style of exhibit as it could." To that end, although many traditionalists insisted on displays of fresh produce, the award system gave preference to exhibits of commercially packaged produce, or of the manufacturing process itself. Thus, there were a number of exhibits showing the methods and machines involved in pomology, floriculture, and arboriculture, with a huge rectangular building annex, the Economical Horticulture Section, lying westward of the Horticulture Palace itself.

The palace was a whimsical confection of architectural excess. Sited prominently at the west end of the South Gardens, the *Official Guide* proclaimed it a French Renaissance structure with garden architecture in the manner of Louis XIV. Its central dome of opalescent glass measured 182 feet high and 152 feet in diameter and featured several smaller domes along its sides.[35] The palace was highly acclaimed, especially when its dome was lit from within at night and shone like a luminescent gem.

Under the great dome, the major exhibits included a huge collection of tropical trees and plants from the largest contributor, Cuba: fourteen carloads of coconuts, tropical lilies, banana trees, mangoes, and more. A "balanced aquarium" display, a novel presentation of water gardening wherein aquatic plants perfectly supplied the needs of the pond's fish, was of great interest to the public. The ancillary domes of the palace enclosed more water gardening displays, as well as a thirty-thousand-dollar collection of orchids from MacRorie & McLaren. Displays of horticulture machinery and the processing of produce such as Hawaiian pineapple and Kona coffee reigned in the palace and the Economic Horticulture Section.[36]

Outdoors, visitors enjoyed the 8 acres of horticultural display gardens sponsored by nurserymen, seedsmen, and florists and arranged by the well-known local nurseryman Carl Purdy. California's amenable climate and growing conditions encouraged participation from exhibitors such as John L. Childs, Vaughan's, Sutton & Sons, Kelway & Son of England, and others. On-site, visitors could exchange ideas with the famed breeder and Santa Rosa resident Luther Burbank, then at the apogee of his success with the publication of the twelve-volume *Luther Burbank, His Methods and Discoveries and Their Practical Application* in 1914–15. Not only did the exposition honor Burbank with his own day, but the "Plant Wizard" himself had office hours for visitors to the Horticulture Palace.

Outdoor garden displays near the Horticulture Palace included evergreens pruned into interesting topiary such as the bird at right. (Author's collection)

The *Official Guide* noted, "As is most appropriate in the State where 'plant wizardry' first gained recognition, there are displays of many new varieties."[37] In one bed, entrants in the International Rose Contest, which offered a one-thousand-dollar prize, bloomed throughout the summer. Major interest centered on the beds of dahlia varieties, particularly during the Dahlia Show in September. According to Todd:

A few years before the Exposition, great interest had begun to center in the dahlia, because of the profitable tendency of the seedlings to vary from the parent plants and so yield new and strange forms. Wonderful variations from the old hard-boiled pompoms of our grandmothers had been produced, and there was a bewildering variety of "singles," and "doubles," and "colarettes," and "peony" and "cactus" and "decoration" and "show" dahlias, in every imaginable shade and combination.[38]

Foreign and State Gardens

Holland's nurserymen occupied a prime space on the western end of the Horticulture Palace display garden, and their exhibits extended more than 800 feet along Administration Avenue. This collection featured sixty thousand spring bulbs including hyacinth, tulips, and daffodils, and later in the season, gladioli, begonias, and dahlias, all framed by shrubs and trees such as rhododendrons and Japanese maples. Both Holland's gardening methods and its new plant introductions drew interest. The *Official Guide* described decorative shrubbery "some of which has been shaped to standard patterns—a development of the trellis idea new to us. Here also box and yews, clipped to resemble birds, bottles, spirals, interlaced hoops and the like."[39]

Most of the other foreign exhibitors' buildings were clustered around the Avenue of the Nations and behind the Palace of Fine Arts. Among the many South and Central American exhibitors reflecting the Panama-Pacific theme were Argentina, Bolivia, Guatemala, and Honduras. The Italian Building featured an inner courtyard formally planted with small trees. The most impressive foreign garden, not surprisingly, was that of Japan.

Japan's 3-acre garden included a characteristic stream, stones, and ornamental trees. Within the garden complex multiple buildings—including the Reception Hall, the Commissioner's Office, and the Main Building—featured now-typical Japanese construction. According to Todd, more than 1,400 trees and 4,400 smaller plants were shipped across the Pacific for this garden, the design for which is attributed to H. Izawa, the Japanese gardener of the World's Columbian Exposition.[40]

Many individual states participated in the PPIE, and their gardens displayed landscaping representative of the region. The Massachusetts garden, designed by Stephen Childs and Carl Purdy, featured dahlias and flowering perennials. The California Garden, occupying a prime location on the north end of the exposition near the boat harbor, re-created the "Forbidden Garden" of the Mission Santa Barbara. Its encircling cypress hedge had been preserved from the former Harbor View public baths.

The horticultural officials at the PPIE were the first to face major plant quarantines in an exposition setting. On August 20, 1912, Congress passed the Plant Quarantine Act and the Federal Horticultural Board was established. With plant specimens arriving from across the nation and, indeed, from around the world, the challenge of balancing rigorous inspection with diplomacy can easily be imagined. The task fell to the Quarantine Division of the California State Commission of Horticulture. Frederick Maskew of that division wrote of hoping to prevent "the entomological aftermath alleged to have followed in the wake of former expositions."[41] Maskew developed his inspection procedure two years in advance of the exposition and published it in February 1913. Thus, exhibitors could plan for the new regulations knowing that any specimen that failed to meet quarantine standards would be rejected. An inspection yard and fumigating house were located on the fairgrounds, and all live plants and fresh fruits and vegetables were examined. Dry material such as seeds and even the dry trunks of coconut palms used in reproducing a Samoan village in the exposition's amusement Zone were scrutinized.

To help ensure that inspections went smoothly, Maskew and his team established relationships with foreign diplomats. Maskew reported that amid all the "fumigating, dipping, stripping of soil, rejecting and actual destruction of specimens," there was no friction among parties concerned. He observed that generally both domestic and foreign exhibits were of high quality, and he singled out the exhibits from the Netherlands and Japan as particularly praiseworthy examples. "In the case of Japan, notwithstanding our most diligent search we failed to find a single live specimen of insect pest on any part of its immense exhibit," he reported.[42] With this success, Maskew hoped that his department's procedure could be adapted for other uses throughout the United States.

Legacies

In December 1915, after a highly successful season, the Panama-Pacific International Exposition closed. As with other popular fairs, many visitors were reluctant to let the Jewel City go. A commemorative planting of trees in Golden Gate Park was permitted, and those states and foreign nations that so desired were allowed, under John McLaren's supervision, to transplant trees from their exhibits. Since the date of the ceremonial planting was repeatedly rescheduled, McLaren found that he could not wait to plant the trees. A planned Memorial Day (then called Decoration Day) planting was deferred, and McLaren reported: "There is no rush about the planting ceremonies of the trees as all are planted except for a few still in the boxes. We can arrange to take away some of the soil from a few of those planted and you may go through the ceremony of planting which will be just as effective as though they were taken from the boxes."[43] Ultimately, thirty-three trees were planted, nine of which were accompanied by commemorative stone tablets.

A number of other artifacts or small structures were proposed for Golden Gate Park, but McLaren, ever protective of the park, was very discriminating. A well that had been included in the Italian pavilion was destined for the park, but McLaren proposed an alternate destination in San Francisco's Washington Square, in the midst of what was at that time a very Italian community. Of the Chinese, Siamese, and Japanese Buildings offered to them, McLaren demurred on the first two, citing lack of funds, but agreed to place the Japanese Building in the Park's Japanese Garden.[44]

On the site of the exposition itself, just as planned, only one permanent building remains today, the Palace of Fine Arts. For many years its fate was uncertain. During the two world wars and the Depression, it fell into neglect and threatened to devolve into a genuine ruin. In the 1960s, however, a movement to rebuild the historic rotunda and colonnade was ultimately successful. Today, thousands visit San Francisco's Exploratorium Museum connected to the former palace.

▲ The Panama-Pacific International Exposition's Japanese Garden included streams and characteristic plantings. The Horticulture Palace dome is in the background. (Author's collection)

The fairgrounds have been taken over by the buildings of San Francisco's Marina District, but the palace lagoon retains a naturalistic landscape in line with the McLaren's original vision. The desire to preserve this beautiful landmark is understandable. As fair visitor Horace Cotton wrote in 1916: "The facade of the Fine Arts Palace itself is a production which exemplifies the ideal possibilities of combining architecture and landscape gardening. The two arts have here been so closely interwoven that no line of division can be drawn between the two; each reflects and emphasizes the charms of the other. This structure shall ever stand as a concrete example of the possibilities for artfully combining these two phases of design when the controlling forces were in harmony with each other."[45] The wedding of architecture and landscape gardening was an element of real progress in the evolution of U.S. world's fairs over the forty years since the 1876 Centennial.

Landscape Lessons from the PPIE

The PPIE's major excavation-and-fill project to create urban space from the sea was a major engineering feat and established a precedent for world's fairs to follow, most notably Chicago's "Century of Progress" World's Fair in 1933. Previous world's fairs had remodeled or annexed existing parkland, but they had not created land from water.

The PPIE brought back the grandeur of the horticulture building, but with a practical twist. Not since the World's Columbian Exposition had such a structure been designated a "palace." The evolution of U.S. horticulture during an era of increasing industrialization was evident in the displays of horticultural commerce at the PPIE. Instead of mounting the typical "five on a plate" displays of perfect apple specimens, exhibitors were now encouraged to demonstrate how produce moved from field to factory. This world's fair marked the transition from small truck-farming outfits to large corporate operations. No future U.S. world's fairs would glorify individual specimens of fruit or vegetables on a display table.

The PPIE was the first U.S. world's fair in which a local landscape designer, John McLaren, was selected to plan the grounds. Although Chicagoan Edward Bennett was commissioned for the overall block plan, McLaren's ideas prevailed in all planting decisions. His successful use of native California plantings paid tribute to the exposition architecture and natural environment. With his ice plant hedge, McLaren showed how landscaping could sometimes be more cost-effective than architectural elements. The illusion of an aged wall, achieved "instantly," demonstrated new possibilities for landscape design.

Through the use of courtyards, McLaren introduced the idea that small-space gardening could be very effective in enhancing existing architecture and bringing mass to scale. Small-space gardens would become particularly relevant to post–World War I America and would be highlights of future U.S. world's fairs.

As a cosmopolitan city, San Francisco attracted a significant number of foreign exhibitors. With the importing of foreign plant material, the PPIE became the first U.S. world's fair to address the quarantine rules, and the efficient and politic process of examination developed there served as a model for future fairs. The PPIE Japanese Garden was perhaps the best to be seen at any U.S. world's fair. It reinforced the popularity of the Japanese Garden in Golden Gate Park—itself a legacy of San Francisco's 1894 Midwinter Exposition that had inspired many area estate owners to install a Japanese garden on their own private grounds.

One of the most famous of these private gardens was that of the industrialist Eugene de Sabla, at his San Mateo estate, El Cerrito. Sometime around 1907, de Sabla hired the chief gardener of the Japanese Tea Garden in the park, Baron Makota Hagiwara, to design a tea garden for El Cerrito. De Sabla and his wife were members of the Japan Society of America, a group organized to combat rising anti-Asian sentiment in the United States during the World War I era of the PPIE. The de Sablas hosted many social events in honor of Japanese culture at El Cerrito's tea house and garden. Today, the de Sabla Japanese garden is listed in the National Register of Historic Places, a reminder of the influence exerted by world's fair gardens.[46]

8

Century of Progress Exposition

Coincident with the Panama-Pacific International Exposition, San Diego sponsored the two-year Panama-California Exposition, a smaller fair in Balboa Park. More than ten years passed before another U.S. exposition was staged, and then it was a return to Philadelphia for the nation's Sesqui-Centennial International Exposition in 1926. The Balboa Park fair turned a profit, but the Sesqui-Centennial proved a financial failure. The dearth of expositions in the United States since the Panama-Pacific raised questions about their relevance in the Jazz Age.

At the close of World War I, the United States entered a period of economic prosperity. Women earned the right to vote, and their numbers and representation in the making of world's fair gardens increased as well. Several national horticulture organizations with mostly female membership emerged during this period, among them the Garden Club of America (1913), the National Garden Club (1929), the Woman's National Farm & Garden Association (1914), and the Wild Flower Preservation Society of America (1915). These groups, with their many local branches, became involved in civic beautification and social issues of the day, and also hosted flower shows and garden walks. Women's influence grew in citywide flower shows even as commercial nurseries' interest in fairs declined.

World's fairs were still hosted by European and South American countries between the 1915 Panama-Pacific International Exposition and the 1933 Century of Progress (COP) World's Fair. Expositions were held in Rio de Janeiro (1922), Paris (1925), both Barcelona and Seville (1929), and other cities. The plethora of fairs led to the creation in 1928 of the Bureau of International Expositions, an international regulatory organization charged with reducing the quantity and increasing the quality of world's fairs. Based in Paris, the organization continues its mission today.

The 1933 Century of Progress Exposition marked Chicago's growth from a military outpost to a city of skyscrapers, but fair boosters recognized the need to broaden the fair's regional theme. (Author's collection)

Paris exerted a significant influence on the character of world's fairs during the 1920s. The city hosted both the 1925 Exposition Internationale des Arts Décoratifs et Industriels Modernes and the 1931 Exposition Coloniale Internationale. The 1925 Exposition is widely credited with popularizing the art deco style that flourished in virtually all branches of the arts through the 1930s.

Chicago's Century of Progress Exposition in 1933–34 adopted a midwestern version of this modern style, in both architecture and landscape design. The boom years of the 1920s had come to a sudden halt with the 1929 crash, yet planning continued for the COP. The result was one of the country's few profitable expositions.

Forty years after the 1893 World's Columbian Exposition and in the midst of the Great Depression, Chicago was again the site of a major world's fair, the Century of Progress Exposition. Although individual European cities often hosted more than one world's fair, Chicago was the first U.S. city to do so successfully.[1] The COP also introduced the practice of an "encore year." Its first fair was held from spring through fall of 1933; the second year, from spring through fall of 1934. With an intervening Chicago winter, this was a test of plants and planners alike.

While the 1933 Fair shared some similarities with its 1893 predecessor,[2] both were clearly products of their times that showcased significant advances in horticultural evolution. In the forty years that elapsed between the two expositions, research and plant hybridizing had increased the number of available garden plants from about five hundred to approximately two thousand. According to the *Chicago Tribune,* "The quadrupling in a century of the number of flowers suitable for planting in Chicagoland is due in part to the organization of seed merchandising and in part to the patient collection of indigenous wild types and the taming of them by breeding and cultivation."[3] The COP deemphasized individual plant specimens and novelties and focused instead on garden design theory and holistic garden plans. Leaving the 1893 Beaux-Arts "White City" behind, the COP's asymmetrical, modernistic design called for color and geometric shapes in architecture and landscapes.

Plans for Chicago's second world's fair began with discussions in the mid-1920s, but, as in many expositions, these talks frequently derailed. By March 1928, the fair's recently formed Architectural Commission approved a plan for an 800-acre fairground located on an artificial island in Lake Michigan that was connected to the mainland via several bridges. (The final size of the fairgrounds, including lagoons, would be just over 425 acres.) The preliminary plan was executed by the Chicago architect Edward H. Bennett, who had worked with both D. H. Burnhams, Senior and Junior, and who had drawn the block plan for the 1915 Panama-Pacific International Exposition. The idea was to complete work on the man-made islands by mid-1931 and allow the filled land to settle for a year before building commenced.[4]

The Architectural Commission, which comprised eight architects from around the United States, decided to adopt a "terrace-type" of architecture for the fair. This style, a midwestern version of art deco, featured multilevel, stepped roofs on buildings that emphasized vertical lines. In order to save construction costs and allow for more interior exhibit wall space, the buildings were to be without windows. At a meeting in Bennett's office in May 1928, the group's chairman, Harvey W. Corbett, announced: "Artificial light, the tremendous progress of which has astonished designers in recent years, will become an inherent component of the architecture. The extraordinary opportunities of the site to use water as an intrinsic element of the composition will be developed to the maximum."[5] This decision had a significant impact on the fair's landscape. Nighttime garden-lighting effects and plantings or waterfalls on rooftop terraces became integral to the design.

As described in a 1928 press release from COP headquarters: "Each of the World's fair buildings will be of two or more stories, set back and terraced. These terraces will be flanked with flowers and overhung with vines. The profusion of water courses, pools, and lagoons throughout the grounds will provide many mirrors to reflect the rainbow colors of the flowers."[6] Gardens were priorities, asserted Edward Bennett: "We will be dealing with great multitudes of people, and therefore must have great expanses of flowers to create a mass impression. Likewise we must have the dainty, exquisite touches. We also propose to get away from the conventional squares, rectangles, and curves by laying out lozenge shaped beds, irregular triangles, and the like."[7]

Internal disagreements on the appointment of the landscape architect Ferruccio Vitale stalled the landscape design process for about six months. D. H. Burnham Jr. and Fair Manager Lenox Lohr preferred Gilmore D. Clarke of Westchester, New York, while the Architectural Commission favored Vitale.[8] A compromise was reached at a COP Executive Committee meeting in June 1930, when Vitale was appointed as part of the Architectural Commission and Clarke was hired as a consultant on landscaping.[9]

As projected, groundbreaking began in the spring of 1930. The Administration, Travel and Transport, Hall of Science, and Electrical Building areas supported "outdoor laboratories" of plantings that were among the first installed in 1931 and 1932. Local and regional nurseries were surveyed on the availability and suitability of plants. According to Lenox Lohr: "Without a complete planting layout, the quantity of materials required could not be definitely fixed. An approximation was found by estimating the acres of landscaping around the buildings called 'intimate' areas, and the quantity of materials required per acre of landscaping in the areas between the buildings, called 'general' or 'park areas.'"[10] Piecemeal planting and estimating, tied to the irregular construction schedule, became normal. Lohr observed that "the asymmetrical architectural plan simplified the landscape design. It made possible the development of the area around each building independently of the others, without preventing a blending of all into a pleasing composition."[11]

Constructing the Modern Fairgrounds

The unimproved fairgrounds required a mammoth landfill project to rival that of the 1915 Panama-Pacific International Exposition. Lenox Lohr noted: "It [the COP site] was entirely 'man made' . . . Part of the site had been filled in by dumping refuse, and under the surface were found rusty bed springs, tin cans, radiators . . . even a submerged scow was encountered while piles were being driven for the Foods and Agricultural Building."[12] A row of Chicago museums, including the newly established Adler Planetarium, connected the mainland with the so-called Northerly Island on the north. Two lagoons separated the man-made Northerly Island from the mainland. South of Northerly Island, along a 3-mile stretch hugging the Lake Michigan shoreline on a 600-foot-wide strip of land, was situated the rest of the exposition.

The landscape architect Alfred Geiffert, Vitale's colleague and successor, commented: "The modern architectural note adhered to in this Fair has no previous counterpart in this country . . . For the landscape architect it has been a source of interesting speculation and an opportunity for collaboration with artists of his sister arts, to adapt his art to meet the requirements of this modern note and yet adhere to the underlying principles of landscape architecture."[13]

Geiffert, along with the local landscape firm Swain Nelson, selected trees and shrubs to provide shapes complementary to the buildings by day and at night, "interesting silhouettes against illuminated surfaces and fantastic shapes in color made possible by the ingenious use of lighting."[14] More than 1,600 trees of considerable size were planted in the winter and spring of 1933 to provide a mature-looking landscape. As Lohr recounted, "These great leafless skeletons, varying in height from twenty-five to fifty feet, were loaded on special equipment, and moved through the city streets under police escort, during the early hours while Chicago slept."[15] Twenty-five thousand shrubs, twenty-four thousand lineal feet of hedging including privet, forsythia, and barberry, and two thousand vines were planted. Seventy-five thousand square feet were devoted to flower beds featuring ageratums, marigolds, petunias, salvia, heliotrope, begonias, and geraniums.[16]

U.S. gardening styles had undergone many changes since the World's Columbian Exposition. Gone were the fanciful floral creations of carpet bedding seen in the parks and large estates around Chicago in 1893. Jens Jensen, an advisor to the 1933 Fair, and other "prairie school" landscape architects had greatly influenced the Midwest and the nation with their interpretations of naturalistic styles. Home lots were smaller, and, with the Great Depression, budgets for country estate landscaping were greatly reduced. A "modern" landscape might reflect a new trend in style and plants, but it also reflected the realities of a depressed economy.

Designs for the bungalow belt housing style shown at the fair included modern touches. A brochure describing the "super-safe brick home" boasted: "There the walks were all straight. There were no winding paths. They went where they were intended to go in the shortest way . . . Flowering trees and bushes in radical and bright color combinations lent life and zest to the yard . . . Straight lines should be the rule, with curves used only where necessary to avoid angularity."[17] Such a design philosophy marked a significant departure from the Olmsted's curved walks on the Wooded Island and the subdued colors seen throughout the fairgrounds at the World's Columbian Exposition.

The Depression also forced landscape architects to streamline their work methods in order to withstand increased competition and reduced client budgets. Such was the case with the 1933 Fair, for which a substantial amount of design work was done in the field. Geiffert commented that "the preparation of a definite hard and fast plan was of necessity early abandoned; however, a number of sketch plans were prepared which have served as guides to an ultimate goal of uniformity in architecture, landscape architecture, color, and lighting."[18]

The innovative use of artificial light—both indoors and out—significantly affected exposition architecture and landscaping. With great fanfare, the 1933 Fair opened with a symbolic beam of light. Telescopes in the nearby Yerkes Observatory transmitted light from the star Arcturus (said to have illuminated the World's Columbian Exposition) to Chicago and turned on the lights of the fair. Buildings bathed in light and color enchanted visitors. One guidebook enthused: "In 1933 the art of lighting has reached such an advanced stage of development that sunlight actually is excluded from the interior of the exhibit buildings as being too inefficient . . . Lighting thus is a determining factor in the architectural treatment, permitting the use of windowless buildings with flat surfaces."[19] Lohr noted: "The color of the buildings would be stirring and the landscaping would accentuate it by providing a restful background. Shrubs and tall cedars would break the monotony of plain walls, and tubbed trees and flower boxes would grace the terraces."[20]

Outside the fairgrounds, civic groups were inspired to beautify Chicago itself in anticipation of the great influx of visitors. The impetus for this civic beatification came largely from Chicago's influential women's clubs. In June 1929, more than fifty women's groups gathered under the umbrella of the newly formed Women's Chicago Beautiful association. The *Chicago Tribune* reported, "If the women have their way, Chicago will be all dressed up in a birthday gown, her back yard cleaned, her front yard mowed, and flowers planted in every nook and corner when she receives visitors for the 1933 World's Fair."[21] The article went on to support the idea that new plantings, billboard removals, and tidying of school and home yards promised "a city-wide housecleaning, but with telling the world that Chicago, instead of being mistress to crime and gangsters, is cultured, religious, [and] has a good business head."[22]

Landscape improvement efforts radiated from the fairgrounds. The Garden Club of Illinois launched a campaign to plant railroad station grounds and vacant lots with flowers and shrubs. State of Illinois agencies cooperated with nurseries to plant trees along outlying roads in cooperative efforts to supply work to the unemployed

Horticultural Building—Concessions versus Education

Idealized gardens were also featured in the Horticultural Building and surrounding grounds. Women had directed Chicago's citywide flower and garden shows since 1927—many of the prominent ladies hailed from garden clubs from the North Shore and other wealthy Chicago suburbs. In May 1932, the COP Executive Committee established a Horticultural Exhibition Committee including the socialite and philanthropist Kate Brewster as chairman, garden club member Tiffany Blake, horticulturist Frank Balthis, and COP director of concessions F. R. Moulton.[23]

Disagreements arose over the vision and goals of the horticulture exhibit as well as the roles and responsibilities of its various committees. Brewster and her committee supported the educational value of exhibits and deplored commercial influence. Her committee hired the Pittsburgh landscape architect Ralph Griswold to prepare plans for the use of Soldier Field as a horticulture venue. Others disagreed with their initiative. COP officials negotiated with groups of professional nurserymen over their participation in the fair. George Asmus, representing the Society of American Florists and Ornamental Horticulturists, and others complained that Soldier Field would not provide ideal conditions for tropical plants. The balance between commercialism and education fluctuated over the summer of 1932. The Horticulture Committee contended that the Florists' Concession was a repeat of all previous fairs, would offer nothing new to attract audiences, and, according to the committee's report, was "a speculative commercial enterprise, subject to all the risks of such ventures regardless of individual integrity. Its primary interest is to make money for itself."[24] Seeing no way to resolve the philosophical differences, Brewster asked that the Horticultural Committee be

GARDEN AND FLOWER SHOW
HORTICULTURAL BUILDING
A CENTURY OF PROGRESS
CHICAGO 1933
SOUVENIR BOOK ♦ TWENTY-FIVE CENTS

◄ The Horticultural Building epito-mized modern design with its sleek lines and sculptural embellishment. (Author's collection)

➤ This "Diorama of Old Japan," like others in the Horticultural Building, provided views of foreign gardens in miniature—an inexpensive way to bring the world to Chicago. (Author's collection)

➤ ▼ The Chinese Moon Garden diorama created the illusion of looking through a window into a small-scale replica of a Chinese garden. (Author's collection)

disbanded, and in October the Executive Committee accepted their resignations.[25]

It wasn't long before fair officials regrouped. Abandoning the proposed Soldier Field venue, they broke ground for a 91,000-square-foot Horticultural Building in the fall of 1932.[26] The Horticultural Building, sited on a peninsula between the northern lagoon and Lake Michigan, featured about twenty-five outdoor garden tableaux dispersed throughout the 5 acres on its Lake Michigan side. Ranging from "A Naturalistic Hillside Garden" to "An Authentic Japanese Garden" and designed by nurserymen, flower societies, or clubs, these garden rooms showed home gardeners some possibilities for their own yards. The building itself housed flower shows and presented dioramas of gardens from around the world. These indoor dioramas offered an economical way in a depressed economy to exhibit international gardens.

Each week, indoor flower shows were held in the Horticultural Building. The lineup of shows for 1933 included peonies in June, gladioli in July, water plants in August, dahlia and autumn harvest shows in September, and chrysanthemums in October. Displays in 1934 were similar, and also included carnations in June, orchids in July, lilies in August, cut roses in September, and a grand finale in October.

Many national flower societies had recently formed, and the fair offered a prime opportunity to display specialty plants. The American Gladiolus Society displayed more than 375 varieties from a planting of 200,000 corms on the southeast and southwest sides of the North Lagoon and along the avenue south of the Hall of Science. One gladiolus grower noted: "The old time gladiolus of grandmother's garden was a short stiff spike of small red flowers. While many folks grew it, it was not considered among the finest garden flowers. But the modern forms range from dainty dwarf growing varieties to immense spikes attaining a height of four to five feet."[27]

The Central States Dahlia Society hosted an immense Dahlia Show, but the season got off to a rocky start. The *World's Fair Dahlia News* reported: "Intense heat was continuous, sulpheric [*sic*] smoke was blowing from nearby railroad locomotives. Indeed, the sight of our garden was truly sickening and heart-rending. We were criticized severely, but unjustly. Our dreams of a beautiful garden were shattered. We felt ashamed of our work."[28] Despite this early melodrama, the Dahlia Society, the climate, and the gardens all rallied in later months, and beautiful dahlia specimens were displayed. The *Dahlia News* reported that until this world's fair, dahlias had not been popular in the Midwest, and that the newly formed Central States Dahlia Society had adopted the motto, "A dahlia in every garden."[29]

Themed and Corporate Gardens

The small, themed garden tableaux revolutionized horticultural displays at world's fairs. Previous outdoor horticultural exhibits tended to feature beds of flowers and shrubs, with plants arranged in mass groupings suitable for public gardens. The PPIE offered smaller courtyard gardens that harmonized with their companion architecture. At the COP gardens, even smaller plant compositions were created, specifically targeted to inspire backyard gardeners. Individual flowers assumed no greater importance than did the landscape design in which they appeared.

James Burdett, publicity director of the Horticultural Exhibition, emphasized the differences between "old-fashioned" gardens and those of 1933. He noted that although gaudy flower colors were disdained in 1893, "today we do not [revile them] because now we know how to use vivid colors harmoniously."[30] Burdett contended that the 1933 gardens used complementary colors in combining flowers, hence adding to their appeal: "In the typical '93 beds, the pattern dominated the flower which was cruelly subordinated and distorted. But most people liked that and would exclaim 'Isn't it wonderful! It looks like a carpet!' But about a decade and a half after the old Fair they began to feel that it might be better to be able to say 'Isn't it lovely! It looks like a flower garden.'" Burdett concluded that color, not pattern, had been the key development over the past twenty-five years.[31]

▲ Indicative of the interest in specialty cultivars, the Central States Dahlia Society sponsored its own periodic bulletin for the fair. (Author's collection)

The outdoor horticultural displays changed between 1933 and 1934, but some themed gardens maintained a consistent popularity. Here is a sampler of favorites:

Victorian Garden: For all the fair's modernity, designers loved old-fashioned gardens. Many of these could have come straight from the yard of an 1893 fairgoer. The 1933 "Mid-Victorian Petunia Garden," for example, had a cross-shaped center lawn with eight clipped ball shrubs surrounding a gazing globe. Thousands of petunias were shipped from California and planted as a multihued groundcover. The 1934 version of the Victorian Garden had a flagstone-bordered circular pool containing a fish-shaped fountain. A statue of Pan surveyed the scene from a shaped plinth. Also traditional were the Old Mill and the Formal Italian Gardens.

Rose Garden: The Century of Progress Rose Garden differed greatly from that of the Columbian Fair. Unlike the 1893 patchwork of roses exhibited by multiple companies, the 1933 Fair's rose display had a single sponsor: Inter-State Nurseries of Hamburg, Iowa. In 1933, there were more than six thousand rose bushes of 104 varieties. This more than doubled in 1934 to fifteen thousand bushes of 300 varieties. An arched trellis marked the entrance to the garden, where beds were arranged in interlocking planting schemes, predominantly pink and red.

Modern Garden: "Saw-toothed" edged beds and angular designs were hallmarks of the Modern Garden displays. In 1933, the Men's Garden Club of Aurora, Illinois, exhibited wedge-shaped beds densely planted with annuals. Vaughan's Seed Store created zigzag garden beds filled with deciduous shrubs and outlined with ribbon plantings. Garden enthusiasts from Oak Park, Illinois, constructed a "Garden Symphony" that combined formal elements such as a flagstone walkway and wide lawns, edged with irregularly shaped ribbon-planted flower beds.

Krider's Diversified Gardens: Contrasting

THE HORTICULTURAL GARDENS

with these parochial displays, Vernon Krider, general manager of Krider Nurseries in Middlebury, Indiana, offered a series of garden tableaux reflecting U.S. regions outside of the Midwest. Designed by landscape architect A. J. Vocke of Tippecanoe City, Ohio, Krider's gardens included New England scenes and Allegheny sections replete with rhododendrons and azalea, and West Coast gardens with a plant-based sundial. In homage to absent foreign nations, Krider also sponsored interpretations of German gardens, French gardens called the "Posies of Picardy" that featured French lilacs and roses, gardens of the Netherlands with a windmill and canal, and a tribute to Ireland's Lakes of Killarney region.

Water Gardens: Water gardens, often seen as luxuries, were popular despite the Depression. The fair's horticultural guidebook proclaimed: "The improvement in gardening and the beautification of the home, as a whole, has shown its greatest progress in the last decade. The back yards, which formerly were, more or less, neglected or partly used for growing vegetables, are fast being transformed into outdoor living rooms . . . The center of the outdoor living room, or modern garden, is the water lily pool."[32]

Gil Lambacher, an employee of Tricker Company's Water Gardens, recalled the challenges involved in constructing Tricker's display. Hauling plants and dirt in a truck

▲ This garden shows the "saw-toothed" edges popular as a modernistic design treatment. (Author's collection)

➤ One of many naturalistic gardens at the Century of Progress Exposition, this water garden also featured popular aquatic plants. (Author's collection)

from the company's home base in Ohio, the nonagenarian Lambacher later remembered, "My tires kept blowing out [from the excess weight], and I had to throw dirt to the side of the road."[33] Aquatic plants were anchored in cedar tubs under the pond. Despite the hardships of construction, the show was a great success and the water garden took a first place.

The 1933–34 Exposition marked a departure from past world's fairs in that private companies' exhibits outshone government-sponsored displays. Rather than advertising horticultural products of the region, as was suitable for a state- or foreign-country-sponsored exhibit, a corporate landscape showcased its own brand. Sinclair Oil, for example, emphasized the source of its petroleum products by creating a tropical paradise as a backdrop for their eye-catching dinosaur exhibits. Herbivores such as the brontosaurus and stegosaurus nibbled on hastily transplanted tropical palms. The automotive industry, so dominant in the Midwest, contributed beautiful gardens. General Motors' grounds incorporated a wide plaza surrounded by hedges and lawn in the center of which "GM" was sculpted in plant material. The Firestone Building had a long reflecting pool in front of it with a "singing" fountain highlighted by colored lights, the "only one of its kind in the world." Ford's display included terraced lawns with formal ranks of evergreens and conifer hedges. The American Radiator and Standard Sanitary Corporation "Garden of Ease" boasted cascading water and clipped hedges.

Across the lagoon from the Horticultural Exhibition, *Good Housekeeping* magazine had installed its pavilion and outdoor garden designed by the landscape architect Annette Hoyt Flanders. Described by the magazine as a "Classic Modern garden," the 175 x 112–foot exhibition plot was a geometric study in green and white. Arborvitae hedges and symmetrical allées of poplars framed the garden, and rows of white flowers provided a tranquil setting. "Although here built and planted in a Modern Classical manner, to harmonize with the modern spirit of A Century of Progress, . . . the basic beauty of a garden is dependent on the design and not on the kind of plants or building materials used," Flanders observed. "To accomplish this, a garden simple in line and flexible in execution was made so that it could be adapted to various types of houses and climates by the use of different plants, and be built at varying costs by changing the materials."[34]

The *Good Housekeeping* Garden made extensive use of uplighting to highlight larger trees, and also spotlighted fountains at night. Special aluminum "lily pads" were built to disguise the lights in the reflecting pools. The effect was quite dramatic, and the magazine boasted: "Daytime visitors return at night to see one of the brightest prophesies of progress—garden lighting. Not that they ever do see much of the lights themselves, because these, like the fairy-tale magician, are practically invisible. What they do see is a beautiful night picture as different from the daytime picture of the garden as you in your garden smock are different from you in a dinner dress. But who shall say which picture is the more pleasing?"[35]

Although corporate garden displays predominated, many state buildings were surrounded by themed gardens. Indiana produced a formal landscape design with a center
pool, fountains, and statuary. Michigan offered a restful, informal patio with beach um-
brellas overlooking its namesake lake. Minnesota re-created one of its state parks by installing hundreds of hard- and softwood trees, miniature streams, and lakes. New York
brought in seven carloads of rocks, tree stumps, and native plants to create a slice of the
Adirondack Mountains. The garden included springs and waterfalls, streams teeming
with rock bass, sunfish, and bluegill, and swamps and bogs filled with rare mosses.

Of all the states, Florida's garden displays most lavishly represented its indigenous
flora. Florida's pavilion had a Spanish walled courtyard filled with tropical plants,
vines, parrots, statuary, native rocks, and fruit trees. The living citrus grove comprised
forty full-sized citrus trees that thrived in 3 acres between the lagoon and Agriculture
Building. In contrast to the few spindly and unimpressive orange trees at the 1893
World's Columbian Exposition, the entire grove had been transplanted from southeast
Florida to Chicago. Each orange was individually wrapped in situ and each limb se-
curely tied to the tree. The combination of cool weather in early June and later weeks
of 100-degree heat caused peculiar blossoms and fruit on the Lue Gim Gong orange
trees, as noted by one reporter: "On one and the same tree are ripe oranges from the
blossom of March, 1932; the green oranges from the blossom of March, 1933; the very
small fruit setting from the blossom of July, 1933, and a scattering of new blossoms in
August."[36]

Foreign exhibits were plentiful at the COP despite the Depression, but few countries displayed horticultural products. Some exhibits were offered in absentia, such as
the dahlia tubers sent to the world's fair from Germany, Holland, Canada, England,
Mexico, Austria, Japan, France, Russia, Belgium, and Czechoslovakia. Perhaps most
interesting was the International Friendship Garden, sponsored by the Stauffer Brothers of Hammond, Indiana. Local leaders and those from foreign lands were polled as
to their favorite flower, and these favorites were then planted together in an eclectic
display of international harmony. The guide to the garden promised that lucky visitors could get autographs from visiting dignitaries. Adolph Hitler's favorite flower was
Edelweiss; Benito Mussolini declared himself a "lover of all flowers"; Sigmund Freud
liked gardenias; and Eleanor Roosevelt's favorites were pansies and roses. The rose
was the clear winner in the International Friendship Garden. Eighty dignitaries from
around the world chose a rose as their favorite. The runner-up was the carnation with
twenty-one votes, and the rest of the votes were split among several other flowers.

While not entering specific horticultural classifications, many foreign countries
hosted displays of commerce and native products in their own stand-alone buildings.
Japan's building, while not near the horticulture exhibits, was surrounded by its char-

acteristically charming gardens. In addition to curved bridges and streamlets, the out-door exhibition included a Japanese teahouse, later transported to the Wooded Island site of the 1893 World's Fair Japanese Garden.

Legacies

Modernistic landscape treatments were not universally well received. One ASLA member, Leon Zach, voiced a popular view of modernism as "the over-plentiful use of architectural and geometric forms; excessive indulgence on paper of the T-square, triangle and compass."[37] Other writers and ASLA practitioners decried the use of saw-toothed edges in bed design, oddly shaped clipped forms, and the inevitable rock garden. Even some organizers of the horticulture exhibition were hostile toward the so-called "modern" trend. James Burdett, the publicist for the Horticultural Exhibi-tion, had this to say in a newspaper interview: "Now sometimes you hear talk about modernistic gardens . . . Well, about all the modernists have done in flower gardens is to cut out beds in triangles. There can be no such thing as a modernistic garden . . . because you haven't the modernistic material to plant. The trees and the flowers don't go modernistic."[38]

After a successful two years as one of the few fairs that actually turned a profit, the Century of Progress closed in November 1934. The Horticultural Building, like all of the temporary buildings, was torn down. Nevertheless, bits and pieces of the fair have survived into the present day. The International Friendship Garden, by the Stauffer Brothers of Hammond, Indiana, was re-created in nearby Michigan City, Indiana, where it flourishes and expands today under the direction of a band of volunteer gar-deners. In Middlebury, Indiana, Krider Nurseries donated land to re-create portions of its own display gardens in the Century of Progress Park. Here visitors will find the windmill, giant mushroom, and even some evergreens that once stood in Krider's Diversified Gardens. Roger Krider, who was five years old when he visited his grand-father's gardens at the exposition, says: "My grandfather had a vision that this might be an opportunity to get some exposure. The Fair gave us a springboard to start the mail order business." He recalls the words of the "Garden Poem" that was reprinted in a Krider booklet: "There's a window in my garden, looking out across the sea." It was garden windows such as these, perhaps more so than the windowless modern build-ings of the fair, which truly gave the best views of the Century of Progress.

Landscape Lessons from the Century of Progress

Like the Panama-Pacific International Exposition, most of the landscaping and buildings for the fair were returned to urban development. The extensive fill project, creating new land from Lake Michigan, resulted in permanent new green spaces, including Meigs Field airport (1948–2003) and, later, the Northerly Island lakefront park. Although a mix of garden styles was exhibited, several efforts at a "modern" design featuring asymmetrical borders or saw-toothed edges were seen at the COP. Container plantings for the terraced buildings also offered new methods and combinations of plants and water features.

The COP was the first U.S. world's fair to feature small gardens that could be appreciated and copied by backyard gardeners. Although grand displays existed in the malls and public areas, the horticultural exhibits concentrated on themed designs. Making the best of a depressed economy, the use of small-scale dioramas filled the void left by a dearth of exhibits showcasing foreign gardens.

The increase in hybridization noted at the Panama-Pacific International Exposition encouraged the development of flower societies devoted to a single species. These societies mounted their own flower shows—a departure from previous world's fairs in which individual nurserymen might showcase a specific plant. The societies helped support the Horticulture Exhibition, relieving individual nurserymen of the total burden.

Advances in indoor and outdoor lighting increased the appeal of COP landscapes. Successful artificial lighting led to windowless exhibit buildings, which in turn necessitated special landscaping effects to soften the harsh walls, which eliminated the need for sightlines from within the buildings. Outdoor lighting effects helped extend the interest of the horticultural displays well into the evening hours.

The COP marked the beginning of an evolution away from state and foreign gardens and toward corporate-sponsored exhibits. This trend would become more noticeable at the bicoastal fairs in 1939 and 1940 in New York and San Francisco. It was the beginning of the end for regionalism in garden displays.

A *Convenient* and *Pleasant Place* ☆

WHERE YOU AND YOUR FRIENDS CAN MEET AND
KEEP IN TOUCH WITH ONE ANOTHER AT THE FAIR

THE GARDEN of SECURITY
EXHIBIT SECTION AT APPROACH
TO THE EMPIRE STATE BRIDGE

FAIRCHILD AERIAL SURVEYS

9

The World of Tomorrow

Fair of the Future

Still battling the effects of the Great Depression and on the brink of World War II, the United States badly needed an infusion of optimism, and New York's 1939–40 World's Fair themes of the "World of Tomorrow" and "Peace and Freedom" promised exactly that. The fact that the fair was sited on the Corona Dump offered the opportunity to transform a trash heap into a first-rate exposition site. To accomplish this intimidating task, the New York World's Fair Corporation assembled a team of experts who gave Americans their last experience of a truly world-class fair.

Conducted just six years after the start of the Century of Progress Exposition, American world's fairs on both coasts courted international and U.S. visitors. Overlapping with New York's event was San Francisco's third world's fair, the Golden Gate International Exposition (GGIE). Constructed on man-made Treasure Island, the GGIE posted very respectable attendance figures, but even so, it had less than half the number of visitors to New York. At 400 acres, the GGIE site was one-third the size of the New York World's Fair.

The New York World's Fair of 1939–40 became the last grand BIE-sanctioned fair in twentieth-century America. Eighty-seven years after the United States first ventured into international expositions with the New York World's Fair of 1853, the last visitor exited the gates of a U.S. World's Fair on October 27, 1940. It would be more than twenty years before a fair of this magnitude returned to the United States. When a world's fair opened in Flushing Meadows, New York, in 1965, it debuted to a more technologically sophisticated visitor who traveled by air or on a nationwide system of interstate highways.[1]

But in 1939, these marvels were still years away, and the fair enchanted visitors with its futuristic vocabulary. The emblematic Trylon spire (a fusion of "tri" for its three sides and "pylon" to suggest a gateway) was connected to the enormous Perisphere, which housed the Democracity, a full-immersion vision of the City of Tomorrow. Futurama, an interactive exhibit from General Motors, extended the prophetic rhetoric to new modes of transportation and communication. These utopian constructions were designed respectively by Henry Dreyfuss and Norman Bel Geddes, leaders in the emerging American industrial design movement. "Streamlining" for utility and beauty became a watchword for the fair's Board of Design.

A comparison of the list of designers involved in the 1876 Centennial Exhibition with that of the 1939 New York World's Fair shows the progression of interest in landscape design. From the solitary participation in 1876 of H. J. Schwarzmann to the lengthy roster of designers in New York, the increasing emphasis placed on landscape design over the decades is evident.

New York City parks commissioner Robert Moses (1888–1981) and a group of New York's industrial titans muscled the world's fair into existence with the objective of creating a new park for the city, while realizing healthy returns. Although the fair was international in scope, the Fair Corporation's Board of Directors, architects, and landscape architects came largely from metropolitan New York.[2] Only one nursery west of New York State participated in the fair's horticultural exhibit.[3] While this uniformity helped create a harmonious look, it may also have contributed to a certain sameness evident throughout the fairgrounds.

By June 1939, fifteen members of the American Society of Landscape Architects and another fourteen landscape architecture or design firms had participated in the design of the grounds.[4] Gilmore D. Clarke, chair of the Board of Design's Landscape Design Committee, served as the fair's chief landscape architect. Private exhibitors could and did hire their own landscape professionals, subject to approval of plans by Clarke.

Clarke was professionally affiliated with at least five of the Fair Corporation's consulting landscape architects (Charles Downing Lay, Arthur F. Brinckerhoff, and Charles N. Lowrie) and collaborators (Alfred Geiffert Jr. and Michael Rapuano).[5]

Interestingly, there are many stylistic parallels between the landscapes of this fair and those of the Centennial. Clarke, in describing the 1939–40 landscape plan, predicted that old-fashioned garden styles would be reinterpreted with a modern twist: "It will demonstrate that the old art of bedding may be adapted to the present modern trends in architectural design and result in securing dramatic compositions of formal ground patterns in wide ranges of color in harmony with the gay colors of the architecture and the murals. Once more we shall use petunias, lantanas, annual phlox, verbenas, tagetes, heliotrope, ageratum and geraniums by the thousands in mass display for dramatic color effects."[6] Clarke did not ascribe a name to this landscape style, although he observed that such elements as the axial formal boulevards radiating from the Theme Center (anchored by the Trylon and Perisphere) lent a suggestion of Versailles to the composition.

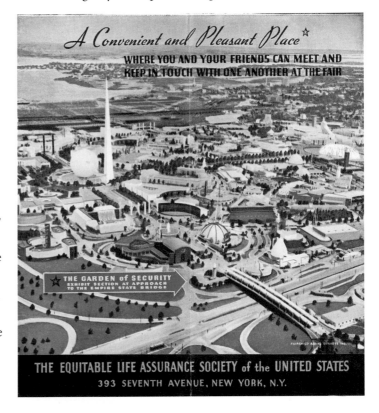

> This stylized map of the fair shows its location on the Flushing River, with the Trylon and Perisphere anchoring Constitution Mall. (Author's collection)

In the May 1939 issue of the *Magazine of Art,* the architectural critic Frederick Gutheim complained of the fair, "If a style is born it is the Corporation Style—a bastard dialect of architectural larceny and advertising." The article prompted an irate Clarke to tender his resignation as a board member of the American Federation of Arts, the sponsoring organization of the magazine, with a blistery retort: "Mr. Gutheim is not, in my opinion, an architect of distinction, and in my judgment his views are not worthy of publication."[7]

Gutheim nonetheless raised an important issue. As world's fairs became more a venue for individual businesses than for national and state buildings, how was the fair landscape to adapt? Regional architecture (expressed in foreign nations' pavilions or state buildings) could readily be complemented with regional plants. But what statement or identity could a corporation make with its landscape?

The *New York Herald Tribune* reported, "Harmony is the keynote of the Fair's architecture: harmony of building with building of architectural pattern with the ideas which the exhibits represent."[8] The emerging field of industrial design offered corporate America the notion of streamlining as a means toward efficiency and aesthetic appeal—not only in the packaging of products, but in the products themselves. Buildings, too, were designed and constructed along these modern lines. The building housing the perfumer Maison Coty, a multitier glass structure, suggested a powder-puff box. The Radio Corporation of America (RCA) edifice was shaped like a radio tube. National Cash Register was topped by 40-plus-foot cash register to ring up the fair's daily attendance in large numbers. The Wonder Bread Building was adorned with its trademark bubbles of red, blue, and yellow. The Hall of Marine Transportation resembled the prow of a ship; and the Aviation Building, a hangar. The building thus became a package designed along clean, modernistic lines. While architects were charged with creating buildings that reflected various corporate missions, landscape architects were required to design gardens that not only captured a corporate culture but also blended seamlessly into the overall landscape.

Raising the Fair

Not since the St. Louis Exposition had a world's fair been built on such an enormous scale. The New York site embraced more than 1,200, acres and extended about 3.5 miles south from Flushing Bay.[9] At its widest point, the fair site stretched to a mile. With Manhattan to the west, and Brooklyn and Queens to the east, the Flushing Meadows–Corona site was the geographical and population center of the city. With ready rail, water, road, and even airport access, the location was attractive.

Location, however, was perhaps the only favorable attribute of its site. This was, after all, what F. Scott Fitzgerald called the valley of the ashes: "a fantastic farm where ashes grow like wheat into ridges and hills and grotesque gardens."[10] The site, once a low-lying marshland, had been polluted with industrial effluent and, since 1908, had served as the city dump for coal ashes and other waste. Towering mountains of coal ashes grew to as high as 90 feet. The New York City Parks landscape architect Francis Cormier described the prefair site:

The waters of Flushing Bay were polluted by the large sanitary sewers which flowed into it and its bottom covered with an increasingly high mountain of raw sewage, leaving foul flats at low tide. The fires from the refuse mountains on Riker's Island filled the air with columns of smoke and smell. This usually drifted over the Flushing Meadow mingled with the smoke and smell of Corona dump and the miasmic odors which at low tide arose from Flushing Bay. The Flushing Meadow was traversed by ill-constructed causeways and faulty bridges which became more inadequate as traffic increased.[11]

Atop a bed of clay, a thick, fibrous mat of marshy grass roots, often 4 feet deep, covered much of the site. In this "meadow mat," the briny waters of the bay and an accumulation of decades of ashes combined to make the seemingly insurmountable task of transforming the "grotesque gardens" into a lush landscape. On June 29, 1936, ground was broken. From the fall of 1936 through early 1937, ground conditions were the subject of detailed investigations.[12] By excavating Fountain and Willow Lakes and improving the flow of Flushing River, adequate drainage was provided. The official fair guidebook claimed that the preparation of the site "was the largest single reclamation project ever undertaken in the eastern United States. The mountains were leveled and the bogs filled in with almost six million cubic yards of ashes. Over the marshes thus filled in, hundreds of thousands of cubic yards of top soil were deposited and leveled."[13]

A massive tide gate and dam were built to control water levels in Flushing Bay and in the man-made waterways. Infrastructural elements including roads, sewer, and electricity were installed to serve not only the fair but also the future park. According to E. J. Carrillo, chief landscape engineer, more than 100,000 cubic yards of additional excavation work was executed during 1937 and 1938 in preparation for planting beds, tree pits, and lawns.[14] In an idea borrowed from the 1907 Jamestown Exposition, more than 10 miles of chain-link fence from 6 to 9 feet high enclosed the fairgrounds. Ahead of schedule, in March 1937, the fairgrounds were ready for construction and planting.

The thoroughly scoured, cut, and filled site presented a blank canvas for planting. No tree or shrub remained. On April 2, 1937, the first three trees were planted in the Transportation sector. These were all Oriental planes (*Platanus orientalis* L.), or sycamores, each weighing 10 tons and stretching 30 feet high, with 28-foot spreads. In all, ten thousand trees were obtained, largely from Pennsylvania, Connecticut, New Jersey, and New York.[15]

American elms, swamp and Norway maples, pin oaks, Oriental planes, honey locust, sweet gum, white willow, katsuras, white flowering dogwood, cockspur thorn, and crabapple cultivars were among the larger specimens transplanted.[16] The Landscaping Department embarked on scouting missions to evaluate trees offered by private landowners and others. Specimens were loaded on flatbed trucks, delivered across planned routes, and covered with a wax emulsion to prevent desiccation after planting.

According to Henry C. Nye, the chief landscape designer, only 2 percent of the trees planted were lost.[17]

Many of the mature trees obtained had interesting backgrounds, and the Fair Corporation maintained photographs and case histories not only of selected trees, but also of trees declined. Near the Consumers' Interests Building thrived a transplanted elm tree descended from the famous Washington elm at Cambridge, Massachusetts (so called because it was sited where George Washington took command of the American army in 1775). Trees came from the Long Island estates of the master glass artist Louis Comfort Tiffany and the banker Otto Kahn, and from unassuming New Jersey sites such as Jack's Service Station in Wycoff and the Hackensack Water Company. From Connecticut, elms arrived from the Supple farm in Brookfield and red maples from the Clark estate at Cornwall Bridge.[18] The exacting tree specifications and daunting expense involved in transportation prompted Gilmore Clarke to comment: "All the large trees are in locations where they will grow on to maturity in the Flushing Meadow Park of tomorrow . . . And so these living reminders of the New York World's Fair of 1939 will be perpetuated for those who visit the park in later years."[19]

Yet, despite all the careful planning, mishaps large and small occurred. On September 21, 1938, the worst hurricane ever recorded in the northeastern United States struck with Category 3 force. Property damage and loss of human life were tragically high. An estimated 2 billion trees were lost throughout New York and New England, and trees that survived the storm later suffered browning from the massive salt spray from wind-blown seawater.[20] For the most part, the fairgrounds were spared; a *Better Homes and Garden* magazine writer reported that on an October 27, 1938, visit, only one dogwood was marked for replacement.[21]

A Tour of the Grounds

The fairgrounds were divided roughly in half by the World's Fair Boulevard between the northern "Exhibit Area" and the southern "Amusement Area." Seven "zones" grouped exhibits thematically to help visitors make sense of the layout. At the west entrance to the Exhibit Area, beyond the Corona Gates, was the Transportation Zone. A visitor would move counterclockwise from here through the remaining five zones of the Exhibit Area: Communications and Business Systems; Community Interests; Government; Food; and the Production and Distribution Zone. The Amusement Zone, surrounding Fountain Lake, dominated the south end of the fairgrounds. In an attempt to keep the physical scale of the fair from overwhelming visitors, the Fair Corporation limited building size to one-story structures—deemed an aesthetic necessity given that the skyscrapers of Manhattan formed the backdrop. The progression of color also helped visitors navigate the fairgrounds. Radiating from the pure-white Trylon and Perisphere, buildings in each zone shared a color palette that moved gradually through deepening tones of primary color.

Landscapes coordinated with this color coding. As Henry Nye had promised: "One of the outstanding features of the landscape treatment will be the flower planting in the Exhibit Area, which is being synchronized with the general color scheme. In the Plaza to the north of the Theme Building, a yellow area, there will be cream-colored lantana and lavender heliotrope. In the Plaza to the south, a blue area, there will be white petunias and red phlox, followed by scarlet sage."[22] Largely responsible for planning the patterns and hues of the bulb and flower displays was Miss M. B. Sprout, a Vitale and Geiffert staff member. To harmonize with the exposition's public buildings and thoroughfares, Sprout orchestrated the planting of more than 2 million annuals, bulbs, and other temporary plantings, particularly geraniums, pansies, narcissi, ageratums, verbenas, scillas, camassia, laurel, and roses.

Water features, including numerous reflecting pools and basins, not only cooled the heat radiating from flat building walls and pavement, but also reflected the sky and trees. Fountain jets amid the basins offered refreshing mists and sprays to passersby during the day and a kaleidoscope of colored lights at night. As a major feature on Constitution Mall, each night the Lagoon of Nations "became a son et lumiere show with fireworks, flames, colored fountains orchestrated by complex mechanisms and a musical accompaniment."[23] A long rectangular reflecting pool formed the centerpiece of the Court of States, with the flag of each state mirrored in the water.

Imaginative lighting figured prominently in the landscape design. Borrowing ideas from the 1937 Paris International Exposition, landscape designers availed themselves of many different lighting techniques to highlight plants, fountains, and sculptures. The master architect of the Paris Exposition, Jacques Greber, retained as a consultant to New York's fair, complimented the lighting and water effects, noting "great quality of color" and "a perfect architectural composition: variety, softness, gaiety and distinction."[24] He called the illumination of trees a "wonderful effect even on bare branches." Referring to the lighting along Constitution Mall, the fair's main thoroughfare, a fair press release noted: "The feature of the plan is illumination by reflection from the stately trees. Each and all of these will be flooded with light from a mercury vapor lamp installed out of sight in the ground and projecting a vertical beam into the foliage. The resultant effect is that of a greenish-white luminescence."[25] Smaller mercury vapor lamps were also concealed in the ground to highlight the flower beds. With these hidden lamps, the designers hoped the mall would be free of distracting lighting poles and lamp standards.

The newly graded fair site was essentially level, a condition that made possible its distinctive broad grass lawns.[26] Large expanses of green turf, worked into rectangles, arcs, and other geometric shapes, complemented the planes of the modern architecture and also framed sculptures. "The lawns of which there're some 250 acres, are particularly effective," wrote Sterling Patterson in *Better Homes and Gardens*. Patterson observed that rather than "rolling, pastoral stretches," the world's fair lawns were "a green plane, an element in a striking design."

Clipped and shaped hedges became the fair's signature landscape treatment and complemented the futuristic architecture. "I predict that there will be a revival of interest in shaped hedges as a result of the New York World's Fair's use of them," commented one member of the National Advisory Committee on Women's Participation. "They are an important element in the design at several points."[27] Hedges framed the streamlined structures in the Theme Center, the Ford Building, Temple of Religion,

and many other attractions. As Sterling Patterson noted, in rejecting the prevailing practice of "customarily grouped shrubs and perennials . . . a foundation planting [at the fair] is a vigorous stroke of a painter's brush, interpreted in clipped privet or dense Japanese Yew."[28]

Hedges also served as a crowd-control and traffic-management mechanism. Shortly after the fair's opening, for example, an internal Fair Corporation memorandum complained: "It has been observed at Corona Gate South that visitors are utilizing the base of the sculpture for many reasons such as sitting down, standing while taking pictures, etc. This is being done to such an extent that the sculpture has been damaged."[29] The solution was to install an 18-inch privet hedge around the Hawkins sculpture.

▲ Like many gardens surrounding corporate buildings, the sharp planes of manicured hedges and lawns complemented sleek building design. (Author's collection)

The Theme Center, with its Trylon and Perisphere, and Constitution Mall attracted the most attention from contemporary writers commenting on the fair's landscape design. One of the most intriguing architectural elements of the Theme Center was the helicline, a 950-foot-long, 18-feet-wide spiraling ramp that connected the iconic buildings. The designs of many gardens were influenced by the spiral shape of the helicline, most obviously the Spiral Garden, also called the Perylon Circle,[30] located southwest of the Theme Center. A foot-high Canadian hemlock hedge unwound from the center of the spiral to 20 feet at its outer ring. The design offered a sense of motion through the graduated sizes of bordering crabapple trees and broadened into a "comet's tail" of bedding plants made of alternating stripes of pink petunias and blue ageratums.[31] Further extending the fluid lines of the helicline, and serving as a backdrop to the Spiral Garden, a serpentine American arborvitae hedge ranging from 5 to 15 feet high wove among mature elm trees.

From the Theme Center, two mirroring courts bracketed the Trylon and Perisphere: the Court of Power and Court of Communications. Flanked on each side by symmetrical patterns of seasonal bulbs and annual flowers inset into smooth lawns, the Court of Power plaza was sharply defined by a zigzag hedge behind the flowers. The hedge framed fluorescent light standards, shaped like the curved and tubular leaves of an exotic plant. Four 65–foot sculptural pylons demarcated the Court of Power as it widened into a cul-de-sac, the Plaza of Light, with its own centerpiece circular fountain and basin.

Near the main theme center, the spiral hedge garden offered visitors a mazelike experience with graduated heights of hedges leading to a central fountain. (Author's collection)

Mirroring the Court of Power on the opposite side of the Perisphere, the formal Court of Communications featured two broad walkways bisected by a wide median of geometric plantings and smooth lawns. A long, rectangular reflecting basin showcased the sculpture of horse and rider, Joseph Renier's Speed, meant to symbolize the speed of communications. Innovative aqualons, upright fountains of moving water, punctuated the tree-lined outer edges of the parallel walkways. After the spring showing of flowering bulbs, the display gave way to a jeweled mixture of bedding plants.[32] Flowering dogwoods and other deciduous trees completed the tableau.

Continuing counterclockwise around the Theme Center, the Rose Court within the

Business and Insurance Building offered yet another treatment of hedges. In June, yellow polyanthus roses replaced the tulips that had been in bloom when the fair opened. Large ornamental wrought-steel trellises displayed two hundred climbing roses of the newly patented 'Golden Glow.' The garden's central turf panel was embellished with scroll-shaped *Taxus* hedging, bordered with white petunias and heliotrope.[33]

The grandest avenue of the fair, Constitution Mall, extended for 1 mile, running northeast from the Theme Center to the Federal Government Building. With its major water features, sculptures, and landscape elements, the mall may have been Gilmore Clarke's favorite landscaped area. Nearly half of his photographic essay on the world's fair for *Landscape Architecture* magazine focused on design elements of the promenade.[34]

Paul Manship's *Sundial* sculpture anchored the promenade on the south. The elegant, white, 80-foot sundial, said to be the largest in the world, rose from a mound of turf. The sculpture was the focal point of a sunken garden encircled by a shallow set of stairs. Clarke devised a rippling planting scheme to suggest water surrounding the monumental *Sundial.* Facing it, but separated by a long, oblong water basin, the Fountain of Time included a heroic 66-foot-tall statue of George Washington. This Washington Square, at the intersection of Constitution Mall and Jefferson and Hamilton Places, functioned as a public gathering place where bands played and performances were held. Audiences sat on wooden benches separated by a series of hedges manicured into loops and circles.

Beyond Washington Square, the main promenade extended toward the Lagoon of Nations, which boasted another long reflecting pool. The Mall was framed in a double allée of swamp maples underplanted with mountain laurel and English ivy. Presented in the half-moon sloped planting beds that lined the Mall were seasonal displays of flowers beginning with spring tulips that progressed from white near the Theme Center to deep red at Rainbow Avenue. Overall, the Central Mall display contained

△ Constitution Mall was formally landscaped in beds of spring tulips followed by seasonal annuals. Mature trees offered shade while huge reflecting pools and fountains provided additional relief from heat. (Author's collection)

500,000 geraniums, lantanas, ageratums, heliotropes, verbenas, annual phlox, and 250,000 pansies.[35]

Trees defined the scale and formality of the other main thoroughfares in the Exhibit Area. Elm trees framed the Bowling Green and Lincoln Square; Oriental planes lined the Avenue of Transportation. Norway maples lined the Court of Railways and Court of Ships, while pin oaks formed the perimeter of the Plaza of Light and Avenue of Labor.[36] Seasonal displays of flowers also made a show on these minor avenues, beginning with tulips and ending several months later with chrysanthemums.

Corporate and Private Gardens

Although corporate pavilions gained prominence in Chicago's 1933 Exposition, by 1939 in New York, they were the fundamental exhibition halls. With regionalism no longer as relevant as it had been in state or national horticulture displays, corporations determinedly impressed their brands upon the landscape. The Wonder Bread Company, for example, displayed a field of grain in front of their building. The lawns surrounding the building of the cigarette manufacturer Lucky Strike were strikingly green, a result of fertilizing the turf with 1.5 tons of tobacco stems. The Eastman Kodak garden endorsed the company's photographic products by providing a scenic backdrop, the precursor to today's "Kodak moments." The garden included props such as scaled-down models of the Perisphere and Trylon, along with a mural of fair scenery, to encourage patrons to experiment with their cameras.

The most extensive landscape treatment surrounded the car manufacturers' buildings in the Transportation Zone. The automobile's influence on American society was steadily growing, and cars were omnipresent at the world's fair. Practical reasons were said to dictate the Transportation Zone's prime location at the Corona gate entrance, but the ascendance of American transportation cannot be overlooked. Veteran railroad companies contended for exhibit space with the airline industry, but in terms of overall square footage, the automobile claimed the largest share.

Car manufacturers provocatively married images of landscape and automotive technology. Chrysler showcased its latest automobile models in a "frozen forest." The 1939 Fair's *Official Guidebook* explained: "In a glittering 'frozen forest' Chrysler Motors uses the science of its Airtemp Division to provide a highly spectacular and imaginative setting for its display of Plymouth, Dodge, DeSoto and Chrysler cars. Here, in the midst of New York's summer heat, is an oasis of snowy palms—a tropic island where moonlight turns mysteriously to snow on each tree it touches, suggesting what city gardens of tomorrow may become when today's science adds its inventiveness to the landscape gardener's ancient art."[37]

Around the General Motors and Ford Buildings, a joint campus of modern landscape design illustrated automotive themes. The front of both buildings faced a pedestrian plaza, while the back, fittingly, overlooked the recently revamped Grand Central Parkway. The Ford gardens, designed by Gilmore Clarke and Michael Rapuano, made lavish use of sheared hedges to complement the modern architecture of the building. More than 1,800 lineal feet of hemlocks ranging from 3 to 18 feet high and from 5 to 20 feet thick, formed a graceful arc across the 2.5-acre lawn. The hemlocks were supplemented by privet, clipped cedar hedges, nearly two thousand deciduous shrubs, and more than twenty-one thousand blue and white verbenas.[38] To the left of the main entrance of the building, a basin of water with several small fountains reflected a coiled ramp of hedges that echoed not only the curves of the building's rotunda, but also Ford's popular "Road of Tomorrow" exhibit, which allowed visitors to drive sample cars along the raised roadway leading to the corkscrew ramp anchoring the Ford display. *Landscape Architecture* magazine noted: "Inspired by the sense of movement and simplicity [in the automotive exhibit] the landscape design grew to emphasize direction."[39]

In the center of the "Road of Tomorrow" exhibit's corkscrew stood the *Chassis Fountain* by the sculptor Isamu Noguchi, a fusion of industrial gears and shafts surrounded by spires of columnar evergreens and set off by annual beds. Encircled by spurs of the "Road of Tomorrow" highway, the Ford Garden Court included hedge-lined panels of turf bounded by umbrella-topped bistro tables. The Garden Court provided the setting for numerous orchestral recitals and other musical entertainments. In the valuable real estate of the center court, Ford executives might have showcased more of their automobile designs, but they instead chose to plant a garden. Landscape was thus integral to the exhibit design: it was the centerpiece of the driving experience, designed for visibility and to provoke interest on many levels.

The adjacent GM Building was surrounded by 2 acres of landscaped grounds designed by Clauss Brothers. On either side of the main entrance, two sunken, reverse-

▲ The auto manufacturers' buildings occupied prime locations at the fair and made extensive use of hedges and sculptural gardens such as those shown in this view of the Ford Motor Building. (Author's collection)

Z-shaped beds of tulips created a look of modern formality. After flowering, the tulips were followed by sixteen thousand wax begonias. A low English upright yew hedge bordered these gardens, and near the street, another reverse-Z-shaped English yew bed announced the exhibit to passersby. Accented with flowering crab trees, block plantings of pfitzer junipers, Belgium begonias, azaleas, dogwoods, rhododendrons, and other plants, the display featured season-long color.

▲ Designed by Geiffert, Equitable Life's "Garden of Security" comprised the company's sole exhibit. (Photography by John Gorman; author's collection)

Also by Otto Clauss, the Firestone Building gardens showcased the letter *F* fashioned from red leaf barberry. Surrounded with rows of formal hedges, the Firestone "Singing Color Fountains," which debuted at the 1933–34 Century of Progress Exposition, made an encore performance. Patterns in a 65-foot-long bed of ageratums suggested the tread of a Firestone farm tire. Lastly, a "rubberized farm" featuring Firestone products anchored another outdoor exhibit including apple, plum, cherry, and pear trees, grapevine arbors, elderberry and huckleberry bushes, and weeping willows alongside an artificial creek.[40]

Alfred Geiffert is credited with the design of landscapes for two other major businesses: the American Telephone and Telegraph Company, which faced the Theme Center, and the Commonwealth Edison structure. The most striking feature of the AT&T Building was its surrounding dense forest planted with 138 full-grown white and Montana pine. This "bosque," as it is labeled in Geiffert's plans, became a favorite picnic spot for fair visitors. *Landscape Architecture* noted: "When first invited to undertake the landscape design of the American Telephone and Telegraph Company exhibit, the landscape architect was asked to do a garden. Realizing the general weakness of a garden with its lack of large scale and structural value, it occurred to him that a forest—and in this instance, of pine trees—would be a strong, appealing spectacle."[41] Immense bowl-shaped containers held delicate Japanese maple trees, along with "great salad bowls of concrete holding 15-foot latticed bamboo spheres with vines trained over them." Geiffert continued this North woods theme with generous plantings of evergreens in his design for the Electric Utilities Exhibit, wherein a huge waterfall representing a hydroelectric dam suggested the source of the utility's energy.

Perhaps the most intriguing use of garden space to symbolize corporate identity was that of the Equitable Life Assurance Society, also designed by Geiffert. Equitable's "Garden of Security" was its sole exhibit—no building housed displays of products or services. Instead, the baseball-diamond-shaped half-acre plot was intended to portray all the values the insurance company purported to offer: solidity, security, and shelter were expressed through the rows of tall, columnar evergreens sheltering a large, triangular lily pool. Rising above the pool, the sculpture of a guardian angel, *Protection,* mounted on a 36-foot-tall obelisk connoted safety.

Geiffert also landscaped the Edward G. Budd Manufacturing Company's garden. Budd, like Equitable, offered only a single display. Whereas Equitable marketed services, Budd was a pioneer in fabricating stainless steel for the automotive and rail industries. This large-scale manufacturer surely could have displayed manufactured products or displayed the assembly process. Instead, the Budd display was a garden. Tall, sheared red cedars formed a backdrop for pools and fountains. A large, irregularly paved gray flagstone plaza offered contrast to the bituminous paving of most of the fair. Modernistic sculptures added interest as well.[42]

Foreign Gardens

Because of the unsettled conditions in Europe, foreign participation in the New York World's Fair fluctuated between 1939 and 1940. With few exceptions, international pavilions were located in the Government Zone, across the Flushing River. The gardens and buildings bordered the Lagoon of Nations and Flushing River and flanked the Court of Peace.

Two years before Pearl Harbor, Japan exhibited a magnificent garden at the 1939 World's Fair, one of the most impressive ever staged at a U.S. exposition. Japan had commissioned one of its best landscape architects, Dr. Tsuyoshi Tamura, to execute the design. Tamura, also a forester, was instrumental in developing the national park system in Japan in the 1920s. Having toured the United States' system of national parks and met with the National Park Service director Stephen Mather, Tamura believed not only in the aesthetic and recreational value of parks but also in their importance in conservation efforts.[43] Thus he designed a garden that was at once for the spiritual seeker and the spectator. Tamura was assisted by Dr. Nagao Sakurai, a former horticultural consultant to Japan's Imperial Household, and Shogo J. Myaida, a Japanese-born landscape architect who had settled in America in the 1920s. Myaida was largely entrusted with the garden installation, and, in his own private practice, artfully blended Asian and American gardens with an understanding of both cultures. He knew that a traditional Japanese garden in America would not last long because of uninformed garden maintenance.[44] But a world's fair garden did not require long-term maintenance—only that needed for high-traffic and exposed conditions.

According to New York World's Fair publicity, "All the fragile charm of the Nipponese countryside with its mountain vistas, winding streams, fragrant foliage and silvery waterfalls has been reproduced about the red and gold Japanese Pavilion, in itself a replica of an ancient Shinto shrine."[45] The publicity described the pavilion as representative of the Great Ise Shrine, the most sacred of the thousands of Shinto shrines in Japan. Within the 25,000 square feet of the exhibit, Tamura replicated the Isuzu River in an 8-foot stream, "curving gracefully in exact simulation of the crooks and bends of the river in Japan."[46] A 5-foot-high mountain was the source for a waterfall, and the river wound around tableaux of stones, rocks, and shrubbery. This impressive construction formed a backdrop for the lilies, chrysanthemums, azaleas, and irises, and finally for a 50-foot-wide lake populated with goldfish and other carp.

The Netherlands Garden, one of the largest foreign displays, was designed by the New York firm of Innocenti and Webel.[47] Their work fused a respect for tradition with modern principles of landscape architecture. The 2.5-acre Netherlands Garden featured long reflecting pools suggestive of the region's famed canals. These were edged with large poplars and willows. *Landscape Architecture* noted: "In making their design the landscape architects kept in mind the large number of people coming from the main exit from the Netherlands Building which leads to the garden area. Instead of planning a plaza scheme, the obvious conception of a direct exit for crowds, they arranged to break up the stream of people into smaller rivulets and circulate them indirectly through the garden . . . This was done effectively by making a definite T-shape to the pool around which everyone must walk, and by diverting the minor circulation to the smaller gardens."[48] These smaller gardens included fountains, hedges, topiary work, and geometric beds.

Because the Netherlands Garden shared some land with the Polish Pavilion, a long reflecting pool connected the two exhibits. In season, sixty-five thousand tulips were in bloom, later replaced by about fifteen thousand bedding plants underplanted with periwinkle and ivy.[49] A critic wrote approvingly, "The horizontality of the beds and enclosing hedges contrasted with the strong verticals of the double row of poplars through the center of the scheme, keeping the spirit of the Holland landscape with its low, flat land, long canals and isolated marching avenues of poplar."[50]

Horticulture Exhibit: "Gardens on Parade"

Across the Flushing River, encircled by foreign buildings and exhibits from Italy, Chile, Venezuela, and Great Britain, the horticultural exhibit "Gardens on Parade" proposed to represent the heart of American landscapes. At "Gardens on Parade," a spectrum of different garden types was displayed on a small scale. There were naturalistic gardens (Wayside Wild Flower Shrine, Woodland Garden, and Informal Garden); gardens that paid homage to other nations (Garden of Nyssa, Parterre Gardens, English Garden, French Parterre Garden); specialty gardens (Rock Garden, Espalier Garden, and Water Garden); and plant connoisseur gardens (Cacti and Succulent Gardens, Parade of Modern Roses, Glories of the Garden, Herb and Knot Gardens, and Fine Turf Grasses).

Organized by a consortium of the Horticultural Society of New York, the New York Botanical Garden, the Brooklyn Botanic Garden, the New York Florists' Club, and the Society of American Florists, "Gardens on Parade" included a 6-acre outdoor display and an indoor exhibit hall. Directors and officers of the nonprofit consortium, incorporated as Hortus, Inc., included many social register names: Henry F. du Pont was chairman of the Board of Directors, and other familiar family names included Auchincloss, Rockefeller, and Marshall Field. The overall garden plan and buildings were designed by a team consisting of the consulting landscape architect Charles Downing Lay and the architect William A. Delano and his son, Richard Delano.[51]

While many were involved with producing the horticultural exhibit, the most influential was its president, Harriet Barnes Pratt. Wife of the industrialist and philanthropist Harold Pratt, she was an avid horticulturist and practitioner on her own estate in Glen Cove, Long Island. Pratt had a reputation for good taste and aesthetic sensitivity

▲ The elaborate gate and tentlike rotunda invited visitors to the extensive "Gardens on Parade" exhibit created by landscape designers and nurserymen alike. (Author's collection)

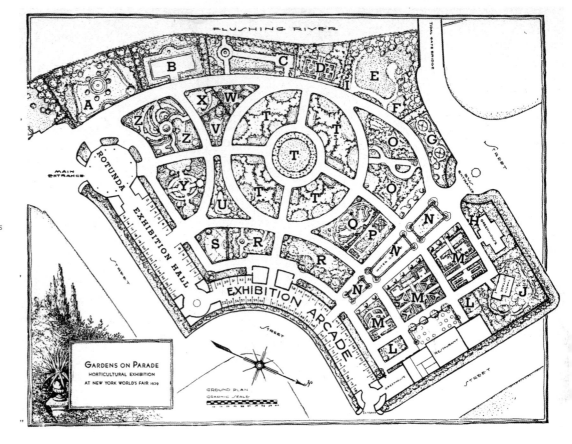

▶ From the central Havemeyer Tribute Garden, a fan-shaped collection of display gardens included Gardens of Today, Yesterday, and Tomorrow. (Author's collection)

PLOT	EXHIBIT TITLE
A	Formal Garden
B	Blue and White Garden
C	Garden of Nyssa
D	In Old New England
E	Anybody's Garden
F	Rock Garden
G	Espalier Garden
H	Cacti and Succulent Gardens and Plant Research
I	Wayside Wild Flower Shrine
J	Woodland Garden and Old English Thatched Cottage
L	Parterre Gardens
M	Parade of Modern Roses
N	Water Garden
O	Glories of the Garden
P	Herb and Knot Gardens
Q	French Parterre Garden
R	Year Round Garden
S	Fine Turf Grasses
T	Havemeyer Tribute Garden
U	Informal Garden
V	Garden of Today
W	Garden of Yesterday
X	Garden of Tomorrow

that was exemplified by her appointment to several White House advisory groups on décor. She was the first secretary of the Garden Club of America, and a fifteen-year member of the National Arboretum Committee. Her expertise and contacts however, came at the price of an uncompromising and exacting temperament. Fair officials anticipated this risk in 1937, while contacting potential leaders of the Horticulture Committee. Wrote one official: "The only fly in the ointment is whether we can get Mrs. Harold I. Pratt to go along. It seems Mrs. Pratt is exceptionally enthusiastic on Horticulture, but at times is hard to get along with as we understand she wants to run the whole show."[52]

Indeed, Pratt relentlessly pursued the details of the exhibit, employing any useful combination of personal energy, persuasion, browbeating, and horse trading. Pratt's idea for the display was a "great Outdoor Flower Show comparable to Bagatelle in Paris," according to a 1937 letter exchange among fair officials.[53] The Parc de Bagatelle, a former private estate purchased by the City of Paris in 1905, grew in renown as a public botanical garden beginning with its selection as the site of the world's first international rose show in 1907. Pratt and the Horticulture Society hoped to bring a comparable fusion of elegance and education to Flushing Meadows. If she perceived that this ideal was compromised in any way, Pratt wrote directly to the president of the New York World's Fair, Grover Whalen, or to park commissioner Robert Moses with complaints or suggestions.

Typical is a 1938 letter to Whalen in which she offered to take five thousand dollars' worth of World's Fair bonds in exchange for the privilege of hosting a garden party at "Gardens on Parade" for the king and queen of England. "Probably you have been, as I have, to the Garden Parties at Buckingham Palace," she wrote. "We could do it at Hortus to the 'King and Queen's taste,' I believe."[54] When the 1938 hurricane caused significant damage to the site, despite an accusatory reference to the fair's faulty tidal gate, she contributed personal funds and plantings from her own estate. Likening "Gardens on Parade" to the "stepchild of the Fair," she aired many grievances about perceived slights to the exhibit, including inappropriate lighting, insufficient access to water, and inaccessibility to bus stops.[55]

Despite initial low attendance, "Gardens on Parade" was well received in the popular press and by those who visited. *House Beautiful* magazine called it the "greatest thing in gardening display in our lifetime."[56] The gardens occupied a fan-shaped wedge with circus-tent-like rotundas at the entrances. The exhibit hall and arcade connecting the rotundas lined one side and the bottom curve of the wedge. Fifty gardens were created, largely by nurseries and gardening clubs. Indoor exhibitors sold everything from flower sachets, garden ornaments, and tools to gourds, dried flowers, fruit juice extractors, magazines, and horticultural microscopes.

Of particular interest were the three Gardens of Yesterday, Today, and Tomorrow. The Garden of Yesterday, by the Long Island landscape architect John Dunkinfield, put a new twist on the old-fashioned knot garden by planting traditional herbs in the shape of the Perisphere and Trylon. The Garden of Today, created by Alice Orme Smith, and other graduates of the Smith College Graduate School of Architecture and Landscape Architecture, was outlined with globular, sheared boxwood. A traditional garden gate framed by two white dogwoods announced the entrance to the space. A single gnarled apple tree formed the focal point of the garden, in the center of a smooth lawn bordered by an informal mix of flowering trees and shrubs (such as crabapples, hawthorns, and lilacs), mixed perennials, and annuals. New introductions included 'Flaming Fire,' 'Harmony,' and 'Early Sunshine' marigolds, 'Indian Spring' hollyhock, 'Blue Moon' scabiosa, and 'Salmon Glory' phlox. Hortus's souvenir program book explained, "This is a simple little garden that anyone could have in a small place without spending much money."[57]

LAVISH DISPLAY OF COLOR

Provided by 7500 Beautiful Plants
in "ROSES ON PARADE"

© N.Y.W.F.

Executed and Maintained by the World's Largest Rose-Growers

Never before have so many lovely Roses—the latest creations of both American and European hybridizers—provided such a lavish display of colors and varieties. "Roses on Parade," a section of the Horticultural Exhibit of the New York World's Fair, is aptly described as the most colorful Rose-garden of the century. It provides the perfect setting for the enjoyment of more than 250 varieties of Roses from 18 different countries—truly an International Rose-Garden.

Jackson & Perkins, the world's largest Rose-growers, and creators of "Roses on Parade," have been in the nursery business for 65 years. You are invited to visit J. & P.'s extensive test and display gardens at Newark, New York State, near Rochester. There you will see 20,000 Rose plants in over 3,000 varieties, including test plantings of

thousands of unnamed varieties from which will be selected the Roses of the future, and fields of over a million growing Rose plants.

J. & P. Roses are known the world over. Now, because of insistent demands from the public, a retail department has been added. You may now obtain these Roses from your local dealer or direct from Jackson & Perkins Company, as you may prefer. *The terms:* Please send cash with order or prior to shipping-time. Shipments prepaid east of Mississippi River; beyond that, add 15 per cent.

WORLD'S FAIR
(*Pat. pend.*)
Striking red blooms in large clusters.
Each $1.00
$10 dozen

© J. & P.

Write for FALL CATALOG

If you wish our new Fall 1939 Catalog, write Jackson & Perkins Company, Department WF, Newark, New York State. Our Fall Catalog will contain detailed descriptions and illustrations in color of the new Rose creations and the best of the older varieties. Also helpful information on planting.

LOOK FOR THIS LABEL

Jackson & Perkins' New Roses are patented for your protection. This label is your guarantee of the genuine.

None Genuine Without This Tag

▲ Jackson and Perkins sponsored "Roses on Parade," and a striking red rose was chosen as the "World's Fair" rose. (Author's collection)

The Garden of Tomorrow, sponsored by nine clubs of the Garden Club of America, offered a modernistic view of gardens that was meant as an exhibition rather than a set of ideas that could be readily translated to a typical backyard. Incorporating an iconic shape of the fair, a curving pathway echoed the spiral so prevalent throughout the grounds. Most interesting was the glass fence, a series of corrugated opaque panels in staggered heights that added a futuristic touch to the garden. The translucent fence permitted ivy to grow on both sides and still allowed sunlight to filter through. According to an approving description in the program booklet, "There is a feeling of motion in this garden with the design done in the manner of a Picasso abstraction, one that integrates all the elements into a moving whole."

Other gardens attempted to demonstrate an avant-garde vision as well. The first garden a visitor encountered after passing through the elaborate main entrance gate was "A Modern Maze of Motion—Tomorrow's Garden" by the nurserymen Bobbink & Atkins of Rutherford, New Jersey. Hedges of various heights swirled around a central planting. The program notes explained: "As we wander through the garden, the curve of the walk and hedges give one the thought of motion. This suggestion of motion is accentuated by the constant graduation of the hedges from the low to high—it's new . . . Tomorrow we will look for ease, speed and efficiency and find it possibly in this modern garden form."[58]

Jackson & Perkins's "Parade of Modern Roses" displayed about eight thousand rose plants of 250 varieties. Striving for an international flair, the exhibit showcased roses that originated in eighteen countries including Ireland's 'McGredy's Sunset' and 'Hector Dean.' Jackson & Perkins is said to have coined the term "floribunda" rose,[59] and the firm dedicated a large portion of space to these at the exhibit. The "'World's Fair' rose" (formerly 'Minna Kordes'), a fully double scarlet floribunda, was introduced at the exhibit in the fall of 1939. 'World's Fair' was planted near the exhibit's pergola and other locations, demonstrating its versatility. So many visitors enjoyed the rose display and wanted to take plants home that Jackson & Perkins began their mail-order business as a result. In their catalogue, *All about the New Roses—World's Fair Edition,* Jackson & Perkins offered planting diagrams for roses. Homeowners were urged not to plant in old-fashioned circular beds in the front yard, but rather near the detached garage—either alongside the driveway or in a formal garden adjacent to the garage.

Krider Nurseries of Indiana displayed "Glories of the Garden," and the souvenir program noted, "Combining various types of plants and plantings with simplicity of arrangement reflects the spirit of tomorrow without departing from certain recognized practices and standards." Krider's display was personally designed by Charles Downing Lay. Within the broad curves of a rock garden, a variety of shrubs, flowers, and conifers were exhibited. Krider parlayed the "Glories of the Garden" exhibit into its sales catalogues in later years. Its forty-fifth anniversary issue, published in 1940, was trademarked *Glories of the Garden,* and featured the Trylon and Perisphere images with the question, "Were you there?" on almost every page. They offered a collection of "the twelve plants which received the most attention and admiration from World's Fair visitors to our gardens." For three dollars, customers could order these prized dozen: forget-me-not (*Anchusa myosotidiflora*); Armeria 'Glory of Holland'; blue bells of Scotland (*Campanula rotundifolia*); columbine 'Crimson Star'; dianthus 'Red Grenadin'; geum 'Fire Opal'; *Heuchera* x *Brizoides;* liatris 'September Glory'; lynchnis (*Viscaria flore pleno*); nepeta 'Six Hills Giant'; stokesia 'Blue Moon'; and viola 'Apricot Gem.'

Krider's exhibit was one of the few from nurseries outside of New England and the Middle Atlantic. Although "Gardens on Parade" aspired to present gardens from around the nation and world, there was no doubt that this was a New York–centered exhibit. The centerpiece theme garden, occupying the most prominent display space, was the Havemeyer Tribute Garden. Sponsored by the Horticultural Society of New York, the garden commemorated one of its own members, former society president Theodore A. Havemeyer. The garden featured a fountain centered in a bowl-shaped circle of turf, surrounded by four equal sectors of shrubs and plantings. Lilacs, a favorite of the late Havemeyer, were prominently featured. Contributors to the memorial garden resided for the most part on Long Island or in other regions of New York, and their names, along with those of their estate's gardeners, were listed in the horticultural souvenir book.

Legacies

Plans for the ultimate disposition of the park were grand and seemed assured when Robert Moses regained authority of the leased land from the Fair Corporation. But the fair had not returned the expected profit, and the public and private funds that could be allocated toward park redevelopment were scarce because of the war effort. Many planned park enhancements were deferred, revamped, or never materialized. Shifting sympathies and alignments among nations in wartime affected the disposition of World's Fair landscape elements. Commitments from international exhibitors to leave landscape specimens behind often needed confirmation, while patriotic Americans lobbied to retain the landscape material of Allied nations.

The disposition of New York World's Fair items, including landscape elements, was of great interest to many parties, and often received high-profile attention. Alfred P. Sloan Jr., chairman of General Motors, even wrote to Moses expressing concern about potential plant poaching from the GM exhibit. Sloan became aware of the plant salvage operation in a roundabout way—his wife had received a circular from a local nursery on Long Island announcing "World's Fair Trees at Bargain Prices."[60]

Often, Robert Moses's thin reserves of diplomacy were tested in fielding the multitude of "helpful" suggestions on dismantling the fair. When a group of "prominent Belgian Americans and distinguished New Yorkers" asked to install a heroic bronze statue of Belgium's late King Albert, Moses received their request favorably.[61] Conversely, after trying to forestall efforts to save the fair's temporary Leif Eriksson statue, Moses instructed George Spargo to "put the kibosh on this," noting that they had "wasted a lot of time, ate a number of rotten dinners [trying to come to an amicable solution], and ended up with nothing."[62]

The Japanese Pavilion and gardens were to be retained as the only foreign structure left in the postfair park. Minor modifications were made to pedestrian pathways on the south end, and an additional teahouse and gardens by Tamura & Sakurai were to be installed on the north end. On September 18, 1940, with a small dedication ceremony, the gardens and pavilion were presented to the City of New York. As Japanese Commissioner General Kaname Wakasugi wrote to Robert Moses, "The retention of the Japanese Pavilion and its garden by the City is greatly appreciated by the Japanese . . . [T]hey will be a monument truly indicative of the friendship between the United States and Japan."[63]

Temporary nurseries were established near the former Aviation Building and Florida Buildings to accommodate relocated trees and shrubs. As buildings were torn down, plant material was salvaged and stored for later use. The south area of the former fair site, near the lakes, was to receive the most immediate attention, particularly since midges plagued the site. Prospective homeowners in the nearby area wrote directly to Commissioner Moses asking for updates on the problem. Entomologists were contacted, insecticides used, and fish were stocked in the lakes to control the insects.

Robert Moses was characteristically blunt in responding to requests. When Jackson & Perkins, who had donated their rose gardens and offered to provide a continuous supply of rose plants and sponsor a rose festival, requested a plaque noting their contributions, Moses was quick to object. In an internal memo, Moses characterized the offer as a "publicity racket" and contended, "Certainly we are not making any arrangements with this company to keep supplying roses as an advertising medium, nor is there going to be any rose festival if I have my health and strength."[64]

Plant salvaging operations were to be completed on a tight schedule. Before the onset of winter, trees and shrubs needed to be lifted and heeled into the park's temporary nurseries. Using hundreds of park employees borrowed from other boroughs, the plant salvage project was completed by December 21, 1940. In the short six or seven weeks between the end of the fair in October and then, nearly five hundred trees and thousands of shrubs were relocated. The most numerous specimens included flowering dogwood, white pine, crabapple, maple (Norway, sugar, and red), and various beech and birch trees. Most of the transplanted shrubs were destined for replanting in Flushing Meadow, with some planned for the GM Parkway. The most popular shrubs for Flushing Meadow included azalea, holly, mountain laurel, yews (more than 3,100 *Taxus cuspidata* and almost 1,200 *T. breuifolia*), barberry, and spirea.[65]

The fate of "Gardens on Parade" hung uncertain for a while. Many visitors or donors were interested in the garden's disposition.[66] Elements of the display were parceled out to various organizations or individuals. The School of Horticulture at the State Institute of Applied Agriculture in Long Island claimed items from Krider's display, and the metal pool and fence sections from the Garden of Nyssa.[67] Four metal murals of flower groups that decorated the exterior walls were to be sent to Dr. William Robbins, director of the New York Botanical Garden.[68]

The inimitable Harriet Pratt was evenly matched with Robert Moses. Pratt lobbied long and hard to maintain the "Gardens on Parade" site as a demonstration garden. She extended social invitations to Moses and personally assisted with planting a trial garden near Corlears Hook Park, a park that had been redesigned under Moses.[69] Pratt was a strong advocate for demonstration gardens in the parks. She tried to convince Park General Superintendent Allyn Jennings that either Central Park or Flushing Meadow should include some trial gardens, contending that both the Bronx and Brooklyn Botanical Gardens were too far from Manhattan. Jennings went so far as to attach a map triangulating the distances to the existing botanical gardens and Pratt's Park Avenue house, demonstrating the ease with which Manhattanites could access existing educational gardens. Robert Moses was more succinct in his memo to Jennings: "Her [Pratt's] backyard idea is completely nutty, and I am opposed to such an exhibit anywhere in the park system or in the Flushing Meadow Park."[70]

Pratt's relentless efforts on behalf of the "Gardens on Parade" began to take their toll on Moses. In attempting to secure funding from her wealthy colleagues, Pratt insisted on various donor recognition plaques and legalistic assurances from the Park Department as to the future of the gardens. In an internal memo to George Spargo, Moses expressed annoyance with socialite interference and confided: "A group of well intentioned, enthusiastic, wealthy, tight and more or less idle women can run us ragged around and around Gardens on Parade. This is a small incident in the development of Flushing Meadow Park, and Flushing Meadow Park is only one of the things we have to attend to."[71] His written response to Pratt was more diplomatic, yet he did allow that "Gardens on Parade" occupied an infinitesimal part of Flushing Meadow Park, and "I have given more personal time and attention to Gardens on Parade than would ordinarily have been justified. I have done so because of my high regard for you and for what you are trying to do."[72]

Moses did accede to fencing in the display gardens and taking proper care for the plants, but he did not agree to retaining the garden layout or establishing demonstration gardens.[73] By the fall of 1941, a transitional redevelopment plan for "Gardens on Parade" was under way. The plan would ameliorate the picked-over look of the scavenged gardens, preserve existing plant material, and develop the ultimate educational community garden envisioned by Pratt. Plant material from other reworked city green spaces was transplanted to fill the gaps in "Gardens on Parade." More than 30 trees and more than 150 shrubs were moved from malls on 225th Street, for example, particularly holly, pine, *Prunus* varieties, mountain laurel, Oregon grape, and rhododendron.

It took almost ten years, but Harriet Pratt finally had her rose festival at the revitalized "Gardens on Parade." On June 5, 1948, "Gardens on Parade" evolved into the Queens Botanical Gardens, which officially opened in Flushing Meadow Park with a rose garden including more than eight thousand bushes of 250 varieties. Robert Moses himself handed over the keys to the garden to the president of the Queens Botanical Gardens Society, and Harriet Pratt was introduced as a guest of honor.[74] The 5-acre gardens retained the original fan shape, and Havemeyer Grove formed the centerpiece of the display, as it had in its incarnation a decade before.

Nearly a generation later, a world's fair brought Robert Moses and Gilmore D. Clarke together again to continue improvements in Flushing Meadows Park. The New York 1964–65 Fair, while not sanctioned by the BIE, remains one of the largest held in the United States. The fair used the same basic outlines of the 1939–40 Fair: Clarke's Unisphere was sited about where the Perisphere and Trylon had once stood, and the main thoroughfares and malls remained the same. And, despite the fair's financial failure, Moses was able to accomplish more improvements in Flushing Meadow. "Gardens on Parade" / Queens Botanical Gardens had to be relocated yet again as a result of the 1964–65 Fair, and was moved east of the fairgrounds to the so-called Kissena Corridor—a contiguous stretch of parkland connected to Flushing Meadows.

 ## Landscape Lessons from the World of Tomorrow

The New York World of Tomorrow Fair introduced modern garden design style and corporate gardens to the American public. Major corporate sponsorship of exhibits began with the 1933–34 Century of Progress Exposition, but reached its apogee at the 1939–40 World's Fair. Corporate landscapes followed suit, with many companies attempting to reinforce their brand image in their landscapes. Critics objected that the lack of regionalism heretofore seen in state-sponsored exhibits rendered the "corporate style" bland and homogeneous.

The modern garden style at this world's fair emphasized manicured and clean lines in garden elements. Hedges, adaptable through shearing to almost any shape, became the perfect foil for the modern architecture of the fair. Spirals, created from hedges or in the design of the planting beds, were an especially popular form.

At the same time, the World of Tomorrow Fair featured planting styles slightly updated from the Centennial Exhibition. Massed plantings of annuals both revived and modernized the Victorian practice of carpet bedding. The shapes of the flower beds tended toward geometric in order to complement the fair's streamlined architecture.

With a team of more than thirty landscape architects, the New York World's Fair clearly demonstrated American acceptance of and support for the profession. In the post–World War II building boom, landscape architects could be found designing corporate campuses, suburbs, and individual yards and gardens across the country.

Earlier fairs made some provisions for the automobile in circulation routes and parking, notably the 1933–34 Century of Progress Exposition. At the 1939–40 World's Fair, which was circumlocuted by major highways, automobile exhibits dominated the main entrance and dictated many design decisions for thoroughfares.

The World of Tomorrow Fair also demonstrated the influence of garden clubs and societies. Their management of the "Gardens on Parade" exhibit—the fair's main horticultural feature—testified to their rising credibility in the United States. Emerging from civic and social women's groups in the early 1900s, garden clubs' relevance equaled that of professional florists and nurserymen at the New York World's Fair.

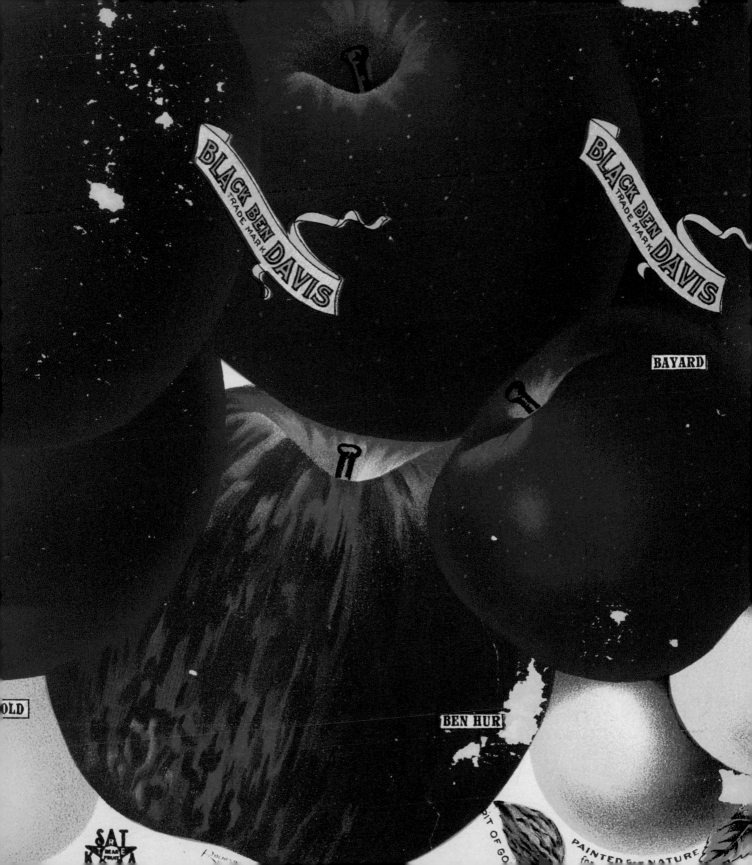

 Epilogue

In May 1940, on the east and west coasts of the United States, the gates finally closed on America's great world's fairs. Who would have predicted that it would be almost a quarter of a century until the next international exposition in the United States? The New York World's Fair of 1964–65 brought back some of the glamour of previous expositions, but it was not sanctioned by the Bureau of International Expositions, and was the last major U.S. world's fair of the twentieth century.[1] From the fairs' seven-decade heyday from 1870 through 1940, what garden and landscape legacies remain?

A walk through one of America's major urban parks can often reveal how the broad outlines of their green spaces have emerged from an exposition—even though the individual gardens may no longer exist. Philadelphia's Fairmount Park, Audubon Park in New Orleans, Chicago's Jackson Park, Buffalo's Delaware Park, Forest Park in St. Louis, and Flushing Meadows in New York all owe a debt to a world's fair. Urban waterfronts such as San Francisco's Marina District and Chicago's Northerly Island also expanded and gained green space through an exposition.

Equally important are the advances in horticultural knowledge and technology that arose from the fairs. Notable improvements include:

* Shipping and storage of perishable produce: With their reputations on the line, nurserymen experimented with shipping, packing, and transportation methods so that their fruits and vegetables arrived in peak condition for an exposition display. Each world's fair, beginning notably with the 1884–85 New Orleans Exposition, offered transportation tips to exhibitors through prefair circulars. Shipping and packaging innovations continued in commerce postfair, and even extended to nonperishable product distribution.

* Diversity of landscape design: Not only did garden styles evolve from, for example, the carpet bedding of the 1876 Centennial to the naturalistic designs at the World's Columbian and Jamestown Expositions, but world's fairs showcased gardening styles from across the nation and world. The gardens surrounding individual state buildings featured indigenous plants, and styles from foreign countries, particularly Japan, England, and France, influenced horticultural tastes in the United States. From the public greenswards at world's fairs, visitors adopted new landscape styles for their own backyards. To observe this, one has only to look at the many seed and flower catalogues marketed to consumers that promoted the flowers and displays in world's fair exhibits.

* Plant culture and hybridization: Early world's fairs celebrated "five on a plate" displays of the finest apples, peaches, and other orchard products. Later, as methods of horticulture improved, visitors admired the latest novelties in plant hybridization. By the 1930s, horticultural societies devoted to particular plants, such as dahlias and cacti, displayed award-winning specimens at fairs. In the days before mass communication, world's fairs fostered the spirit of competition in hybridization and disseminated the results to the widest audience.

* Lighting and water effects: The use of nonplant material to enhance a landscape attracted popular attention and was adopted in both public and private gardens. Outdoor lighting improved from the simple outlining of the 1884 Horticulture Palace to the electric light show of the Pan-American Exposition to the aqualons and underlighting of the 1939–40 New York World's Fair. Water effects also evolved from simple garden fountains at the 1876 Centennial to the lagoons of the World's Columbian Exposition to the Cascades of the Louisiana Purchase Exposition.

The New York World's Fair of 1939–40 embodied all of the changes in America's gardens since Horace Greeley wandered about the 1854 New York Crystal Palace in search of better horticultural specimens than old dried potato tubers. Instead of the wizened potatoes shown in 1854, a fully electrified, life-sized model farm exhibit displayed modern agriculture processes and products. Whereas New York's Crystal Palace housed exhibits from all departments in a single structure, the campus of the 1939–40 world's fair encompassed hundreds of acres, with landscaping assuming a role as important as that of architecture. Landscaping, in fact, was critical in the effort of

▶ Stark's Nursery consistently displayed exhibits in world's fairs, including this example from their 1904 fruit catalogue which emphasizes their variety of apples. (Author's collection)

New Yorker Robert Moses to catalyze park redevelopment. Horticulture displays had also evolved from preserved specimens of fruit to the elaborate "Gardens on Parade" exhibit of 1940, where homeowners were able to view plant displays for aesthetics rather than utility.

Advances in technology, communication, and transportation affected the types of displays in American world's fairs, and also challenged their relevance. Beginning in the 1890s, chromolithographed catalogues enabled seedsmen to describe their flowers and fruit without actual exhibition displays. American radio programs from about

Look At FRONT and BACK Covers At Same Time To See Whole Tree Picture. READ Complete Story on Page 8

$2,400.00 CROP FROM 122 YOUNG GOLDEN DELICIOUS APPLE TREES

And that happened the year of deepest Depression—when farm prices were rock bottom. Photo above shows Les Anderson, Pike Co., Ill., farmer, standing beside one of these 122 trees only 11 years old that bore 1140 bu. of great, big, glorious Golden Delicious that made him $2,400.00 in cold cash. Planted on only 2½ acres, these few Golden Delicious "brought me as much money the same year as if I had planted 266 acres of good land to corn."

STARK BRO'S NURSERIES—119 Years Old At LOUISIANA, MO.

◀ Stark's Nursery continued to showcase their "World's Fair Fruits" in connection with the 1933 Century of Progress World's Fair. (Author's collection)

1920 included farm and garden segments discussing the latest horticultural developments. Improvements in growing methods and railroad shipping made oranges from California and even bananas from the tropics commonplace on a New Yorker's breakfast table. Leisure travel by way of trains, automobiles, and later, airplanes closed the distance between gardens coast to coast. An avid gardener no longer needed to visit a world's fair to see a demonstration of advances in landscape design or fruit and flower production.

Fairs thrived in Europe and other continents after World War II, but had "fair fatigue" finally descended on the United States? Doubts about the effectiveness of the fairs began to surface in the 1930s. In 1927, prior to the Century of Progress Exposition, a *Chicago Tribune* editorial predicted popular disenchantment: "The increase in foreign travel has gratified much of the nation's curiosity about the lives and handiwork of men and women in other lands. The movies have done more in the same direction. The uses of electricity and improved methods of power generation which were of absorbing interest thirty-five years ago, are today commonplace."[2] A Century of Progress mayoral advisory committee initially recommended against the fair, "deciding that under twentieth century conditions such an event is provincial and would prove unsuccessful . . . With rapid transportation facilities and with American's habit of travel developed to a high degree, the committee predicted that a fair in which was congregated objects from distant lands would no longer have the nineteenth century allurement."[3]

Despite the success of the Century of Progress Exposition four years later, cost-benefit questions arose about the 1939–40 World's Fair. Some critics suggested fairs might be obsolete: "Compared with earlier expositions, this problem of [exposition] size has taken on staggering dimensions. Once it was possible to gather products from home and abroad, put them under a roof, and hold a successful fair. Today the radio, film and press have made the fairgoing public pretty familiar with almost anything a fair can show them, and it has become the practice to try to kill the bird with four barrels instead of one."[4]

Membership in professional horticultural societies concomitantly declined with the rising popularity of less scientifically oriented, locally focused garden clubs. Whereas membership in the earlier societies had appealed to professional nurserymen, florists, and seedsmen, the twentieth-century garden club movement drew amateur gardeners interested in social status as well as gardening. Whereas professionals had sought national exposure and information exchange, amateur clubs encouraged local camaraderie, which could be satisfied without world's fairs. The advent of plant patents in the 1930s protected new introductions and undercut the importance of being first to market at a costly exposition.

Through the latter half of the twentieth century, U.S. interest in expositions, as measured by congressional support and funding, steadily dwindled. From 1939 through 2010, the BIE sanctioned thirty-seven expositions,[5] of which only five were in the United States. The last, the 1984 Louisiana World Exposition in New Orleans, had the dubious distinction of being the only exposition to declare bankruptcy during operations. Both disappointing results and instability in international relations prompted the U.S. Senate Foreign Relations Committee to recommend that the United States withdraw as a member of the BIE in 2001: the recommendation was carried out.

Nor has the United States been an active participant in the international horticultural expositions, a form of specialized exhibition also sanctioned by the BIE since 1960. Sponsored largely by foreign contingents, eighteen international horticultural exhibitions were held between 1960 and 2010. Similarly, the International Association of Horticultural Producers, established in Switzerland in 1948, included twenty-five countries from five continents in 2000, but did not include the United States.[6]

The emergence of U.S. public botanical gardens and arboreta further undermined the rationale for international floral displays. Public gardens have increased substantially both in number and size in the latter half of the twentieth century. The American Association of Botanical Gardens and Arboreta (now the American Public Gardens Association, or APGA) was formed with about seventy-five members in 1940, the same year that America hosted its last great world's fair. Currently, the APGA boasts about five hundred members representing all fifty states. At a public garden,

Ideas and displays at world's fairs became part of our national culture when propagated through nursery catalogues. (Author's collection)

visitors may enjoy the hands-on experience they once would have obtained at a world's fair. APGA-affiliated institutions often hold seminars and classes, thus fulfilling the educational mission of a world's fair.

Still, public gardens cannot offer the global experience available through a world's fair or international horticulture exposition. Although many arboreta and public gardens display trees from around the world, sponsor classes on global trends in garden design, or even have permanent exhibits such as Japanese gardens, none can hope to have as many participating nations simultaneously exhibiting their own latest trends in garden design. Nor does a permanent public garden have the same transformative power on an urban landscape, encouraging renewal through a temporary exposition.

Although federal support for U.S. world fairs has declined, this has not dampened interest in them in many large American cities. BIE-sanctioned Expo 2020 sparked many grassroots efforts to apply as host cities such as in Houston, Los Angeles, and New York. California made its interest official with then governor Arnold Schwarzenegger's 2010 announcement of a planned bid for the 2020 World's Fair to be held in the San Francisco Bay area. In addition to noting the innovation in Silicon Valley, Schwarzenegger emphasized California's traditional agricultural and horticultural pursuits: "We are ready to showcase our world-class leadership in so many different areas, if it is entertainment, environmentalism, agriculture, our great, great wines . . . the list goes on and on and on."[7]

As history has shown, there are many pitfalls and delays between submission of bid proposals and the actual groundbreaking for a World's Fair. Whether Expo 2020 or another future world's fair revitalizes the United States landscape remains to be seen. Until then, our world's fair gardens remain hidden in plain sight with lessons and legacies for all to treasure.

 Key Names

The years of the world's fairs in which individuals participated appear in parentheses at the end of each listing.

Berkmans, Prosper Julius (1831–ca. 1910): Berkmans, of Augusta, Georgia, operated an orchard and nursery, Fruitland Nurseries (today the site of Augusta National Golf course). The Berkmanses' nursery, a father-and-son affair, imported much of their stock from Europe, and these business relationships likely helped P. J. Berkmans in his additional role coordinating foreign exhibits for the 1884–85 New Orleans Exposition. (1884–85, 1901)

Brinckerhoff, Arthur F. (1880–1959): Brinckerhoff partnered with Ferruccio Vitale and Alfred Geiffert Jr. from 1917 through 1924. In 1924, Brinckerhoff left the partnership to form an independent practice. The 86-acre Arthur F. Brinckerhoff Nature Preserve in Redding, Connecticut, was established in 1967 in his memory. New York World Fair sites attributed to Brinckerhoff included the Administration Building Area and the court between the New York City Building and the Theme Building.[1] (1939–40)

Clarke, Gilmore D. (1892–1982): A native New Yorker, Clarke grew up in the family florist business in the Bronx. He graduated from Cornell's Department of Rural Art in 1913 and went to work for Charles Downing Lay. His next job, in 1915, was with the New Jersey landscape architect Charles N. Lowrie. Both of Clarke's former mentors were commissioned landscape architects to the New York World's Fair. Clarke's design of the Bronx River Parkway using native, weathered stone bridges received popular acclaim.[2] These commissions, along with his work on Virginia's Mount Vernon Memorial Highway (1929- 31), consultation with the National Park Service, and work with the New York City Department of Parks, earned Clarke national prominence. President Hoover appointed him a member of the National Commission of Fine Arts in 1935, and, at the time of the 1939–40 New York World's Fair, Clarke's other positions and honoraria included Fellow and vice president of the American Society of Landscape Architects, dean of Cornell's College of Architecture, and advisor to Harvard's School of Landscape Architecture, and numerous other consultancies. Clarke served as the ASLA president from 1949 to 1951. Among the NYWF landscapes attributed to Clarke were: Court of Communications, Court of Power, Rose Court, Spiral Garden Court, portions of Constitution Mall, Washington Square,[3] New England Building (1939),[4] and National Advisory Committees Building (1939).[5] (1939–40)

Earle, Parker (1831–1917): Earle was responsible for the Horticulture Department of the 1884–85 Exposition in New Orleans. Affectionately dubbed the "Earl of Horticulture" by colleagues,[6] Parker Earle hailed from Cobden, Illinois, where he managed a fruit farm. Having previously served as a judge for the Horticulture Department at the 1876 Centennial Exposition, Earle, a savvy businessman, is largely credited with inventing the refrigerated railroad car to transport his produce to markets. After the 1885 exposition, Earle continued as president of the American Horticultural Society. (1876, 1884–85)

Geiffert, Alfred, Jr. (1890–1957): Geiffert assumed responsibility for the landscape design of Chicago's 1933–34 World's Fair upon the death of his partner, Ferruccio Vitale. Without a formal education in landscape architecture, Geiffert had apprenticed at the side of Vitale from 1908 until Vitale's death in 1933. Along with Arthur Brinckerhoff, Geiffert was made a partner in the firm in 1917.[7] His firm retained the Vitale name, and at one point during the world's fair project, the firm letterhead appeared as Vitale, Geiffert, and Gilmore Clarke. Among the NYWF landscape designs attributed to Geiffert are: Administration Building (1936),[8] Consolidated Edison Company, Petroleum Industries Inc., Devoe & Reynolds, American Radiator Company, Carrier Corporation, Inc. (1938).[9] Public areas included: Central Mall—Planting Plan, Main North and South Esplanades, Business Systems Building, and Transportation Sector circulation areas.[10] (1933, 1939–40)

Kessler, George E. (1862–1923): Park engineer for Kansas City, Kessler was hired as landscape architect for the Louisiana Purchase Exposition based on recommendations from prominent businessmen in the St. Louis brewery business. Born in 1862 in Frankenhausen, Thuringia, Germany, Kessler moved at age three to the United States with his family and then returned to Germany when he was sixteen. In Weimar, Germany, he worked as a gardener's apprentice and took courses in botany and engineering at local universities. He returned to New York in 1881, building a private landscaping practice. The Kansas City, Fort Scott, and Gulf F.S.& G. Railway hired him to build and maintain a park in Kansas City in 1882. Kessler was largely responsible for the landscape design of the Kansas City Park System from its inception in 1892. In addition to his design of the World's Fair, Kessler worked in Baltimore, Cleveland, Topeka, and, of course, Kansas City.[11] (1904)

Lay, Charles Downing (1877–1956): Named for Charles Downing, brother of Andrew Jackson Downing, and son of portrait painter Oliver I. Lay, Charles Downing Lay seemed destined for the art of landscape architecture. A founding member of the ASLA, Lay helped to establish the society's official magazine, *Landscape Architecture,* in 1910. Lay maintained an independent practice in New York for more than forty years, and was appointed the landscape architect for New York City's Parks Department in 1913–14, following in the legendary footsteps of Samuel Parsons Jr. Lay has been described as a very practical designer who emphasized aesthetics and preferred "evidence of human occupation" in idealized natural landscapes, but also produced formal designs that "avoided harsh symmetry and cold formality."[12] Lay's New York World's Fair attributions include the Administration Building Area, Court between the New York City Building and Theme Building,[13] Means of Production Court (1937),[14] Food Center Court, Pharmacy south and east façade, Industrial Science, Building Q11 (1938),[15] and "Gardens on Parade." (1939- 40)

Lowrie, Charles N. (1869–1939): As a landscape architect for the Hudson County Park Commission for thirty years, Charles Lowrie was the 1910–11 ASLA president. Lowrie was responsible for designing the areas around the 1939–40 New York World's Fair Amusement Zone, which included Fountain and Willow Lakes. An early president of the ASLA, he died after a brief illness during the World's Fair of 1939–40. (1939–40)

Manning, Warren H. (1860–1938): Warren Manning, a protégé of Frederick Law Olmsted, adopted Olmsted's naturalistic style and worked for him at the World's Columbian Exposition. Son of a Massachusetts nurseryman, Manning was known as a superb plantsman as well as a landscape designer. (1893, 1907)

McLaren, John (1846–1943): The Scottish-born McLaren worked as San Francisco's superintendent of parks for more than fifty years. McLaren immigrated to the United States in 1870 after studying horticulture at the Edinburgh Royal Botanical Gardens. He created the landscape design for the famous California estates of individuals such as the banker George Howard in San Mateo and Leland Stanford in Palo Alto. He achieved fame in San Francisco for developing the city's Golden Gate Park, a formerly barren dune land rejected even by Frederick Law Olmsted as being unplantable. A friend of the environmentalist John Muir, McLaren preferred naturalistic designs using native California plants, with judicious use of plants from around the world. As John D. Barry noted in *The City of Domes* (1915): "There was no difficulty in finding a man best suited to plan the garden that was to serve as the Exposition's setting. For many years John McLaren had been known as one of the most distinguished horticulturists in this part of the world."[16] (1894, 1915, 1939–40)

Meehan, Thomas (1826–1901): Englishman Meehan formed Philadelphia's Meehan's Nurseries in 1853, having worked with William Saunders and at Bartram's Garden. With Saunders, he built America's first greenhouse with a fixed roof in 1854. He served as editor of *Gardener's Monthly,* and later founded *Meehan's Monthly.* Meehan oversaw the exhibits in the Agriculture Building at the 1876 Centennial. (1876)

Miller, Charles H.: Superintendent of the 1876 Centennial Horticulture Department, Miller, a self-styled landscape gardener, co-owned Miller & Yates, of Mount Airy Nursery in Philadelphia's Mount Airy neighborhood. (1876)

Mississippi Valley Horticultural Society: Regular correspondents to the society included high-profile individuals such as the pomologist Robert Manning of Massachusetts; nurserymen James Vick and Patrick Barry, both of Rochester, New York; nurseryman Charles Downing of Newburg, New York; U.S. entomologist C. V. Riley of Washington, D.C.; and fruit grower William Parry of New Jersey. (1885)

Olmsted, Frederick Law (1822–1903): The "Father of American Landscape Architecture" worked in several careers before landscape architecture. As a journalist, farmer, and merchant seaman, Olmsted traveled the country and world, observing social conditions and the influence of the natural environment. Olmsted's first major work in landscape architecture, the redevelopment of New York's Central Park with colleague Calvert Vaux, created a new vision for American landscapes. Where European styles and sensibilities had previously held sway with many of America's foreign-born gardeners and landscape designers, the American-born Olmsted created landscapes that harmonized with the nation's growing cities and paid respect to U.S. native plants.

Olmsted's style is often deemed naturalistic, with massed plantings of native plants and open greenswards. His major public works include park systems for New York City, Buffalo, and Boston; numerous campuses including Harvard, Cornell, Smith College, Stanford, and the University of California, Berkeley. His private client list includes names such as Vanderbilt, Rockefeller, and other prominent citizens.

Prior to the 1893 World's Columbian Exposition, Olmsted completed a number of major commissions in Chicago. In 1868, Olmsted and his partner, Calvert Vaux, were engaged to develop the general plan for Riverside, Illinois, a suburb of Chicago. This community, a national historic landmark village today, became a national model for urban planning. In 1869, when Chicago established its parks commissions, Olmsted and Vaux were subsequently chosen to design the South Parks, which included two large pleasure grounds, Washington Park and Jackson Park. His contacts with members of Chicago's elite, many of whom were themselves from the East Coast, led to private estate commissions. (1893)

Ragan, W. H.: A pomologist from Greencastle, Indiana, Ragan also participated in many horticultural societies. (1884)

Rapuano, Michael (1904–1975): The youngest member of the New York World's Fair 1939–40 landscape design team, Rapuano acquired an early background in public parks as the son of the superintendent of parks in Syracuse, New York. Studying landscape architecture at Cornell University, Rapuano won the Rome Prize in 1927, and two years later began working with the Westchester County Park Commission, where he met Gilmore Clarke. He worked part-time with Clarke's office in the early 1930s, and became a partner in the firm in 1939. His career is associated with large public works, and highway design.[18] (1939–40)

Saunders, William (1822–1900): Saunders oversaw the plantings around the United States Government Building at the 1876 Centennial. Saunders, the USDA's first botanist and landscape architect, was a Philadelphia landscape gardener with national commissions for cemeteries, campuses, and residences. (1876)

Schmitt, Herbert W.: Also of Vitale's office, Schmitt served as the supervisor of landscape design in Chicago. (1933)

Schwarzmann, Hermann: (1846–1891): German immigrant Schwarzmann had been hired as an assistant engineer for Fairmount Park in 1869, a year after he arrived in America. Just twenty-three years old, Schwarzmann became invaluable to the park's chief engineer. Schwarzmann was soon supervising more than 450 men in building park infrastructure after the recent accessions to park land. During 1871, he voluntarily developed plans for the older, east portion of Fairmount Park. Promoted to engineer of design in July 1872, Schwarzmann was commissioned to develop the plans for the Zoological Gardens in West Park, the first of its kind in America. The few biographical sketches that remain about Schwarzmann suggest that his engineering and architectural skills were gained in his military training and service in Germany. His skills as a landscape gardener appear to have been self-taught. The biographer John Maass reports from the 1871 minutes of the Commissioners of Fairmount Park: "Since the head gardener, Mr. Harding, ceased to occupy that position, the laying out of the planting has been under the immediate supervision of Senior Assistant Engineer H. Schwarzmann, who gave much of his leisure time to the assiduous study of the subject as presented in many standard works, especially in those of France and Germany, for which his familiarity with European languages gave him peculiar facilities."[19] (1876)

Taylor, Frederic: Professor Taylor, of the University of Nebraska's Horticulture Department, was secretary of that state's horticultural society. He had supervised Nebraska's fruit exhibit in the World's Columbian Exposition and, with Rudolph Ulrich, designed the Trans-Mississippi Fair. On May 17, 1899, Taylor was appointed as the Pan-American director of concessions and superintendent of horticultural and food products, with a salary of five thousand dollars. (1893, 1898, 1901, 1904)

Tracy, Samuel Mills (S. M.) (1847–1920): A professor of botany at the University of Missouri, Mills served in various horticultural societies and published many horticulture-related articles.[17] (1885)

Ulrich, Rudolph (1840–1906?): German-born Ulrich worked on several European estates in Italy and England before immigrating to America in 1868. By the 1870s, he was working as a gardener on estates in the San Francisco area. Leland and Jane Stanford hired Ulrich to design and tend their Palo Alto country estate of about 450 acres. It is likely that Ulrich met Frederick Law Olmsted through his work on these estates and such premiere properties as the Hotel Del Monte. When Olmsted was hired by the Stanfords to work on the Leland Stanford Junior University, he and Ulrich exchanged letters regarding local plant material.[20] Their collaboration seems to have been mutually satisfactory since Olmsted offered Ulrich the landscaping position at the World's Columbian Exposition, and was influential in his hiring as superintendent of the Brooklyn Parks System after the fair.

Ulrich's work at the Trans-Mississippi Exposition in 1898 enhanced his qualifications for the Pan-American Fair, as did the recommendations he received from previous employers. World's Columbian Exposition architect D. H. Burnham wrote: "Mr. Ulrich is a man of sterling character, untiring energy and industry, and has proved himself to be a master of his profession in every detail . . . There is no one in the country who compares with him in handling the preliminary work and finishing the landscape for such a thing as you have in hand. He has judgment, very large experience, tremendous energy, can handle men better than anyone I ever knew and he can be relied upon perfectly."[21]

Ulrich's designs for carpet bedding at the Stanfords' Palo Alto farm and at the Hotel Del Monte display a liberal use of color and geometric plantings. (1893, 1898, 1901)

Vitale, Ferruccio (1875–1933): Italian-born Vitale came to the United States as a military attaché to the Italian embassy. With a background in engineering and architecture, he began his practice of landscape architecture in New York in 1904. He was a founding member and trustee of the Foundation for Architecture and Landscape Architecture at Lake Forest, Illinois. As such, he secured strong relationships not only with Chicago architects, but also with the wealthy industrialists and philanthropists of Chicago's North Shore communities. The foundation was based on the ideal of integrating architecture with landscape architecture—a premise that served Vitale well in working with the fair's Architectural Commission. (1933)

 Notes

INTRODUCTION

1. John E. Findling and Kimberly D. Pelle, eds., *Historical Dictionary of World's Fairs and Expositions, 1851–1988* (New York: Greenwood Press, 1990), 376–81.

2. This book covers a period from the 1850s through the 1940s during which the profession of landscape architecture gradually emerged. The individuals responsible for creating the world's fair landscapes titled themselves with a variety of names including landscape engineer, gardener, landscape architect, and more. I use the term "landscape designer" to cover those periods when the differences among the titles were blurred or nonexistent.

3. The American Horticulture Society debuted at the New Orleans World's Industrial and Cotton Centennial Exposition of 1884–85.

4. Although the United States has not recently hosted a world's fair, the tradition has continued strongly in other parts of the world. Hannover, Germany, hosted the first world's fair of the millennium in 2000, and Japan secured the right to host the 2005 World's Fair. The 2008 World's Fair was held in Zaragoza, Spain, and the 2010 Fair in Shanghai, China. San Francisco put in a

bid to host a world's fair in 2015, but Milan, Spain, secured the Bureau of International Expositions (BIE) approval (www.bie-paris.org).

5. Deciding what to include in a count of world's fairs can be troublesome since many countries hosted large expositions. I have used the classifications of world's fairs as presented in Findling and Pelle's *Historical Dictionary of World's Fairs,* 376–81. Significant scope, attendance, and international presence were the major criteria for inclusion in this book.

6. Some world's fairs are commonly abbreviated in contemporary literature and by world's fair historians whereas others are not. Where applicable, I will introduce those abbreviations.

7. Mrs. Potter Palmer, for example, an influential Chicago socialite and passionate Francophile, invited leading landscape designers and nurserymen from Paris and Versailles to design plantings for the Women's Building at the Columbian Exposition. Outdoor displays of Mexican horticulture were prominent at the 1884–85 New Orleans Exposition, honoring the budding diplomatic ties with this neighboring country.

8. *General Report of the Judges of Group XXIX,* International Exhibition, 1876 (Washington, D.C.: Government Printing Office, 1880), 7.

9. *Official Catalogue of the New York Exhibition of the Industry of All Nations* (New York: George P. Putnam, 1853), 51.

10. Horace Greeley, ed., *Art and Industry as Represented in the Exhibition at the Crystal Palace* (New York: Redfield, 1853), 108.

11. Ibid., 110.

12. Entrants in this group were defined as "hothouses and horticultural materials, flowers and ornamental plants, kitchen-garden plants, fruit trees, seeds and useful forest plants and hothouse plants" (William P. Blake, ed., *Reports of the United States Commissioners to the Paris Universal Exposition,* vol. 1, *1867* [Washington, D.C.: Government Printing Office, 1870], 179–80).

13. *Garden and Forest,* August 30, 1893, 362.

14. Warren H. Manning, "The Influence of American Expositions on the Out-Door Arts," *Massachusetts Horticultural Society Transactions* (March 8, 190): 75.

15. John Manbeck, "*Historically Speaking:* Manhattan Beach Memories," *Brooklyn Eagle,* September 11, 2008, www.brooklyneagle.com/categories/category.php?category_id=23&id=23070.

16. Seattle hosted the 1962 World's Fair, and New York returned to its 1939–40 site with the World's Fair of 1963–64. The Knoxville Fair was held in 1982, and the last major American fair of the twentieth century was held in New Orleans in 1984.

17. All data from Findling and Pelle, eds., *Historical Dictionary of World's Fairs,* 375–81.

18. The 1909 Alaska-Yukon Pacific Exposition, for example, is not profiled, even though the site at today's University of Washington retains exquisite elements from the Olmsted firm's landscape design. The 1905 Lewis and Clark Exposition in Portland, Oregon, while a horticultural marvel, is not described because the entire site has been lost to industrialization.

1. CENTENNIAL EXHIBITION

1. U. P. Hedrick, *A History of Horticulture in America to 1860* (New York: Oxford University Press, 1950), 230.

2. Ibid., 261.

3. Quoted in James D. McCabe, *The Illustrated History of the Centennial Exhibition*

(Philadelphia: National Publishing, 1876;), 20. The original plan included public squares in each of the city's four quarters, and streets were named after native trees: Vine, Mulberry, Chestnut, Walnut, etc.

4. The 1867 Exposition Universelle in Paris comprised about 170 acres and included gardens; however, most exhibits were housed in one main building with smaller foreign pavilions nearby. The 1873 Vienna Exposition, with a Machine Hall, Art Hall, two Agriculture Halls, and a main Rotunda, served as a better model for the Centennial.

5. George William Johnson and David Landreth, *A Dictionary of Modern Gardening* (Philadelphia: Lea and Blanchard, 1847), http://chestofbooks.com/gardening-horticulture /Dictionary/index.htmlChest of Books; http://chestofbooks.com/gardening-horticulture /Dictionary/index.html.

6. Frank J. Scott, *Suburban Home Grounds* (1870; repr., New York: American Life Foundation and Study Institute, 1982).

7. Virginia Scott Jenkins, *The Lawn: A History of an American Obsession* (Washington, D.C.: Smithsonian Institution Press, 1994), 31.

8. John E. Findling and Kimberly D. Pelle, eds., *Historical Dictionary of World's Fairs and Expositions, 1851–1988* (New York: Greenwood Press, 1990), 61.

9. B. S. Olmstead, "Who Shall Lay Out Our Ornamental Grounds?" *Gardener's Monthly,* June 1876, 164–65.

10. "Landscape Gardening," *Gardener's Monthly,* August 1876, 226.

11. Lemon Hill was purchased in 1799 by Henry Pratt, whose greenhouses sheltered the estate's namesake lemon trees. Strawberry Mansion was built around 1750 and acquired its name from a subsequent owner who sold strawberries and cream in the 1840s. In 1795, Samuel Breck built Sweet Briar, with its lavish grounds and lawns extending to the Schuylkill River.

12. Lemon Hill, with its exquisite gardens created by Henry Pratt, was Fairmount Park's first estate purchase in 1844. In the late 1860s, several others followed: Mount Pleasant (1868); Laurel Hill, Ormiston, Sweetbriar (1867); Woodford, Strawberry Hill, Belmont Mansion (1869); and Solitude (1867).

13. Aaron Wunsch, Historic American Building Survey, Schuykill River Villas HABS No. PA-6194, 1995, 12.

14. This estate was originally owned in 1773 by John Penn, grandson of William Penn and cousin of John Penn of Solitude, a nearby estate in Fairmount Park that became the site of the Zoological Gardens.

15. John Maass, *The Glorious Enterprise* (Watkins Glen, N.Y.: American Life Foundation, 1973), 22. Although the Olmsted and Vaux firm had dissolved by the time of the actual exposition, the men were still in partnership during the design competition.

16. Hermann J. Schwarzmann to Committee of Plans and Designs of the Fairmount Park Commission, July 4, 1874, City Archives of Philadelphia.

17. Hermann J. Schwarzmann to Committee of Plans and Designs of the Fairmount Park Commission, August 7, 1875, City Archives of Philadelphia.

18. Hermann Schwarzmann, *Report of the Chief Engineer of the Exhibition Grounds, United States Centennial Commission,* vol. 1 (Washington, D.C.: Government Printing Office, 1880), 286.

19. Grading the area for the three major buildings (Main, Machinery, and Agricultural Halls) required the removal of more than two hundred thousand cubic yards of earth. Grading the remaining areas of the grounds for avenues, walks, railroads, and lakes required crews to move an additional three hundred thousand cubic yards. A 9-foot-high wooden fence was constructed around the fairgrounds, totaling 2.78 miles in length. More than 16 miles of avenues, roads, and walks were created, and about 3.5 miles of railway tracks were laid (Hermann Schwarzmann, *Report of the Chief Engineer of the Exhibition Grounds, United States Centennial Commission,* 1:287–99).

20. *American Agriculturist,* April 1876.

21. Among the U.S. states exhibiting, only Mississippi—the sole representative from the former Confederate States of America—showed a bit of regional architecture and vegetation in its log building made of sixty-eight types of native lumber and dressed with Spanish moss eaves. A few of the foreign nations showed some regionalism in architecture: the British buildings were constructed in Elizabethan style; the Swedish schoolhouse was made of native wood; and the Brazilian government building included an open piazza, as might be favored in a tropical climate.

22. The Japanese American National Museum's exhibit (June 17, 2007–January 6, 2008) of the influence of Japanese gardens in America highlighted the 1876 Centennial as introducing the garden style to America ("Landscaping America: Beyond the Japanese Garden," www.janm.org).

23. J. S. Ingram, *Centennial Exposition Described and Illustrated Being a Concise and Graphic Description of This Grand Enterprise Commemorative of the First Centenary of American Independence* (Philadelphia: Hubbard Brothers, 1876), 344.

24. Francis A. Walker, ed., *United States Centennial Commission International Exhibition 1876,* vol. 7, *Reports and Awards* (Washington, D.C.: Government Printing Office, 1880), 40.

25. Nearly one hundred U.S. exhibitors displayed more than 3,800 plant specimens in about 18,000 of the total 22,000 square footage used indoors. The remaining indoor space featured plants from Spain and England. Spain was the next-largest country with indoor exhibits: four exhibitors showed 427 articles. England, with three exhibitors featuring 239 articles, was the third-most prolific. Individual entrepreneurs from Jamaica, Bermuda, Victoria, New Zealand, the Sandwich Islands, St. Domingo, France, and Germany rounded out the competition.

26. Thomas Meehan, "Opening of the Centennial Exhibition," *Gardener's Monthly and Horticulturist,* June 1876, http://chestofbooks.com/gardening-horticulture/Gardener-Monthly-V18/Opening-Of-The-Centennial-Exhibition.html.

27. W. D. Brackenridge, Walker, ed., *United States Centennial Commission International Exhibition 1876,* vol. 8, *Reports and Awards,* 30.

28. Ingram, *Centennial Exposition Described,* 114.

29. Dorsey Gardner, ed., *United States Centennial Commission International Exhibition 1876,* vol. 9, *Grounds and Buildings of the Centennial Exhibition,* 107.

30. Thomas Meehan, "Horticulture at the Centennial #2," *Gardener's Monthly and Horticulturist* 18, no. 212 (September 1876): 287.

31. George Thurber quoted in Walker, ed., *United States Centennial Commission International Exhibition 1876,* vol. 8, *Reports and Awards,* 8.

32. Meehan, "Horticulture at the Centennial #2," 287.

33. Ibid., 256.

34. As with many contemporary accounts, discrepancies exist in accounts of the exact nature

of this planting. George Thurber in the commission's *Reports and Awards* identifies this as *Aralia papyrifera.*

35. Meehan, "Horticulture at the Centennial #2," 285.

36. Thurber quoted in Walker, ed., *United States Centennial Commission International Exhibition 1876,* vol. 8, *Reports and Awards,* 11.

37. Ibid., 8:14.

38. Meehan, "Flora at the Centennial—May," *Gardener's Monthly and Horticulturist* 18, no. 211 (July 1876): 219.

39. The rhododendron exhibit was the only flower show of merit. Meehan hinted at the uncertain planning: "We suppose there will be special exhibitions of various classes of fruits and flowers during the several months that the exposition will continue, but . . . nothing definite is decided on, at this moment of writing" (Meehan, *Gardener's Monthly and Horticulturist,* January 1876, 30).

40. Meehan, "The Centennial Exposition," special issue, *Gardener's Monthly and Horticulturist* (October 1876), http://chestofbooks.com/gardening-horticulture/Gardener-Monthly-V18/The-Centennial-Exposition.html.

41. Thurber quoted in *United States Centennial Commission International Exhibition 1876,* vol. 8, *Reports and Awards,* 8.

42. Gardner, ed., *United States Centennial Commission International Exhibition 1876,* vol. 9, *Grounds and Buildings of the Centennial Exhibition,* 107.

43. Ibid., 9:108.

44. Eli K. Price, *Report to the American Philosophical Society and to the Fairmount Park Commissioners,* December 15, 1876, 4–5, Fairmount Park Archives.

45. Warren H. Manning, "Influence of American Expositions on Outdoor Arts," *Brush and Pencil* 10, no. 3 (June 1902): 170–76.

46. Ibid.

47. Clay Lancaster, *The Japanese Influence in America* (New York: Abbeville Press, 1983), see esp. "Japanese Exhibition at the Philadelphia Centennial," 37–50.

48. Smithsonian Institution website, www.sil.si.edu/SILPublications/seeds/bergerh-h.html.

49. *Vick's Illustrated Monthly,* May 1883, 151.

50. Donald G. Mitchell. "Japanese Gardens" as reprinted in *Prairie Farmer,* November 4, 1876, 354.

51. *Scribner's Monthly,* June 1879, *Scribner's Monthly (1870–1881),* American Periodicals Series Online.

52. Meehan, *Gardener's Monthly and Horticulturist,* July 1876, 221.

53. Interestingly, Bartholdi Park at the U.S. Botanic Garden—according to its website, the oldest American botanic garden located in Washington, D.C.—features geometric plantings around the Bartholdi Fountain for which it is named. This fountain, removed from the Centennial to a temporary location on the grounds of the Capitol Building in 1877, formed the centerpiece of the outdoor U.S. Botanic Garden for many years.

54. Many concurrent influences shaped the beginnings of U.S. public gardens, including European trends and the advancement of U.S. horticultural societies.

55. Galen Cranz, *The Politics of Park Design—A History of Urban Parks in America* (Cambridge: MIT Press, 1982), 13–24.

56. Meehan, *Gardener's Monthly and Horticulturist,* June 1876, http://chestofbooks.com/gardening-horticulture/Gardener-Monthly-V18/Opening-Of-The-Centennial-Exhibition.html.

2. WORLD'S INDUSTRIAL AND COTTON CENTENNIAL EXPOSITION

1. www.encyclopedia.com/topic/Railroads.aspx.

2. Eugene V. Smalley, *Century Illustrated Magazine,* June 1885, 187, *Century Illustrated Magazine (1881–1906),* American Periodicals Series Online.

3. The 1876 Centennial in Philadelphia and San Diego's 1915–16 Exposition also included permanent structures for horticulture.

4. City Ordinance 452CS, as described on the website of New Orleans Public Library Archives, Department Synopsis of Ordinances, 1841–1937, www.nutrias.org/~nopl/inv/synopsis/synopsis.htm.

5. "The City Speaks," *New Orleans Times-Democrat,* January 9, 1885, 3.

6. "The World's Exposition—Tree Planting Begun on the Grounds," *New Orleans Times-Democrat,* October 10, 1885, 5.

7. D. Clive Hardy, "New Orleans 1884–1885, The World's Industrial and Cotton Centennial Exposition," in *Historical Dictionary of World's Fairs and Expositions, 1851–1988,* ed. John E. Findling and Kimberly D. Pelle (New York: Greenwood Press, 1990), 88.

8. Although scarce information is available about Gilman and Ogden, S. H. Gilman is listed as a captain of Company E—Crescent City Rifles Co. B of Orleans Parish, and an obituary for Ogden identifies his military service as a general also in the Crescent City Rifles Co. (*Monroe Bulletin,* June 2, 1886, 1, reprinted in Rootsweb, http://ftp.rootsweb.com/pub/usgenweb/la/ouachita/obits/mb1886.txt).

9. "World's Exposition" column, *New Orleans Daily Picayune,* January 17, 1885.

10. W. H. Ragan, "An International Exhibition of Horticultural Products," appendix, *Transactions of the Mississippi Valley Horticultural Society—1884* (Indianapolis: Carlon and Hollenbeck, 1884), 261.

11. Parker Earle, "An International Exhibition of Horticultural Products," appendix, *Transactions of the Mississippi Valley Horticultural Society—1884,* 262.

12. "The World's Exposition—An Interview with Hon. Parker Earle," *New Orleans Times-Democrat,* October 14, 1884, 4.

13. "World's Exposition" column, *New Orleans Times-Democrat,* September 12, 1884, November 6, 1884, and November 14, 1884.

14. *Visitor's Guide to the World's Industrial and Cotton Centennial Exposition* (Louisville: Courier-Journal Job Printing Co., 1884), 13.

15. This "Plan No. 1 . . . Situation Plan," printed by the Southern Lithographic Company ca. 1884 (but lacking a specific designer's attribution), depicts a large Agricultural Hall and related exhibits covering virtually the entire expanse of the fairgrounds north of the Main Building. Two rectangular vegetable gardens, approximately 325 x 260 feet, each fronted the entrance to the planned Agricultural Hall, and even larger plots were marked off for experimental gardens and other agricultural purposes. The Central American Garden and Mexican Gardens were shown west of Horticultural Hall, and California and Florida Gardens were drawn at the main east entrance. In addition to designating several lakes and winding pathways, this preliminary plan identified specific locations for groves of tropical and subtropical trees: the banana grove

in the Central American Garden, and groves of mesquite near the Mexican Garden, coconut in the Florida Garden, orange near the Art Gallery, palms at the Main Building entrance, lemons, magnolias, pomegranates, and pine groves on the north end of the site (plan available through the Williams Research Center, New Orleans).

16. "World's Exposition" column, *New Orleans Daily Picayune,* October 13, 1884, 1.

17. *Visitor's Guide to the World's Industrial and Cotton Centennial Exposition,* 8–9.

18. "World's Exposition" column, *New Orleans Times-Democrat,* April 2, 1885, 3.

19. Ibid., December 26, 1884, 3.

20. Ibid., December 12, 1884, 3.

21. "Hauling Gigantic Plants," *New Orleans Daily Picayune,* January 11, 1885.

22. *New Orleans Times-Democrat,* December 10, 1884, 3.

23. "Those Live Oaks," *New Orleans Times-Democrat,* May 23, 1885, 3. It is likely that the paper is referring to the nurseryman William Perry.

24. *Visitors' Guide to the World's Industrial and Cotton Centennial Exposition,* 15.

25. *American Architect and Building News,* April 5, 1884, 15, 432, *American Architect and Building News (1876–1908),* American Periodicals Series Online.

26. Thomas Meehan, "Glazing without Putty," *Gardener's Monthly and Horticulturist* 28 (1886), http://chestofbooks.com/gardening-horticulture/Gardener-Monthly-V28/index.html.

27. "Horticultural Hall under the Electric Light," *New Orleans Times-Democrat,* December 21, 1884, 3.

28. Reports of Herbert S. Fairall, Commissioner, to the Governor of Iowa, in *Iowa at the World's Industrial and Cotton Centennial and the North, Central and American Expositions New Orleans, 1884–G* (Des Moines: Geo. E. Roberts, State Printer, 1885).

29. "Bring Flowers," *New Orleans Daily Picayune,* December 15, 1884.

30. "World's Exposition—The Great Fruit Show," *New Orleans Daily Picayune,* January 17, 1885.

31. "Horticultural Premiums," *New Orleans Times-Democrat,* February 2, 1885.

32. Ibid.

33. "World's Exposition" column, *New Orleans Times-Democrat,* April 6, 1885.

34. "Horticultural Hall," *New Orleans Times-Democrat,* January 8, 1885.

35. "World's Exposition" column, *New Orleans Daily Picayune,* November 12, 1884.

36. "The Horticultural Reunion," *New Orleans Daily Picayune,* January 14, 1885.

37. "The American Horticultural Society," *New Orleans Daily Picayune,* January 18, 1885.

38. "American Exposition—Purchase of the Plant from the Old Organization," *New Orleans Times-Democrat,* July 14, 1885, 3.

39. The article noted that an Audubon Park Commission had been formed and had paid five hundred dollars for a park plan from one John Bogart of Chicago—likely John Bogart of the architectural firm, Jenney, Schermerhorn, and Bogart, founded by William Le Baron Jenney.

40. Catharine Cole, *New Orleans Daily Picayune,* January 10, 1892, reprinted on the website Catharine Cole's Louisiana, www.catharinecole.com/index.html.

41. *1897 Year Book of Audubon Park, New Orleans* (New Orleans: Audubon Park Association, 1897), 30.

42. Atlanta hosted a fair in 1881, and Louisville in 1883, but these were both relatively minor fairs with fairgrounds of fewer than 50 acres and total attendance of fewer than 1 million.

43. During the Civil War, severed supply lines from the North cut, among other things, the availability of naturally harvested ice. Many artificial ice alternatives and industries emerged in the South, including the Louisiana Ice Manufacturing Company in the late 1860s.

44. *Harper's Bazaar,* January 24, 1885, 67.

45. Smalley, *Century Illustrated Magazine,* June 1885, 190.

3. WORLD'S COLUMBIAN EXPOSITION

1. Janice L. Reiff, "Chicago's Social Geography," *Encyclopedia of Chicago History,* www.encyclopedia.chicagohistory.org/pages/11409_em.html.

2. Chicago History Museum, "The Great Chicago Fire," www.chicagohs.org/history/fire.html.

3. Cathy Jean Maloney, *Chicago Gardens: The Early History* (Chicago: University of Chicago Press, 2008), 84–91.

4. Mayor's Office of New York City to Frederick Law Olmsted, November 16, 1889, Frederick Law Olmsted Papers, Manuscript Division, Library of Congress, Washington, D.C. (hereafter cited as LOC: FLO). This letter thanks Olmsted for a one-hundred-dollar contribution to the Preliminary Expense Fund for the International Exposition of 1892.

5. "The General Design of the Columbian Exposition," *Garden and Forest,* August 30, 1893, 361. This article quotes a report from Frederick Law Olmsted, *Report upon the Landscape Architecture of the Columbian Exposition,* to American Institute of Architects.

6. Frederick Law Olmsted to Harry S. Codman, April 21, 1892, LOC: FLO.

7. Frederick Law Olmsted to Lyman J. Gage, President of the Board of Directors of the World's Columbian Exposition, August 28, 1890, LOC: FLO.

8. Ibid.

9. Ibid.

10. Frederick Law Olmsted to Clarence Pullen of New York, January 7, 1891, LOC: FLO.

11. The architecture of the World's Columbian Exposition is covered at great length in many other books. Daniel H. Burnham, chief architect of the fair, selected architects from around the country and Chicago including Adler & Sullivan, S. S. Beman, Richard M. Hunt, Henry Ives Cobb, and Peabody & Stearns.

12. Warren H. Manning, "The Influence of American Expositions on the Out-Door Arts," *Massachusetts Horticultural Society Transactions* (March 8, 1902): 73.

13. "Memorandum as to what is to be aimed in the planting of the lagoon district of the Chicago Exposition, as proposed March, 1891," LOC: FLO

14. Frederick Law Olmsted to D. H. Burnham, December 1891, LOC: FLO.

15. Frederick Law Olmsted to D. H. Burnham, January 28, 1891, LOC: FLO.

16. Frederick Law Olmsted to D. H. Burnham, December 28, 1891, LOC: FLO.

17. "Memorandum as to what is to be aimed in the planting of the lagoon district of the Chicago Exposition, as proposed March, 1891," LOC: FLO.

18. Ibid.

19. Ibid.

20. Ibid.

21. Frederick Law Olmsted to Harry Codman, March 23, 1891, LOC: FLO.

22. Frederick Law Olmsted, "Report upon the Landscape Architecture of the Columbian Ex-

position to the American Institute of Architects," read before the World's Congress of Architects at Chicago and reprinted in *American Architect and Building News,* September 1893, 41.

23. "Memorandum as to what is to be aimed in the planting of the lagoon district of the Chicago Exposition, as proposed March, 1891," LOC: FLO.

24. Rudolph Ulrich, Report of Landscape and Miscellaneous Departments to Mr. D. H. Burnham, December 15, 1893, unpaginated.

25. Ibid.

26. Ibid.

27. Rudolph Ulrich to H. S. Codman, March 14, 1891. LOC: FLO.

28. Frederick Law Olmsted Jr. to Frederick Law Olmsted Sr., July 16 1891, LOC: FLO. Olmsted Jr., who, like many easterners, found the hot Chicago summer enervating, opted for wearing a pith helmet to ward off the heat. He was also concerned about malaria and took a grain of quinine each night "so as to (be) on the right side while in the neighborhood of the swamp." Olmsted Jr. questioned a doctor about the prevalence of malaria on the exposition site itself and was relieved to hear the physician's view that the strong lake breeze prevented a high incidence of the disease.

29. Rudolph Ulrich, Report to Olmsted, Frederick Law & Co., May 21, 1891, LOC: FLO.

30. Frederick Law Olmsted to Partners, July, 1892, LOC: FLO.

31. Frederick Law Olmsted to Rudolph Ulrich, March 11, 1893, LOC: FLO.

32. Henry Codman and John Wellborn Root, D. H. Burnham's partner, both died unexpectedly in the course of the exposition's planning. Codman died on January 10, 1893, just four months shy of the exposition's opening.

33. The WCE landscape involved huge numbers of plants. Ultimately, the Landscape Department under Rudolph Ulrich provided: 7,300 trees, 37,000 shrubs, 100,000 willow cuttings, 156,000 herbaceous plants, 177,000 bedding plants, 61,000 hardy and ornamental plants, 10,000 clumps or crates of aquatic plants, and 200 creepers and vines. To add more ambience, waterfowl including about 500 aquatic birds like swans, geese, gulls, and ducks were imported at a total cost of $2,400. During the three-year construction period, 355,521 cubic yards of sand were moved, and 149,120 cubic yards of black soil handled. In each year, the workforce grew and shrunk according to seasonal needs: the peak in 1891 was in December with 315 men and 73 teams, 1892's peak was November with 372 men and 83 teams, and, with just a month to go before the exposition's opening, a whopping 918 men and 183 teams worked in April 1893 (Rudolph Ulrich, "Report of Landscape and Miscellaneous Departments to Mr. D. H. Burnham," December 15, 1893, unpaginated).

34. Frederick Law Olmsted to Rudolph Ulrich, March 11, 1893, LOC: FLO.

35. L. H Bailey, *Annals of Horticulture in North America for the Year 1893* (New York: Judd, 1894), 32.

36. In 1889, one Chicago park superintendent acknowledged: "Floriculture at the present time occupies a conspicuous position in park mis-adornment. With questionable taste our parks are filled with gymnastic caricatures of the art; it is hard sometimes to tell where the menagerie ends and where the flower garden begins" (J. A. Pettigrew, "Landscape Gardening in Its Application to Public Parks," *Transactions of the Horticultural Society of Northern Illinois* [1889]: 364).

37. Frederick Law Olmsted to Rudolph Ulrich, March 11, 1893, LOC: FLO.

38. Edgar Sanders, "Japanese Gardening," *Prairie Farmer* (1893): 7. Isawa is sometimes spelled "Izawa." This likely refers to the Japanese gardener Izawa Hannosuke.

39. L. H. Bailey, "Japanese Horticulture at the Fair," *Garden and Forest,* August 30, 1893, 369.

40. F. C. Seavey, "Frederick Law Olmsted, Notes from the Fair," *Gardening,* August 15, 1893, 373.

41. M. C. Robbins, "Gardening at the World's Fair," *Garden and Forest,* July 19, 1893, 303.

42. Jenney is perhaps best known as the "father of the modern skyscraper," based on his plan for the Home Insurance building in Chicago.

43. Bailey, *Annals of Horticulture in North America for the Year 1893,* 72.

44. "Crystal Cave at the Fair," *World's Columbian Exposition Illustrated* (Chicago: World's Columbian Exposition, 1893), 72.

45. Johanna S. Wisthaler, "By Water to the Columbian Exposition," 1894, www.fullbooks.com/By-Water-to-the-Columbian-Exposition2.html.

46. L. H. Bailey, "The Plant Effects in the Horticultural Building," *Garden and Forest,* August 16, 1893, 349. The diagram is adapted from this article.

47. M. C. Robbins, "Gardening at the World's Fair," *Garden and Forest,* July 19, 1893, 302.

48. Report by Frederick Law Olmsted, presumably to his partners, April 1892, LOC: FLO.

49. Frederick Law Olmsted to J. C. Olmsted and Harry Codman, April 29, 1892, LOC: FLO.

50. Frederick Law Olmsted to John C. Olmsted, from London, May 19, 1892, LOC: FLO.

51. Frederick Law Olmsted to partners from Wargrave, Berks, July 19, 1892, LOC: FLO.

52. Frederick Law Olmsted to Harry S. Codman, April 21, 1892, LOC: FLO.

53. L. P. Bryant, "Observations at the Fair," *Transactions of the Horticultural Society of Northern Illinois* (1894): 276.

54. "The Horticultural Congress at Chicago," *Garden and Forest,* August 23, 1893, 359.

55. Frederick Law Olmsted to D. H. Burnham, June 20, 1893, LOC: FLO.

56. Ibid.

57. Ibid.

58. "Art Societies and City Parks," *Garden and Forest,* July 12, 1893, 292.

59. Frederick Law Olmsted to Mr. Stiles, October 7, 1892, LOC: FLO.

60. Ibid.

61. M. C. Robbins, "A Glorified Park," *Garden and Forest,* July 12, 1893, 294.

62. James R. Grossman, Ann Durkin Keating, and Janice L. Reiff, eds., *The Encyclopedia of Chicago* (Chicago: University of Chicago Press, 2004), 902.

63. J. G. Jack, "The Columbian Exposition, Plants around the Lagoons of Jackson Park," *Garden and Forest,* October 4, 1893, 419.

64. *Youth's Companion,* April 25, 1901, 222, *Youth's Companion (1827–1929),* American Periodicals Series Online.

65. Clay Lancaster, *The Japanese Influence in America* (New York: Abbeville Press, 1983); see 189–215 for an excellent discussion of Japanese gardens and landscapes in U.S. history.

4. PAN-AMERICAN EXPOSITION

1. The Buffalo and Erie County Historical Society, http://bechsed.nylearns.org/.

2. In March 1899, the exposition's Joint Committee of Architects and Engineers suggested a hand-picked list of fifty-three architects, landscape architects, and engineers to recommend

the best site and plot plan for the fair. The recommended landscape architects on the list were Warren H. Manning, the Olmsted Brothers, Parsons & Pentecost, S. W. Langdon, Secy. of the American Association of Landscape Architects, and O. C. Simons [presumably Ossian Cole Simonds] (Edward B. Gurthene to Executive Committee of the Pan-American Exposition Company, March 31, 1899, Buffalo & Erie County Historical Society Library and Archives).

3. Olmsted Sr. and Burnham were well known for their collaboration on the World's Columbian Exposition, and Manning, who had also worked on that fair, had already worked with Buffalo's civic leaders on exposition matters (*Buffalo Commercial,* April 3, 1899).

4. Most candidate sites were eliminated due to poor accessibility, small size, or distance from Buffalo. The three sites remaining were "The Front," a park along Lake Erie, the "Riverside site," 350 acres adjoining Niagara River, and the "Rumsey site," an area north of the existing Delaware Park.

5. At the Trans-Mississippi Exposition, Taylor served as the director of horticulture, and Ulrich was in charge of landscape design.

6. Local newspaper accounts announcing Ulrich's appointment were quite positive, although a worrisome headline in the September 3, 1899, *Buffalo Express* declared, "Ulrich Not Dead." Reports of the rumor of Ulrich's untimely drowning near Rock Island had identified the wrong man.

7. *Buffalo Courier,* December 26, 1900.

8. According to the Village of Corfu website (www.corfuny.com/history.htm), Scott's greenhouse is the oldest business still operating and is now using the name Don Scott, Florist and Garden Center. The website states that in the mid-1900s, Scott's was the largest importer of bulbs from Holland in the United States.

9. William Scott, *The Florists' Manual: A Reference Book for Commercial Florists* (Chicago: Florists' Publishing, 1906), 32.

10. This included the director of works, Newcomb Carlton; H. S. Kissam, supervising architect; and Samuel J. Fields, chief of engineering and construction.

11. *Buffalo Courier,* October 31, 1900.

12. In her essay "Rudolph Ulrich and the Stanford Arizona Garden," Julie Cain notes that Ulrich preferred formal gardens and carpet bedding, as seen in his designs for such Californian estates as the Stanfords' Palo Alto Farm and Linden Towers, the James C. Flood estate in Menlo Park (Sandstone & Tile Stanford Historical Society, Spring-Summer 2003).

13. William Welles Bosworth, "Gardening," from *The Official Pan American Art Hand Book,* reprinted at http://panam1901.bfn.org/documents/gardeningbosworth.html.

14. *Buffalo Express,* February 25, 1900.

15. Edwin Fleming to Newcomb Carlton, November 28, 1899, Buffalo and Erie County Historical Society Library and Archives.

16. *Harper's Weekly,* 1901.

17. The U-shaped connection with the other buildings seemed a bit incongruous, but one news account explained, "The exigencies of the general plan caused some deviation from the idea of progression from the conception of nature and primitive man through the achievements of industry and art" (*Harper's Weekly,* March 9, 1901).

18. *Buffalo Courier,* January 7, 1901.

19. California secured the lion's share of the space with eight of the twenty-five display slots.

New York was next with three display slots. The rest of the displays were divided among fifteen other states, some private exhibitors, and six foreign exhibitors (Costa Rica, Guatemala, Jamaica, Mexico, Nicaragua, and Ontario).

20. *Buffalo Courier,* May 1, 1901.

21. California promised a poppy flower vehicle. The fair's jinrikishas (a type of rickshaw) were to be lined with flowers, and the concession's rolling chairs would also be adorned with floral arches. About one hundred members of bicycle clubs decorated their bicycles' wheels with flowers.

22. This was the first time the group (which had originated as the National Pomological Convention) had reconvened in Buffalo since its inception in 1848 (*Buffalo Commercial,* August 7, 1901).

23. Of the three major classifications in the exposition's horticulture exhibits, pomology received the most entries and awards: 1,347 gold, silver, or bronze medals out of a total 3,661 entries. Floriculture awarded 251 total medals, and Viticulture awarded 111 (Frederic W. Taylor, "Report of the Superintendent of Horticulture," 5, Buffalo & Erie County Historical Society Library & Archives).

24. *Buffalo Commercial,* May 14, 1900.

25. *Buffalo Courier,* May 12, 1901.

26. Henry A. Dreer also contributed fifteen smaller beds of tulips, hyacinths, and narcissus. Their total exhibit of 31,000 square feet included these spring bulbs, plus aquatics and herbaceous plants throughout the exposition grounds. Peter Henderson & Co. displayed 70,000 spring flowering bulbs and occupied the entire arc-shaped space between the Horticulture Building and north of the canal. Other major contributors included J. C. Vaughan of Chicago with seventeen beds of hardy phlox, pansies, geraniums, and begonias; Conard Jones with cannas; Thomas Meehan with seventy-five specimen evergreens; Vick's with six beds of spring and summer flowering plants; and Atlee Burpee with five beds of summer roses, begonias, and coleus. William Scott himself showed two hundred althea plants including the new French altheas. The Mexican government sponsored a cactus garden across the canal near the Mines Building.

27. This special exhibition of 'Crimson Rambler' roses was in addition to the roses already on display. Among the crimson roses was a new variety, never before displayed, the 'Admiral Schley' (*Buffalo Express,* June 29, 1901).

28. "Floriculture at the Pan-American Exposition," *Ledger Monthly,* December, 1901, reprinted at http://panam1901.bfn.org/documents/gardeningbosworth.html.

29. William Welles Bosworth, "Gardening," in *The Art Handbook: Official Handbook of Architecture and Sculpture and Art Catalogue to the Pan-American Exposition,* ed. David Gray (Buffalo, N.Y.: David Gray, 1901), reprinted at http://panam1901.bfn.org/documents/gardeningbosworth.html.

30. Twenty-four Vases de Borghese (presumably after Rome's Villa Borghese) adorned the circular flower beds south of the Fountain of Abundance, and at the north and south entrances to the Electricity, Machinery, and Liberal Arts Buildings. Almost one hundred Vases des Tuileries (after Paris's Jardin des Tuileries) could be found in the Rose Garden, in the East and West Esplanade fountain gardens, plaza, pergolas, and East and West mall gardens. More than fifty Vases Amphitrite, named for the Grecian goddess of the sea, were distributed among the Rose Garden, pergolas, bowers, and parterres near the Court of the Cypresses and the Court of Lilies.

Other styles included vases in the style of Louis XIV and Medici ("More Flowers Being Planted at the Exposition," *Buffalo Evening News,* May 30, 1901, in *The Art Handbook: Official Handbook of Architecture and Sculpture and Art Catalogue to the Pan-American Exposition,* reprinted at http://panam1901.bfn.org/documents/gardeningbosworth.html).

31. The Southern Exposition of 1883 in Louisville, Kentucky, used incandescent lighting for building interiors. Some buildings at the 1876 Centennial were lit with gas lamps. The World's Columbian Exposition used a mix of incandescent and arc lights, a harsh lighting source, to outline its buildings.

32. Luther Stieringer, "The Evolution of Exposition Lighting," *Western Electrician* 29, no. 12 (September 21, 1901): 187+, quoted at http://ublib.buffalo.edu/libraries/exhibits/panam/sel /stieringer.html.

33. *Buffalo Courier,* July 21, 1901.

34. *Buffalo Express,* August 24, 1901.

35. *Worcester Spy,* December 4, 1901, reprinted in "Do the Pan," www.panam1901.org/thisday /decemberarchives.html.

36. *Buffalo Evening News,* December 6, 1901, reprinted at www.panam1901.org/thisday /decemberarchives.html.

37. Ibid., December 12, 1901, reprinted at www.panam1901.org/thisday/decemberarchives .html.

5. LOUISIANA PURCHASE EXPOSITION

1. Mac Griswold and Eleanor Weller, *The Golden Age of American Gardens: Proud Owners, Private Estates 1890–1990* (New York: Abrams, 1991), 13.

2. David Rowland Francis, *The Universal Exposition of 1904* (St. Louis: Louisiana Purchase Exposition Co., 1913), 46.

3. Ibid., 48.

4. George E. Kessler, "Landscapes of the Louisiana Purchase Exposition," Papers of George E. Kessler, Missouri History Museum (hereafter cited as MHM: GEK).

5. Francis, *The Universal Exposition of 1904,* 206.

6. George E. Kessler to Isaac S. Taylor, October 15, 1901, MHM: GEK.

7. Isaac S. Taylor to George Kessler, October 29, 1901, MHM: GEK.

8. Francis, *The Universal Exposition of 1904,* 207.

9. George E. Kessler to Isaac S. Taylor, March 16, 1902, MHM: GEK.

10. George E. Kessler to Isaac S. Taylor, October 11, 1902, MHM: GEK.

11. Francis, *The Universal Exposition of 1904,* 207.

12. *Outdoor Floral Exhibits,* Division of Works Landscape Department manuscript, unsigned, undated, p. 436, Missouri History Museum Louisiana Purchase Exposition Collection.

13. Francis, *The Universal Exposition of 1904,* 470.

14. *Outdoor Floral Exhibits,* 438.

15. Ibid., 100.

16. Ibid., 359.

17. Francis, *The Universal Exposition of 1904,* 466.

18. George E. Kessler to Isaac S. Taylor, September 16, 1902, MHM: GEK

19. Manuscript marked, "To Mr. D. Cholt," 3, MHM: GEK.

20. Louisiana Purchase Exposition Company, *Official Guide to the World's Fair* (St. Louis: Official Guide Co., 1904), 38–39.

21. *Final Report of the Louisiana Purchase Exposition Commission* (Washington, D.C.: Government Printing Office, 1906), 222, retrieved from United States Louisiana Purchase Exposition Commission, United States Department of State.

22. From MHM: GEK, no date or page.

23. Caroline Loughlin and Catherine Anderson, *Forest Park* (Columbus: Junior League of St. Louis and University of Missouri Press, 1986), 82.

24. Ibid., 83.

25. Ibid. See 82–105 for a thorough discussion of the park's recreation facilities and capabilities.

26. George Kessler biography, www.georgekessler.org/index.php?option=com_content&view=article&id=79:missouri&catid=36:locations-by-state&Itemid=61.

27. *Town and Country,* September 12, 1903, 10, *Town and Country (1902–1913),* American Periodicals Series Online.

28. The West Princes Street Gardens floral clock in Edinburgh dates to 1903 or 1904.

6. JAMESTOWN EXPOSITION

1. At the beginning of the twentieth century, world's fairs proliferated. St. Louis had just celebrated the 1904 World's Fair, Portland hosted the 1905 Louis and Clark Exposition, and Seattle was already planning the Alaska Yukon Pacific Fair for 1909, not to mention the various European fairs under way. It was not until 1928, with the establishment of the Bureau of International Expositions, that some attempt was made to coordinate world's fair schedules.

2. Robin Karson notes that Manning's penchant for wild gardens predates his experience in the Olmsted firm (Karson, *Nature and Ideology: Natural Garden Design in the Twentieth Century,* www.doaks.org/Nature/natur007.pdf).

3. Warren H. Manning, "Report of the Landscape Department to the Director of Works," in *The Official Blue Book of the Jamestown Ter-Centennial Exposition,* by Charles Russell Kiehy (Norfolk, Va: Colonial, 1909), 734.

4. *Virginian Pilot,* June 30 and July 2, 1906.

5. William H. Lee, *Guide to Historic Virginia and the Jamestown Centennial* (Chicago: Laird and Lee, 1907), 130.

6. *Chicago Tribune,* January 5, 1907, 3.

7. Manning, "Report of the Landscape Department to the Director of Works," 734.

8. Manning observed numerous abandoned pump dredges and old cars near the hundred-acre Lake Sanford, which, while distant from the exposition site, was included in the scope of work. Lake Sanford and several other large areas of standing water near the fairgrounds were successfully drained in an attempt to ward off mosquitoes (Manning, "Report of the Landscape Department to the Director of Works," 734).

9. *Guide to the Jamestown Exposition and Map of Grounds* (Washington, D.C., Norfolk & Washington Steamboat Co., no date), unpaginated.

10. Warren H. Manning, "Civic Horticulture and Civic Improvement," *Proceedings of a Congress of Horticulture Held at Jamestown Exposition, by the National Council of Horticulture* (September 23, 1907): 82.

11. Frank Eberle, "Exposition's Crowning Feature," *Jamestown Magazine,* September 1906, 3–5.

12. William M. Dixon and Warren H. Manning, "Report of the Director of Works," in *The Official Blue Book of the Jamestown Ter-Centennial Exposition,* by Kiehy, 730.

13. Ibid.

14. Ibid., 731.

15. Manning, "Report of the Landscape Department to the Director of Works," 734.

16. "Preliminary Plans of the Jamestown Exposition," *Jamestown Bulletin,* June 1, 1905.

17. Manning, "Report of the Landscape Department to the Director of Works," 734.

18. Ibid., 735.

19. Manning, "Civic Horticulture and Civic Improvement," 84.

20. Ibid.

21. "Landscape at the Exposition Site Is Beautiful," *Jamestown Bulletin,* April 1906.

22. Frank Eberle, "Exposition's Crowning Feature," *Jamestown Magazine,* September 1906, 6.

23. Manning, "Report of the Landscape Department to the Director of Works," 735.

24. Manning, "Civic Horticulture and Civic Improvement," 84.

25. Ibid.

26. Eberle, "Exposition's Crowning Feature," 1–2.

27. The only notable exception to the Colonial style was the Larkin Building, designed by Frank Lloyd Wright.

28. Manning, "Report of the Landscape Department to the Director of Works," 734.

29. Ibid.

30. Eberle, "Exposition's Crowning Feature," 2.

31. Manning, "Report of the Landscape Department to the Director of Works," 734.

32. *Virginia Gazette,* August 11, 1906, magazine section, 1.

33. H. Augustine, "Report of Delegate to Horticultural Meetings held at Jamestown, VA, Sept 23–30, 1907," *Transactions of the Illinois State Horticultural Society* (1907): 156.

34. The eight-man judging team also included Earley Vernon Wilcox, professor and author of agriculture books; Fred R. Crane, instructor in Farm Mechanics at the University of Illinois Extension; USDA agrologist Frank Lamson-Scribner; and USDA employee and Floridian transplant Marcus L. Floyd, noted for his experimental tobacco crops in Connecticut.

35. "Department of Agriculture," in *The Official Blue Book of the Jamestown Ter-Centennial Exposition,* by Kiehy, 621.

36. *Virginia Gazette,* August 11, 1906, 1–2.

37. Jessie M. Good, *Chautauquan; A Weekly Newsmagazine,* December 1900; *The Chautauquan; A Weekly Newsmagazine (1880–1914),* American Periodicals Online Series.

7. PANAMA-PACIFIC INTERNATIONAL EXPOSITION

1. Clay Lancaster, *The Japanese Influence in America* (New York: Abbeville Press, 1983), 197-215.

2. Currently under restoration by Shofuden, LLC (see www.shofuden.com).

3. After San Francisco's 1906 earthquake, the Burnham and Bennett team finished the plan and worked on the 1909 Plan of Chicago.

4. Edward H. Bennett, "List of Books," Series VI, Box 52, San Francisco Pan-Pac Exposition Correspondence, Edward H. Bennett Collection, Ryerson and Burnham Archives, Art Institute of Chicago.

5. "Preliminary Notes for the Analysis of the Location of the Exposition with Regard to the Sites Selected," Series VI, Box 52, San Francisco Pan-Pac Exposition Correspondence, Edward H. Bennett Collection, 10.

6. Ibid.

7. Frank Morton Todd, *The Story of the Exposition* (London: Knickerbocker Press, 1921), 300.

8. Ibid., 168.

9. Edward H. Bennett to C. C. Moore, December 21, 1912, Edward H. Bennett Collection.

10. John D. Barry, *The City of Domes* (San Francisco: John J. Newbegin, 1915), 11.

11. Todd, *The Story of the Exposition*, 308.

12. John McLaren, *Gardening in California Landscape and Flower* (San Francisco: A. M. Robertson, 1909), 90.

13. Todd, *The Story of the Exposition*, 309.

14. Deep trenches were cut on the sides of each tree, severing the plant's side roots. Boxes, 3–6 feet square and 2½–4 feet deep, were fitted in the trenches around the sides of the tree. Fresh loam was added in a three-inch space between the side roots and the walls of the crate. For four to six months, sometimes longer, the trees grew side roots in situ and continued to gain nutrients from their tap or bottom roots.

15. Todd, *The Story of the Exposition*, 309.

16. Ibid., 311.

17. Horace G. Cotton, "The Landscape Development of the Panama Pacific International Exposition at San Francisco and the Panama California Exposition at San Diego," A.B. thesis, University of California, Berkeley, 1915, Environmental Design Archives, University of California, Berkeley.

18. *Official Guide Panama-Pacific International Exposition* (San Francisco: Wahlgreen, 1915), 35.

19. Juliet James, *Palaces and Courts of the Exposition: A Handbook of the Architecture, Sculpture and Mural Paintings with Special Reference to the Symbolism* (San Francisco: California Book Company, 1915), 50, reproduced in Project Gutenberg, www.gutenberg.org/catalog/world/readfile?fk_files=12048&pageno=41.

20. Louis Christian Mullgardt, *The Architecture and Landscape Gardening of the Exposition* (San Francisco: Paul Elder and Company, 1915), 64.

21. Cotton, "The Landscape Development of the Panama Pacific International Exposition," appendix C, 24. The quantity of flowers planted may have been substantially reduced with budget cuts or design changes: appendix B in Cotton's thesis indicates that 17,000 daffodils and 17,000 anemones were planted, and only 52,000 pansies.

22. Ibid., 34.

23. Ibid., 32.

24. Ibid.

25. Other trees included the evergreens blue gum (*Eucalyptus globules*), and white gum (*E. viminalis*), swamp mahogany (*E. robusta*), and shrubby evergreen viburnum, *Laurestinus* (Juliet James, *Palaces and Courts of the Exposition*).

26. Cotton, "The Landscape Development of the Panama Pacific International Exposition," 51.

27. James, *Palaces and Courts of the Exposition.*

28. Cotton, "The Landscape Development of the Panama Pacific International Exposition," 53.

29. Mullgardt, *The Architecture and Landscape Gardening of the Exposition*, 134.

30. Barry, *The City of Domes*, 58.

31. *Official Guide Panama-Pacific International Exposition*, 67.

32. James, *Palaces and Courts of the Exposition*.

33. Barry, *The City of Domes*, 62.

34. Todd, *The Story of the Exposition*, 310.

35. *Official Guide Panama-Pacific International Exposition*, 77.

36. Todd, *The Story of the Exposition*, 312.

37. *Official Guide Panama-Pacific International Exposition*, 77.

38. Todd, *The Story of the Exposition*, 315.

39. *Official Guide Panama-Pacific International Exposition*, 28.

40. From F. M. Todd's *Story of the Exposition*, quoted in Lancaster, *The Japanese Influence in America*, 213.

41. Frederick Maskew, "The Work of the Quarantine Division in Connection with the Panama-Pacific International Exposition," *Monthly Bulletin* (California State Commission of Horticulture), 4, no. 8 (August 1915): 353.

42. Ibid., 357.

43. John McLaren to Joseph M. Cumming, June 1, 1916, PPIE Collection, Bancroft Library, University of California, Berkeley.

44. J. M. Cumming to President of Exposition, March 10, 1916, PPIE Collection, Bancroft Library, University of California, Berkeley.

45. Cotton, "The Landscape Development of the Panama Pacific International Exposition," 44.

46. National Park Service website, www.cr.nps.gov/nr/feature/asia/2010/sabla_tea_house.htm.

8. CENTURY OF PROGRESS EXPOSITION

1. San Francisco (1894 and 1915 expositions) and Philadelphia (1876 and 1926) could also be contenders for this honor. However, San Francisco's first fair, the Midwinter Exposition of 1894, was relatively small (about 160 acres and just over 1 million visitors), and Philadelphia's Sesqui-Centennial Fair in 1926, while large, lost more than $5 million (John E. Findling and Kimberly D. Pelle, eds., *Historical Dictionary of World's Fairs and Expositions, 1851–1988* [New York: Greenwood Press, 1990], 376–81).

2. Both fairs were located on the lakefront, on the south side of the city. Many fair exhibitors, such as Vaughan Seed Company, Lord & Burnham greenhouses, and Philadelphia's Henry A. Dreer nurseries, participated in both fairs. The architect Daniel H. Burnham Jr., son of the Columbian Fair architect D. H. Burnham, served as the director of works for the 1933 Fair.

3. "Five Acre Garden at Fair an Outdoor Idyll," *Chicago Tribune*, June 22, 1933, 4.

4. "Chicago's Fair to Center on 800 Acre Island," *Chicago Tribune*, March 17, 1928, 19–20.

5. "Terrace Type of Architecture Picked for Fair," *Chicago Tribune*, May 26, 1928, 15.

6. "World's Fair Board Will Mobilize Garden Experts to Add Beauty," *Chicago Tribune*, December 26, 1928, 27.

7. Ibid.

8. Unsigned, potentially undelivered letter from Chairman of COP Architectural Commis-

sion to Chevalier Ferruccio Vitale, January 10, 1939. See also D. H. Burnham to H. W. Corbett, telegram, April 15, 1930, Century of Progress Collection, Special Collections and University Archives, University Library at the University of Illinois at Chicago (hereafter cited as UIC-COP Collection).

9. "Excerpts taken from Minutes Executive Committee Meeting, June 27, 1930," UIC-COP Collection.

10. Lenox R. Lohr, *Fair Management* (Chicago: Cuneo Press, 1952), 84.

11. Ibid., 83.

12. Ibid., 56.

13. Alfred H. Geiffert, "Landscaping for the Fair," manuscript dated 11/30/32, p. 3, UIC-COP Collection.

14. Ibid., 3.

15. Lohr, *Fair Management,* 85.

16. Ibid.

17. Brochure for the "Super-safe" brick home, p. 21, Collection of the Museum of Science and Industry.

18. Alfred Geiffert, "Landscaping for the Fair," November 30, 1932, 3, typescript, UIC-COP Collection.

19. *Chicago World's Fair Guide* (Chicago: American Autochrome, 1933), 7.

20. Lohr, *Fair Management,* 83.

21. "Women of 50 Groups Uniting to Clean Chicago," *Chicago Tribune,* June 27, 1929, 31.

22. Ibid.

23. C. W. Fitch to Colonel Van Deventer, interoffice memo, May 16, 1932, 5/137, UIC-COP Collection.

24. "Report of Horticultural Committee—A Century of Progress," September 12, 1932, 5/136, UIC-COP Collection.

25. Kate L. Brewster to F. R. Moulton, September 30, 1932, 5/135; and F. R. Moulton to Assistant Secretary, interoffice memo, October 11, 1932, 5/137, UIC-COP Collection.

26. "Officials of Fair Disclose Plans for Horticulture Group," *Chicago Tribune,* October 26, 1932, 15.

27. Harold D. Platt, "The Romance of the Gladiolus," in *Horticultural Exhibition and Garden and Flower Show at a Century of Progress International Exposition, May 26th to November 1st, 1934* (Chicago: The Exposition, 1934), 64.

28. *World's Fair Dahlia News* 2, no. 4 (November 1933): 34.

29. Rev. P. Oswald, "The Increasing Popularity of the Dahlia," *World's Fair Dahlia News* 2, no. 4 (November 1933): 2.

30. "5 Acre Flower Garden at Fair an Outdoor Idyll," *Chicago Tribune,* June 22, 1933, 4.

31. Ibid.

32. J. T. Charleson, "Water Gardening and Its Exotic Charms," in *Horticultural Exhibition and Garden and Flower Show at a Century of Progress International Exposition, May 26th to November 1st, 1934,* 24.

33. Gil Limbacher, phone interview by the author, May 1999.

34. Helen Koues, "Good Housekeeping Exhibition Classic Modern Garden and Pavilion at a Century of Progress—Chicago," *Good Housekeeping,* August 1934, 55.

35. C. M. Cutler and G. R. La Wall, "Garden Lighting Brings Magic by Night," *Good Housekeeping,* November 1934, 73.

36. "Oranges Mix Their Dates," *Official World's Fair Weekly,* August 19, 1933 (Chicago: A Century of Progress International Exposition), 12.

37. Leon Henry Zach, "Modernistic Work and Its Natural Limitations," *Landscape Architecture* 22, no. 4 (1932): 293.

38. "5 Acre Flower Garden at Fair an Outdoor Idyll," The *Chicago Tribune,* June 22, 1933, 4.

9. THE WORLD OF TOMORROW

1. The automobile was a huge factor in designing this fair. The American automobile giants Ford, GM, and Firestone exhibited prominently at the fair's main gates. Highways were rerouted and expanded around the perimeter, and inner circulation routes were designed to accommodate vehicular traffic.

2. Gilmore D. Clarke to Robert D. Kohn, January 3, 1938, New York World's Fair 1939/1940 Collection, Manuscripts and Archives Division, New York Public Library (hereafter cited as NYPL-NYWF).

3. According to the nursery's catalogue, *Krider's Glories of the Garden for 1940.*

4. Thomas D. Price to Gilmore D. Clarke, June 1, 1939, NYPL-NYWF.

5. Clarke's formalized many of these associations with partnerships. As of May 1937, "Vitale & Geiffert, Gilmore D. Clarke" was the official letterhead of the landscape architecture firm with offices at 101 Park Avenue in New York.

Vitale & Geiffert et al. to C. L. Lee, May 4, 1937, NYPL-NYWF.

6. Gilmore D. Clarke, "The Design of the Landscape," October 17, 1938, typescript, NYPL-NYWF.

7. Gilmore D. Clarke to Mr. Robert Woods Bliss, June 27, 1939, NYPL-NYWF.

8. *New York Herald Tribune,* April 30, 1939, 19.

9. Some references show the acreage as 1,260 acres, but 1,216 acres is generally accepted as the size of the final developed area.

10. F. Scott Fitzgerald, *The Great Gatsby.*

11. This plan also showed the intended design for the postfair park: the fair's Transportation sector, with its GM and Ford exhibits, was to become playing fields and baseball diamonds; the Communications exhibit and Administration Building were destined for "pitch putt golf"; the area that would be the fair's horticulture exhibit, "Gardens on Parade," was planned for community gardens (Francis Cormier, "Flushing Meadow Park: The Ultimate Development of the World's Fair Site," *Landscape Architecture,* September 1939, 168).

12. E. J. Carrillo, "Land Development and Landscaping," NYWF press release, December 20, 1938, NYPL-NYWF.

13. *Official Guidebook New York World's Fair 1939* (New York: Exposition Publications, 1939), 24.

14. Carrillo, "Land Development and Landscaping."

15. The Construction and Landscape Department published very detailed specifications on desired trees, complete with graphical drawings indicating tree height, spread, and shape. The requirements for American elms (*Ulmus americana*), for example, included three separate spec sheets for 12″-, 14″-, and 17″-caliper specimens. The minimum requirements for the 17″-caliper

tree included: height 48–55 feet; spread 34–40 feet; branching 10–15 feet above ground; root ball 13½–14½ feet in diameter. Specifications indicated that a vase shape was preferred to the so-called wine-glass shape, and that the tree should be free from crooked branch forms or flat, spreading heads (tree specifications from Construction and Landscape Department manuscript in NYPL-NYWF).

16. Henry C. Nye, "Horticulture at the Fair," World's Fair press release dated December 19, 1938, NYPL-NYWF.

17. Ibid.

18. NYWF Department of Press, 1939, NYPL-NYWF.

19. Gilmore D. Clarke, "The Design of the Landscape," October 17, 1938, NYWF Publicity, February 21, 1939, NYPL-NYWF.20. Suffolk County Community College website, www2 .sunysuffolk.edu/mandias/38hurricane/damage_caused.html.

21. Sterling Patterson, "Miracle of the Marshes," *Better Homes and Gardens,* April 1939, 20. With later plant failures, this figure would reach a highly respectable 2 percent damage, which included factors other than the hurricane.

22. Henry C. Nye, "New York World's Fair 1939 Inc. Landscaping," World's Fair press release dated January 10, 1939, NYPL-NYWF.

23. Stanley Appelbaum, *The New York World's Fair 1939/1940 in 155 Photographs* (New York: Dover, 1977) 102.

24. Jacques Greber to NYWF 1939 Vice President and Chief Architect, April 11, 1939, NYPL-NYWF. The New York City Building was built on the highest point of the exhibit area—22 feet— which then gradually sloped down to about 1.5 feet at the Lagoon of Nations.

25. Release No. Landscape 1, NYPL-NYWF.

26. Cormier, "Flushing Meadow Park," 172.

27. "Landscape Design and Horticulture at the New York World's Fair 1939," February 21, 1939, Department of Feature Publicity for National Advisory Committee on Women's Participation, NYPL-NYWF.

28. Sterling Patterson, "Miracle of the Marshes," *Better Homes and Gardens,* April 1939, 88.

29. J. L. Hautman to Barclay Johnson, June 20, 1939, NYPL-NYWF.

30. *Official Guidebook of the New York World's Fair 1939,* 180.

31. Nye, "New York World's Fair 1939 Inc. Landscaping."

32. This mixture included more than 57,000 pansies "Lord Beaconsfield," and almost 50,000 white and pale yellow pansies, 8,000 petunias, 8,000 scarlet *Phlox drummondii,* and later, 2,700 chrysanthemum 'Fortuna' and 5,000 chrysanthemum 'Niobe' ("Bedding Plants Allocated by Areas," December 6, 1938, NYPL-NYWF).

33. NYWF 1939 Department of Feature Publicity, publicity release dated April 17, 1939, NYPL-NYWF.

34. *Landscape Architecture,* July 1939, 153–65. Clarke did not write extensively of the fair's landscaping in this article, but commissioned John G. Gass, a photographer who specialized in landscapes, and with whom Clarke frequently worked. Gass's photographs of the fair are interesting in that they relegate the iconic architecture as backdrops to the landscape.

35. NYWF 1939 Department of Feature Publicity, no date, unpaginated, NYPL-NYWF.

36. "Gardeners in the Fair," undated manuscript, NYPL-NYWF.

37. *Official Guidebook New York World's Fair 1939,* 210.

38. "The Flowers That Bloom at the Fair," NYWF 1939 Department of Feature Publicity, NYPL-NYWF.

39. "Landscape Architecture at the New York World's Fair II," *Landscape Architecture,* October 1939, 2.

40. "The Flowers That Bloom at the Fair."

41. "Landscape Architecture at the New York World's Fair II," 6.

42. Ibid., 25.

43. Lawrence Culver, "The Economic Aspirations and the Politics of National Park Creation in Jackson Hole, Wyoming, 1919–1929," in *People and Place: The Human Experience in Greater Yellowstone,* ed. Paul Schullery and Sarah Stevenson (Yellowstone National Park, Wyo.: National Park Service and Yellowstone Center for Resources, 2005), 180–94.

44. Hillwood Museum and Gardens website, www.hillwoodmuseum.org/gardens/shogobio.html.

45. "The Flowers That Bloom at the Fair."

46. Ibid.

47. Umberto Innocenti and Richard K. Webel formed a partnership in 1931, after having both worked for the Vitale and Geiffert firm.

48. "Landscape Architecture at the New York World's Fair II," 8.

49. Ibid., 11.

50. Ibid.

51. "Gardens on Parade" benefited not only from the altruistic endeavors of socially prominent individuals, but also from experienced show management including the sponsoring Society of American Florists and Ornamental Horticulturists and John A. Servas, who managed the 1933 World's Fair horticulture exhibit.

52. Mr. Gregory to Mr. Morrisey, March 4, 1937, NYPL-NYWF.53. W. Earle Andrews to the President and General Manager, "Outdoor Flower Show at Fair, March 25, 1937, NYPL-NYWF.

54. Mrs. Harold Pratt to Grover A. Whalen, November 9, 1938, NYPL-NYWF.

55. Mrs. Harold Pratt to Grover A. Whalen, May 8, 1939, NYPL-NYWF.

56. As quoted in "The Flowers That Bloom at the Fair."

57. *Gardens on Parade: The Horticultural Exhibition at the New York World's Fair, 1939* (New York: Hortus), 23.

58. Ibid., 9.

59. University of Illinois Extension website, www.urbanext.uiuc.edu/roses/kinds/floribunda.html.

60. The hapless nurseryman whose brochure landed at the Sloan estate had apparently misunderstood the GM agreement to donate all landscaping material to the park. Moses assured Sloan that no one should be selling fair landscape material on the open market (Alfred P. Sloan to Robert Moses, October 31, 1940, City of New York Municipal Archives, Record Group N.Y.C., Department of Parks (hereafter cited as NYMA–Dept. of Parks).

61. Net Stevenson to Robert Moses, March 20, 1940, NYMA–Dept. of Parks

62. Robert Moses to George E. Spargo, October 16, 1940, NYMA–Dept. of Parks.

63. Kaname Wakasugi to Robert Moses, September 6, 1940, NYMA–Dept. of Parks.

64. Robert Moses to George E. Spargo, January 3, 1941, NYMA–Dept. of Parks.

65. Andrews to Oliver I. Lay, December 26, 1940, NYMA–Dept. of Parks.

66. For example, Julian D. Smith inquired as to the health of a Mary Washington boxwood that was transplanted from its original site in Mary Washington's garden at Fredericksburg, Virginia: "Being familiar with the local controversy associated with sending the plant to the Fair, I am anxious to know where that piece of boxwood is now, and what sort of condition it is in." Smith was assured that the boxwood in question was in very good condition, and that "Gardens on Display" was to become a model garden (Julian D. Smith to Robert Moses, July 5, 1941, and James A. Dawson to Julian D. Smith, July 7, 1945, NYMA–Dept. of Parks).

67. James A. Dawson to Carl Wedell, April 10, 1941, NYMA–Dept. of Parks.

68. Francis Cormier to James Dawson, December 3, 1940, NYMA–Dept. of Parks.

69. This experimental garden was intended to educate residents of the surrounding lower-income neighborhoods in the arts of gardening (Harriet Pratt to Robert Moses, June 15, 1941, NYMA–Dept. of Parks).

70. Robert Moses to Allyn Jennings, January 9, 1940, NYMA–Dept. of Parks.

71. Robert Moses to Sparge, December 30, 1940, NYMA–Dept. of Parks.

72. Robert Moses to Mrs. Harold I. Pratt, October 11, 1949, NYMA–Dept. of Parks.

73. In late June 1941, park officials were considering treatments of "Gardens on Parade" that would retain elements of the original gardens, but add sample backyard treatments for typical Queens yards. It was hoped that various Queens garden clubs might be interested in the design and maintenance of these demonstration gardens (M. Dean to Stuart Constable, June 26, 1941, NYMA–Dept. of Parks).

74. *Long Island Daily,* June 6, 1948, 1.

EPILOGUE

1. Other fairs in the United States included Seattle (1962), San Antonia (1968), Spokane (1974), Knoxville (1982), and New Orleans (1984). While these fairs certainly had iconic structures and some fairs posted a profit, none exceeded 100 acres in size (unlike the NYWF of 1964–65, which boasted more than 600 acres).

2. "The Second World's Fair," *Chicago Tribune,* December 15, 1927, 10.

3. "Cancel 1933 World's Fair; Plan Subways," *Chicago Tribune,* August 2, 1927, 1.

4. "World's Fairs: New York, San Francisco," *Architectural Forum,* June 1939, 393.

5. Per the BIE website, those expositions included: 1947, Paris, France; 1949, Stockholm, Sweden; 1949, Port-Au-Prince, Haiti; 1949, Lyon, France; 1951, Lille, France; 1953, Jerusalem, Israel; 1953, Rome, Italy; 1954, Naples, Italy; 1955, Turin, Italy; 1955, Helsingborg, Sweden; 1956, Beit Dagon, Israel; 1957, Berlin, Germany; 1958, Brussels, Belgium; 1961, Turin, Italy; 1962, Seattle, USA; 1965, Munich, Germany; 1967, Montreal, Canada; 1968, San Antonio, USA; 1970, Osaka, Japan; 1971, Budapest, Hungary; 1974, Spokane, USA; 1975, Okinawa, Japan; 1981, Plovdiv, Bulgaria; 1982, Knoxville, USA; 1984, New Orleans, USA; 1985, Tsukuba, Japan; 1985, Plovdiv, Bulgaria; 1986, Vancouver, Canada; 1988, Brisbane, Australia; 1991, Plovdiv, Bulgaria; 1992, Genoa, Italy; 1992, Seville, Spain; 1993, Taejon, Korea; 1998, Lisbon, Portugal; 2000, Hannover, Germany; 2005, Aichi, Japan; 2010, Shanghai, China (Bureau of International Expositions website; www.bie-paris.org/site/en/expos.html).

6. International Association of Horticultural Producers website, www.aiph.org/site/index_en.cfm?act=teksten.tonen&parent=4683&varpag=4936.

7. Office of the Governor website, http://gov.ca.gov/speech/15975.

1. Agreement between Arthur F. Brinckerhoff and New York World's Fair 1939 Incorporated, March 8, 1937, NYPL-NYWF.

2. Domenico Annese, "Gilmore D. Clarke," in *Pioneers of American Landscape Design,* by Charles Birnbaum et al. (New York: McGraw-Hill, 2000), 56.

3. Gilmore D. Clarke, "Landscape Architecture at the New York World's Fair," *Landscape Architecture* 29, no. 4 (July 1939).

4. S. F. Voorhees to Gilmore D. Clarke, January 6, 1939, NYPL-NYWF.

5. Ibid.

6. "New Orleans Exhibition," *Transactions of the Mississippi Valley Horticultural Society—1884* (Indianapolis: Carlon and Hollenbeck, 1884), 144.

7. Laurie E. Hempton, "Alfred Geiffert, Jr.," in *Pioneers of American Landscape Design,* by Birnbaum et al., 132.

8. S. F. Voorhees to Vitale et al., December 4, 1936, NYPL-NYWF.

9. C. L. Lee to Vitale et al., May 12, 1938, NYPL-NYWF.

10. Voorhees to Vitale et al., July 1, 1937, NYPL-NYWF.11. From George E. Kessler Papers, no date, unpaginated, Missouri Historical Society.

12. Birnbaum et al., *Pioneers of American Landscape Design,* 221.

13. Agreement between Charles D. Lay and New York World's Fair 1939, March 8, 1937, NYPL-NYWF.

14. NWWF 1939 Board of Design Minutes, April 2, 1937, 2, NYPL-NYWF.

15. J. L. Hautman to Charles D. Lay, January 22, 1938, and January 4, 1938, NYPL-NYWF.

16. John D. Barry, *The City of Domes* (San Francisco: John J. Newbegin, 1915), 11.

17. Texas A & M University website, http://botany.cs.tamu.edu/FLORA/taes/tracy/TRACY.htm. The S. M. Tracy herbarium at the University is named in Samuel Tracy's honor.

18. Bradford M. Greene, "Michael Rapuano," in Birnbaum et al., *Pioneers of American Landscape Design,* 308–9.

19. John Maass, *The Glorious Enterprise* (Watkins Glen, N.Y.: American Life Foundation, 1973), 21.

20. Julie Cain, "Rudolph Ulrich and the Stanford Arizona Garden," *Sandstone & Tile,* published by the Stanford Historical Society (Spring/Summer 2003): 10.

21. *Express,* August 13, 1899.

Recommended Reading

Bailey, L. H. *Annals of Horticulture in North America for the Year 1893: A Witness of Passing Events and a Record of Progress: Comprising an Account of the Horticulture of the Columbian Exposition.* New York: Orange Judd, 1894.

Bancroft, Hubert Howe. *The Book of the Fair: An Historical and Descriptive Presentation of the World's Science, Art, and Industry, as Viewed through the Columbian Exposition at Chicago in 1893.* New York: Bounty, 1894.

Barry, John D. *The City of Domes: A Walk about the Courts and Palaces of the Panama-Pacific International Exposition.* San Francisco: John J. Newbegin, 1915.

Bell-Knight, C. A. *The Crystal Palace: The 1851 Exhibition.* [Bath]: British Nostalgia Publications, 1983.

Beveridge, Charles E., Paul Rocheleau, and David Larkin. *Frederick Law Olmsted: Designing the American Landscape.* New York: Rizzoli, 1995.

Birnbaum, Charles A., and Robin S. Karson. *Pioneers of American Landscape Design.* New York: McGraw-Hill, 2000.

Burnham, Daniel Hudson, Joan E. Draper, and Thomas S. Hines. *The Final Official Report of the Director of Works of the World's Columbian Exposition.* New York: Garland, 1989.

Clary, Raymond H. *The Making of Golden Gate Park: The Early Years, 1865–1906.* San Francisco: Don't Call It Frisco Press, 1984.

Findling, John E., and Kimberly D. Pelle, eds. *Encyclopedia of World's Fairs and Expositions.* Jefferson, N.C.: McFarland, 2008.

Flinn, John J. *Official Guide to the World's Columbian Exposition in the City of Chicago, State of Illinois, May 1 to October 26, 1893 . . .* Chicago: Columbian Guide, 1893.

Girvan, Aikman Tom. *Boss Gardener: The Life and Times of John McLaren.* San Francisco: Don't Call It Frisco Press, 1988.

Hales, Peter B., and C. D. Arnold. *Constructing the Fair: Platinum Photographs by C. D. Arnold of the World's Columbian Exposition.* Chicago: Art Institute of Chicago, 1993.

Hedrick, U. P., and Elisabeth Woodburn. *A History of Horticulture in America to 1860.* Portland, Ore.: Timber, 1988.

Hill, Thomas E. *Hill's Souvenir Guide to Chicago and the World's Fair.* Chicago: Laird and Lee, 1892.

International Exhibition: 1876 Official Catalogue. Philadelphia: published for the *Centennial Catalogue* by John R. Nagle, 1876.

Jenkins, Virginia Scott. *The Lawn: A History of an American Obsession.* Washington, D.C.: Smithsonian Institution Press, 1994.

Lillard, John B. *Visitors' Guide to the World's Industrial and Cotton Centennial Exposition, and New Orleans. Commencing Dec. 16, 1884, and Ending May 31, 1885.* Louisville, Ky.: Courier-Journal Job Print., 1884.

Loughlin, Caroline, and Catherine Anderson. *Forest Park.* St. Louis: Junior League of St. Louis, 1986.

Louisiana Purchase Exposition. St. Louis: Official Photographic, 1904.

Maass, John. *The Glorious Enterprise: The Centennial Exhibition of 1876 and H. J. Schwarzmann, Architect-in-chief.* Watkins Glen, N.Y.: published for the Institute for the Study of Universal History through Arts and Artifacts, by the American Life Foundation, 1973.

MacPhail, Elizabeth C. *Kate Sessions: Pioneer Horticulturist.* San Diego: San Diego Historical Society, 1976.

Maloney, Cathy Jean. *Chicago Gardens: The Early History.* Chicago: University of Chicago Press, 2008.

Mattie, Erik. *World's Fairs.* New York: Princeton Architectural Press, 1998.

McCabe, James Dabney. *The Illustrated History of the Centennial Exhibition: Held in Commemoration of the One Hundredth Anniversary of American Independence: With a Full Description of the Great Buildings and All the Objects of Interest Exhibited in Them . . . to Which Is Added a Complete Description of the City of Philadelphia.* Philadelphia: National, 1876.

McLaren, John. *Gardening in California, Landscape and Flower.* San Francisco: A. M. Robertson, 1909.

Minkin, Bertram. *Legacies of the St. Louis World's Fair: A Compilation of Articles.* St. Louis: Virginia Pub., 1998.

Monaghan, Frank. *Official Guide Book of the New York World's Fair, 1939.* New York: Exposition Publications, 1939.

Mullgardt, Louis Christian, Paul Elder, Maud Wotring Raymond, and John Hamlin. *The Architecture and Landscape Gardening of the Exposition: A Pictorial Survey of the Most Beautiful of the Architectural Compositions of the Panama-Pacific International Exposition.* San Francisco: P. Elder and, 1915.

Official Guide: Book of the Fair, 1933. Chicago: Century of Progress, 1933.

Official View Book: A Century of Progress Exposition. Chicago: Reuben H. Donnelley, 1933.

Pan-American Exposition: Thirty Minutes from Niagara Falls; Buffalo, N.Y. from May 1, to Nov. 1, 1901. Buffalo, N.Y.: Matthews-Northrup, 1900.

Punch, Walter T., and William Howard Adams. *Keeping Eden: A History of Gardening in America.* Boston: Bulfinch, 1992.

Rydell, Robert W. *All the World's a Fair: Visions of Empire at American International Expositions, 1876–1916.* Chicago: University of Chicago, 1984.

1607, Jamestown Exposition, 1907, Hampton Roads, Virginia. Norfolk, Va.: W. T. Barron, 1907.

The World's Columbian Exposition Illustrated. Chicago: J. B. Campbell, 1892.

World's Fair Authentic Guide: Complete Reference Book to St. Louis and the Louisiana Purchase Exposition. St. Louis: Official Guide, 1904.

The World's Fair, St. Louis, 1903. St. Louis: Louisiana Purchase Exposition, 1901.

Wurts, Richard, and Stanley Appelbaum. *The New York World's Fair, 1939/1940 in 155 Photographs.* New York: Dover, 1977.

 Index

Page numbers in italics refer to illustrations.